Glimpses of our Ancestors in Sussex ;

Charles Fleet

Glimpses of our Ancestors in Sussex:

and

Gleanings in East and West Sussex.

THE PELHAM MONUMENT, IN ST. MICHAEL'S CHURCH, LEWES.

GLIMPSES

OF

OUR ANCESTORS IN SUSSEX;

AND

GLEANINGS IN EAST & WEST SUSSEX.

BY

CHARLES FLEET,

Author of "Tales and Sketches," "The City Merchant," &c.

ILLUSTRATED.

" I have some rights of memory in this ' County,'
Which now to claim my vantage doth invite me."
—*Shakspeare.*

SECOND SERIES.

LEWES:

FARNCOMBE & CO., PRINTERS, "EAST SUSSEX NEWS" OFFICES.

1883.

PREFACE.

HE favor with which the first Volume of GLIMPSES OF OUR ANCESTORS IN SUSSEX was received by the Public and the Press has encouraged the Author to issue a Second Volume, partly devoted to the same class of subjects which fill the first volume and partly to subjects of a more descriptive and topographical character.

Trusting that an equal measure of indulgence will be extended to this as was received by the former publication, the Author leaves it to the kind judgment of the Public.

ERRATUM.

———

At page 13, line 27, of "A NOBLE SUSSEX FAMILY," read,—

  "This Ducal Pelham married the Lady Mary Godolphin,
"a grand-daughter of John Churchill, the great Duke of
"Marlborough."

DEDICATED, BY PERMISSION,

TO

THE RIGHT HONOURABLE

HENRY THOMAS PELHAM

(EARL OF CHICHESTER),

LORD LIEUTENANT OF THE COUNTY OF SUSSEX.

LIST OF ILLUSTRATIONS.

———

CONTENTS.

GLIMPSES OF OUR ANCESTORS IN SUSSEX.

GLEANINGS IN EAST AND WEST SUSSEX.

GLIMPSES OF OUR ANCESTORS, &c.

A Noble Sussex Family.

HE FAMILIES, in Sussex or elsewhere, who can trace their descent from a follower of the Conqueror may, at the present day, be counted on our fingers. They are, indeed, "few and far between." The Wars of the Roses made sad havoc with them. The Seventh Henry did not spare them. But it was Thomas Cromwell, Earl of Essex, the ruthless minister of Henry VIII., who put the finishing stroke to the work of destruction—almost of extermination. Then fell those deadly blows on the old nobility which drew from one of them, Lord Darcy, as he stood at the Royal Council Board, the fierce and despairing hope "that, ere thou (Cromwell) die, though they wouldst procure all the noblest heads within the realm to be stricken off, yet there shall one head remain that shall strike off thy head." The hope was realized; but not less effectual was the fatal work, and when England at length settled down into something like peace and social order, it was with a newly-created order of nobility. "Those families," says Hallam, "who are now deemed the most considerable, will be found, with no great number of exceptions, to have first become conspicuous under the Tudor line of kings." The Russells, the Cavendishes, the Fitz-williams all date from that period. Even the Howards and

B

the Stanleys are comparatively modern families, only emerging from obscurity by virtue of alliances with older and higher houses.

There are, however, a few exceptions ; and Sussex can still boast amongst the noble families who reside on its soil two or three who carry back their origin to almost the earliest historic period. First and foremost amongst these stand the Pelhams, the representative of whom in Sussex (for the family extends into other counties), the Earl of Chichester, holds the highest official rank in the county, that of Lord Lieutenant, and fills a place in the respect of his fellow-Sussexians which none of his forefathers over-topped.

It is an open question whether the Pelhams came in with the Conqueror or whether they are of Saxon descent. The latter theory is favoured, and was doubtless suggested, by the Anglo-Saxon etymology of the family name, Pelham signifying in Anglo-Saxon a settlement or estate surrounded with pales. But that only serves to connect the family with a place, and to point to the common circumstance of the family assuming the name of the place. Now, it is well determined that amongst the followers of William the Conqueror was William, Baron of Bec-Crespin, in Normandy, who received, as his portion of the spoils of victory, twenty-five lordships in Hertfordshire, one of which bore the title of " Pelham," and this descending to his second son, Ralph, that branch of the family assumed the distinctive title of " Pelham," which, by an easy process in those days, quickly passed into the family name. Thus, Ralph de Pelham, in 1165, held a Knight's fee in Hertfordshire from the Bishop of London, and his son was Hugh de Pelham, and he had a numerous family, one of whom fell back on the old patronymic of de Bec, and, in 1194, was defendant in a suit for Middleton, Cambridgeshire, which his father, Ralph de Bec, or Pelham, had in 1068 held from Picot of Cambridge, and which the said Robert Picot now claimed.

Thus the connection between, or rather the identity of, the de Becs and the de Pelhams is clearly shown. They were de Becs in Normandy, de Pelhams in England, taking both names from their lands, as the good old fashion was, when land made the man—at least, the free man.

To proceed with the Pelham genealogy. In 1218, Petrus or Peter de Pelham returns to his allegiance as such. His elder son, Walter de Pelham, lived in the reign of John, and he, too, was a defendant (the Normans always were fond of litigation !) in a suit for dower brought by the widow of Ralph Fitz-Hugh. In 1199 there were further law proceedings between Walter and Elias de Pelham on the one side and the Abbot of Eynesham on the other. The sons of Walter de Pelham lived (but whether they flourished or not we do not know, though, as a rule, Pelhams always did flourish) in the reign of Henry III. If a Walter Pelham mentioned in the Peerages as living in 1265 were one of them, they *had* flourished. But several members of the family are mentioned about 1272. And it is curious that at this period the de Becs and the de Pelhams again come together; Walter de Pelham (probably the son of him of 1265) holding from Walter de Bec, styled le Chamberlain, two hides of land in Cottenham; and from this Walter de Pelham, who became Lord of Pelham, came all the succeeding branches of the Pelhams as they figure in the English Peerage. Henceforward the family tree grew up straight and broad, and without a rotten branch in it.

It was in the reign of Edward I. that the Pelhams began to hold land in Sussex, chiefly in its eastern extremity, at Hailsham, Huseye (near Pevensey), Ashton, Waldron, &c. The reason of their migration from Hertfordshire to Sussex is not known; but in the 14th century their Sussex lands extended a length of three miles from Hailsham to Horseye, including what are called "the Lands of the Eagle"—the meaning of which high-sounding title the late M. A. Lower (in the genealogical memoir of the Pelhams drawn up by him) declares " he does not quite understand, though they must have been a portion of the great Lordship or 'Honour of the Eagle,' the *caput Baroniæ* of which was Pevensey." Not many years later the office of Constable of Pevensey Castle (the most important fortress, and a Royal one, in the east of Sussex) was conferred on a Pelham.

The Pelhams now begin to stand out as warriors and statesmen. With the third Edward had recommenced the struggle between England and France which for 100 years was to call out all the energies and consume the feudal resources of both countries until they both lay at the feet of absolute Sovereigns, preparatory to the appearance upon the scene of the people. We now fully admit that Edward's title to the French crown was a bad one; but we also see that he had a real cause of grievance against France in the continual stirring-up by that country of dissensions between England and Scotland. But the 100 years' war was a disastrous one for both countries, rich as it was in glory to the English; and none shared more fully in that glory than the Pelhams.

John de Pelham (whose figure in armour, with the three pelicans of the family on the surcoat, was introduced in one of the painted windows of the Chapter House of Canterbury) accompanied the King to France, and was with the Black Prince at the battle of Poictiers, in which the French King, John, was taken prisoner. No less than ten knights and esquires challenged him as their prize; but the King surrendered himself to two Sussex warriors, John de Pelham and Roger la Warr, as his real captors. To these he gave up his sword, and each of the noble knights introduced into their armorial bearings a memento of the deed: La Warr assuming the *crampet* or termination of a scabbard, and Pelham the buckle of the sword-belt (by which, probably, he had seized the luckless King). These badges are used to this day by the Earls de la Warr and the Earls of Chichester; the Pelhams wearing the buckle as an adjunct to their original arms of the three pelicans: sometimes as part of their crest, a cage between two buckles, in allusion to the captivity of the French monarch—and sometimes simply on their great seals still appendent to old deeds. Henceforth the buckle figures in many an ecclesiastical building, both in Hertfordshire, the Pelhams' mother-county, and in Sussex, and wherever it is found it is accepted by archæologists as a proof of the work and presence of the Pelhams. In Sussex the Pelham Buckle is still to be seen, either in the windows or stone-work of the parish churches of Waldron, Laughton, Chiddingly, Rype, Easthoathly, Crowhurst, Burwash, Ashburnham, Penhurst, Dollington, and Wartling, and it was to be seen (until removed to mend the roads !) in the stone-work of Robertsbridge Abbey (of which the Pelhams were benefactors), and is still visible on a chimney-back at Warbleton Priory. In numerous domestic buildings, as at Laughton Place, Halland Place, and on old houses at Hastings, Westham, &c., and on the iron chimney backs in Sussex farm-houses, was the Pelham Buckle a familiar badge and ornament, and it even figured on the backs of sheep ! So popular was it.

Indeed, the feat of arms by which it was won was well supported by the whole career of its winner, who was knighted by Edward III., and not less by that of his son, who bore the same name, and was not less famous as a warrior. Both father and son attached themselves to the persons and fortunes of Edward's younger son, John of Gaunt, "time-honoured Lancaster," and of his aspiring son, Henry of Bolingbroke, Earl of Derby and Hertford, afterwards Duke of Lancaster, and ultimately Henry IV. As the father had been esquire to John of Gaunt, so the son became esquire to Bolingbroke, and, in all probability, accompanied him in his exile after the quarrel between Bolingbroke and Mowbray, Duke of Norfolk. At all events, he landed with Bolingbroke at Ravenspur when he came back, at the invitation of a large number of the English nobility, ostensibly to reform the Government of Richard, but in reality to seize on the Crown. In this he was supported not only by John de Pelham, but by John de Pelham's wife— a lady who anticipated the glory due to those noble dames who, like Dame Douglas and that La Tremouille who was a

Countess of Derby, have defended their husband's castles and honour in their absence. John de Pelham, like his grandfather, had been made Constable of Pevensey Castle for life, and it was here that he left his wife and family whilst absent with his patron on the continent. She was here attacked and besieged by the adherents of Richard, and whilst gallantly and successfully defending the Castle against them, she did as great a feat for a lady of that day as to wield a sword, or even greater; she wielded a pen, and wrote, *in English,* the following epistle :—

"My dere Lord, I recommande me to your hie Lordeschipp wyth hert & body, & all my pore mygth ; and wyth all this I think zow, as my dere Lorde, derest & best yloved of all erthlyche Lordes ; I say for me, and thanke yhow, my dere Lord, with all thys (things?) that I say before, off your comfortable lettre that ze send me from Pownefraite * that com to me on Mary Magdaleyn day; ffor by my trowth I was never so gladd as when I herd by your lettre that ye warr stronge ynogh, wyth the grace off God, for to kepe you fro the malyce of your ennemys. And dere Lord iff it lyk to your hyee Lordeschipp that als son als (as soon as) ye mycht that I mygth her off your gracious spede, whyche God Allmyghty contynue and encresse. And my dere Lord, iff it lyk zow for to know off my ffare, I am here ly layd in manner off a sege, with the counté of Sussex, Sudray, & a great parcyll off Kentte, so that I ne may noght (go) out nor none vitayles gette me, bot wt myche hard (difficulty) Wharfore my dere iff it lyk zow, by the awyse off zowr wyse counsell, for to sett remedye off the salvation off yhower Castell, and wtstand the malyce off thes schires forsayde. And also that ye be fullyche enformed off these grett malyce wyrkers in these schyres whych yt haffes so dispytffully wrogth to zow, and to zowr castell, to yhowr men, and to zour tenaunts, ffore this cuntree have yai (they) wastede, for a gret whyle. Farewele my dere Lorde ; the Holy Trinyté zow kepe fro zour ennemys, and son send me gud tythings off yhow.

"Ywryten at Pevensay in the castell on Saynt Jacobe day last past,
"By yhowr awnn pore
"J. PELHAM.

"(Addressed)
"*To my trew Lorde.*"

Let no fair reader smile at the spelling of this letter or think lightly of its phraseology. *It is the first letter ever written in the English language by a lady.* Such is the opinion of the great historian, Hallam. Previous to this period all those members of the upper classes who could write corresponded in French ; and even this was a rare accomplishment.

---

*Pontefract, in Yorkshire, where Rich. II. was imprisoned and afterwards murdered.

It was a happy inspiration in Dame J. Pelham (she was the daughter of Sir John Escures, and must, surely, have come from a good English stock), when acting so nobly the part of an English wife and helpmate, to make use of the English language—then springing into flower with the genius of Chaucer; and it has given her a place in letters not less exalted than that of her husband in arms.

The successful defence of Pevensey Castle by Dame " J. Pelham " was rewarded by the Constableship of that Royal fortress* being conferred by Henry IV. on John de Pelham and his heirs male, with the " Honour " of the Eagle, this " Honour " (so named from Gilbert de Aquila, a follower of William the Conqueror, who received the gift of the Rape of Pevensey for his services at the Conquest) comprehending a sixth part of the county of Sussex. Sir John was also created a Knight of the Bath at the coronation of Henry IV., and the King, "moved by his special grace, and in good consideration of the grateful services of his beloved and faithful knight, John Pelham, heretofore done," granted to him for life the honour of bearing the Royal sword before him in all places and at all requisite times.

The services of Sir John de Pelham during a long life, both at home and abroad, in peace and in war, justified the confidence of the King. Sir John sat for Sussex in the several Parliaments called by Henry, along with the de Prestons, the Lewknors, the Husseys, the Delyngryges, and other Sussex worthies, receiving the expenses which were then paid by constituencies to their representatives. He defended the Sussex coast against the French, who threatened it with invasion under the Count de St. Pol; he fortified it against the attacks of a still more formidable enemy—the sea—which threatened in those days to swallow up a large part of the coast of Sussex; and he accompanied the fifth Harry in his

---

* The ruins of the Castle of Pevensey, so gallantly defended by Dame J. Pelham, still stand, within the area of the great fortified Roman station of Anderida; but, of course, like other Norman fortresses, its uses, for home protection or foreign defence have long passed away.

expeditions against France. His absence from the field of Agincourt is accounted for by the fact that he had been appointed a Commissioner to array all the defensible men, nobles, and archers in Sussex for the defence of the realm during the King's absence, and to be in readiness as well to expel and repulse any attempts of the enemy as to go beyond seas, if necessity required—a necessity which actually did arise. But he assisted at the terrible siege of Rouen, which lasted a whole year, and in which 50,000 of the inhabitants of that city died of famine. It was whilst engaged in this terrible service that the charge of Queen Joan of Navarre, mother-in-law of the deposed Richard, and who was accused of sorcery, was entrusted to him, and the royal lady remained in custody at Pevensey Castle until 1423. He had been previously made the custodian of Edward, Duke of York, and of the two sons of the Earl of March, who, as the descendants of an elder brother of John of Gaunt, were the lineal inheritors of the crown of England, and in whose cause Harry Hotspur had already raised the standard of revolt against Henry IV. A more welcome and honourable duty fell to John de Pelham in being made the guardian and governor of the youthful King of Scotland, James I., who, captured at sea, and not too honourably detained by Henry V., was so well educated, not only in all courtly accomplishments, but in letters and music, "tongues and sciences," that he became one of the first poets of the day, and, when he returned to Scotland, taking with him as his wife the fair Joan of Beaufort, ruled with a wisdom and spirit that gave twelve years of too short-lived peace and prosperity to that land. Such a fact as this is not less honourable to the memory of Sir John de Pelham than was the capture of John of France by his father; and one of the most gratifying features of the good knight's career must have been to have assisted, as he did as the Representative of Sussex, in the act of that Parliament by which James of Scotland was set at liberty, after a captivity of 18 years, and restored to his country.

Though a Pelham does not figure among Shakspeare's

dramatis personæ, one of their close associates does, namely, " old Sir Thomas Erpingham," to whom the hero-King, on the eve of Agincourt, so kindly said—

> "A good soft pillow for that good white head
> Were better than a churlish turf of France."

And to which Sir Thomas so bravely replied—

> "Not so, my liege ; this lodging likes me better,
> Since I may say : now lie I like a King."

Sir Thomas Erpingham, as Constable of Dover Castle, was joined with the second Sir John de Pelham in commission to view and repair the banks in Pevensey Marsh, between Bexley and Beachy Head, " for its due governance and salvation thereof in the time to come."

It has been a matter of surprise with English annalists that such distinguished men as the two John de Pelhams were not raised to the Peerage.   Collins looks upon it as an "uncommon instance of self-denial."   It may have been such; for a man who enjoyed the high personal favour of Henry V. (he was one of the executors to his will, as he had been to that of his father); who was made, in the very beginning of the new King's reign, one of the Ambassadors to France to treat of the marriage of Henry with the French King's daughter, Katherine ; who was addressed by foreign kings like John of Portugal as " noble and prudent," and solicited to extend his care and kindness to the King's daughter, widow of the Earl of Arundel; who was held in high esteem by the King's brothers as well as by the King himself, and was popular with the people as well as at Court—such a man as this, the guardian of captive Kings and Queens and Princes, a warrior and a statesman, could not have failed to attain the honours of the Peerage had he desired them.   His fortune certainly could have supported the dignity.   In Sussex alone his rent-roll was £876. 5s. 3d. —equal to at least £17,500 in the present day.   Perhaps prudence restrained him, and to this we may owe the descent of the House to this day, without any of those terrible gaps in it which break the line of descent of so many others.

Whilst Sir John de Pelham shared in and largely contributed to the glories of the fifth Harry's reign, he did not live to see the reverses of the ensuing one.   He died in the 7th year of Henry VI., "full of honour," and without a blot on his name as a warrior, diplomatist, or statesman.

It is not known whether the brave wife of Sir John, the defender of Pevensey Castle and the earliest English lady letter-writer, survived her husband.   But she had borne him three children, two daughters (who became the wives of John Colbrand, of Boreham, and Sir John de St. Clerk, or Seynclere)—and a son, who bore his father and grandfather's name, and, like them, went to "the wars" in France and was Constable of Pevensey Castle.   He, too, enjoyed the Royal favour : he was chamberlain in the household of Harry's French consort, Katherine, and to mark her favour to him and his wife, Joan de Courcey (one of her own attendants), the Queen made a grant to him of fifty marks per annum. She also, at a later period, when she was the wife of a Welch gentleman, Owen ap Tudor (by whom came the Tudor dynasty), gave to John de Pelham and to her own husband (with priority to Pelham) power to survey and repair all her towns and castles.   John de Pelham was also master of the Queen-Dowager's Royalties and forests in Normandy; but whether these survived the loss of the English dominion in that Province of France, we are unable to say.   Doubtless the Pelhams, like other English families, were losers by the adverse course of events in France after the appearance on the scene of Joan of Arc ; but they managed, unlike many of their contemporaries, in the troublous days that followed, to keep their English estates, and even, by marriage with such Sussex families as the Lewknors, the Challoners, the Coverts, the Colbrands, the Popes, the Morleys, the Fynes, &c., &c., to extend them.   They also inter-married with the Wests, Lords de la Warr, the Sackvilles, the Carews, the Shirleys, the Sydneys, &c.   Indeed, they are connected, by their numerous alliances, with the best blood of England. Still, during these earlier generations the Pelhams kept steadily to the knightly class. John, knighted by Henry VI., followed the three warriors we have spoken of, but he dying without male issue, the line was now varied by a William Pelham—a simple Esquire—and he, in like manner, gave way to a Thomas Pelham, Esq., after whom we come once more to a John Pelham, his eldest son, but he also dying without issue, a William Pelham succeeds. And in him, after a period of repose for the Pelhams in the troublous and dangerous days of the Wars of the Roses, which saw half the old nobility of England swept off, the Pelhams again came to the front. Sir William Pelham was with King Henry VIII. in his famous interview with Francis the First on the Field of the Cloth of Gold, was knighted by the King, who only knighted men, and, for his services to the King, was permitted to empark 700 acres of land in Laughton, Easthoathly, Chiddingly, and the adjoining parishes. At the former place, Laughton, he built the great mansion, Laughton Place, which figures so conspicuously in the after-history of the parish. He had two wives (a Carew and a Sandys), and families by both, and his eldest son and successor, Sir Nicholas Pelham, renewed the military glories of the House —not, like his ancestors, indeed, by invading France, but in the more legitimate way of defending his own shores against French attack. This, in fact, was *that* Pelham who, as the inscription on his monument at St. Michael's Church, Lewes, quaintly tells us, " did repel 'em back aboard;" that is, the French expedition under Claude d'Annabant, which, after descents at Brighthelmston and Meeching (Newhaven), attempted to land at Seaford, and was here met by Sir Nicholas, at the head of a force consisting chiefly of the neighbouring townsmen and gentry and yeomen, with which he drove the invaders in confusion and much slaughter back to their ships. This brave soldier was also a learned man, and a favourer of the Reformation. He also, like his ancestors, represented his native county in Parliament, and, though he lived in the dangerous days of Mary, and sat in two of the Parliaments called by that Queen, he knew how to couple loyalty with truth to his faith. He lived to see the accession of Elizabeth, and, dying in his 44th year, left his estates unimpaired to his son.

Doubtless, the alliance of Nicholas Pelham with the Sackvilles (he married Anne, daughter of John Sackville, Esq., ancestor of the Earls and Dukes of Dorset, and had by her ten children) gave strength to the Pelhams in the reign of Queen Elizabeth. He attended the Queen in her progress through Sussex, was knighted by her, and, like his ancestors, represented Sussex in Parliament. So did his son, Sir Thomas Pelham, who allied himself by marriage to the Walsingham family, his wife being a niece of Elizabeth's great Secretary of State, and was compelled by James the First's greed to pay for the Baronetage which he had to "take up" instead of receiving that knighthood which his ancestors had so often won on the field of battle. His son— another Thomas— sat in four successive Parliaments, from 1624 to 1640—a memorable era in the history of this country, for it marked the revival of Parliamentary Government after the Tudor despotism—and he constantly voted, with the Essex branch of the family, with the patriotic party. In the extreme acts, however, of the Long Parliament, and in the Civil War which followed, he took no part. During this and the Protectorate of Cromwell he retired into private life, living and dying at Laughton, like his immediate ancestors, having, like them, a numerous family, and being succeeded, also like them, by a son. This son, Sir John Pelham, was elected, with his brother Nicholas, to the Parliament that restored Charles the Second; and it is a unique fact in the history of English Parliaments that these two brothers were returned by the same constituency, and for four successive Parliaments they so sat together. At the same time a son of Sir John also sat for Lewes and East-grinstead, and there were Pelhams from other counties in Parliament. They were, in fact, a "power" in Parliament. Their leaning was, as it always has been, to Liberalism, or, to use the language of that day, to Whiggism. Sir John, in fact, married the sister of the celebrated patriot, Algernon Sydney, and had, like most of the Pelhams, a large family by her. He outlived her 17 years, and died in 1703, at Laughton, at the patriarchal age of 80.

It is remarkable how, in the career of the Pelhams, the two currents of arms and politics run side by side. They were always statesmen as well as soldiers, and from the time of Henry IV. they are to be found representing Sussex in Parliament. In the peaceable days, internally, at which we have now arrived—the 17th and 18th centuries—the Pelhams come more prominently to the front as Parliament-men. Of the three sons of Sir John Pelham the eldest had already sat in Parliament for Lewes and Eastgrinstead in the life-time of his father, and he continued to do so during the reigns of Charles II., James II., and William and Mary (when he was appointed a Lord of the Treasury), up to Anne, when he was created Lord Pelham, Baron Pelham of Laughton, in Sussex, and so attained that point of greatness which, if eminent services could have purchased them, should have been enjoyed by a Pelham ages before. His second wife was a daughter of Gilbert Holles, Earl of Clare, and sister of John, Duke of Newcastle, and by her he had five daughters and two sons, the eldest of whom, and his successor in the Peerage, Thomas, was created Duke of Newcastle, and was left heir by his uncle, the last Duke of Newcastle of the Holles family (sprung from a Lord Mayor of London, *temp.* 1540), heir to his vast estates. This ducal Pelham married the eldest daughter and co-heiress of the great Duke of Marlborough; he held many of the highest offices of State, and stood godfather to George II. He was a Knight of the Garter, Chancellor of Oxford—in fact, supped full of honours, and for 46 years was the acknowledged leader of the Whig party when that party was at the height of its fortunes. Amongst other favours showered on him, he received the additional title of Baron Pelham, of Stanmer, Sussex, with remainder, in failure of heirs male of his own body, to Thomas Pelham, of Stanmer, Esq., a descendant from the third Baronet, and whose father (and it is a notable fact in the history of the House) had been a merchant at Constantinople, but, inheriting Stanmer from an elder brother (Henry), sat in the Parliaments of the two first Georges and left a son, named Thomas after himself, who was destined to be the first Earl of Chichester, and a daughter who was married successively to Henry, Viscount Palmerston, and George Neville, first Earl of Abergavenny—both historic families.

Going back to Duke Pelham—if we may be permitted so to call him—he was the only Duke of his family, for he left no son to inherit his many honours and great wealth, and the Dukedom of Newcastle went to Henry Clinton, Earl of Lincoln. Never did the greatness of the Pelhams shine forth in Sussex so conspicuously as in his day and under his reign—for such it might be called. He resided at Halland —so the great house at Easthoathly was called—more like a Sovereign Prince than a subject. He travelled with gorgeous state from one to another of his Sussex houses—he had several of them—kept open house—gave sumptuous feasts to the grandees of the county and to distinguished foreigners, and was in every respect " the Great Duke of Newcastle." He was very popular both with his tenants and the neigh-bouring townsmen and villagers, and traditions of his progresses and his doings at Halland, Laughton, and Bishopstone yet hang about those neighbourhoods. As to the grand funeral (at Laughton) which closed his career, is it not set down in due fullness in the diary of Thomas Turner, general shopkeeper, of Easthoathly, who was both delighted, amused, and, albeit benefited, yet a little scandalised at the profusion and pomp of the Duke's life and the closing scene of it at Halland !

The career of the first Lord Pelham's second son, Henry, the brother of the Duke, was scarcely less distinguished than that of the great Duke himself—perhaps more so. He began his career like the first Pitt, by being a Captain of Dragoons (Pitt was a Cornet—" that terrible cornet of

Dragoons," as Walpole used to call him), and was present at
the defeat of the Scotch Rebels at Preston Pans. Then,
turning to the Pelham's second love, politics, he entered
Parliament; sat first for Seaford, then for the Shire; was
soon appointed to a Lordship of the Treasury, next made
Secretary of War, sworn of the Privy Council, and, at last,
was appointed First Lord of the Treasury, succeeding to and
carrying out the peace policy of Walpole, one of whose
disciples he was—loving peace, though often dragged into
war by the more restless spirit of his brother. By a curious
fatality all of his six children who survived childhood were
females, so that this branch of the Pelhams soon came to an
end; but one of the daughters married her cousin, the Earl
of Lincoln, and so became Duchess of Newcastle.

It was, however, in the Stanmer branch of the family that
its Sussex greatness was to continue to flourish. We have
seen how the title of Baron Pelham passed to the Duke
of Newcastle, and through him to Thomas Pelham, Esq.,
of Stanmer, grandson of the first Lord Pelham. Thomas
Pelham, like all the members of his family, took to Parliamentary and public life as spaniels take to water. He sat for
the county of Sussex, and filled various offices, for which, in
1801, he was rewarded with an Earldom, and chose for his
title the oldest city of the county, Chichester. Dying in
1805, he was succeeded by his eldest son, who was appointed
Postmaster-General in 1807, and who, marrying a daughter
of the Duke of Leeds (thus allying the Pelhams to the
Osborne family), kept up the good old Pelham practice by
having a family of ten children, four sons and six daughters.
The second of the former (the eldest died in infancy)
succeeded his father in 1826, and still, we rejoice to say,
lives to enjoy the fame, honours, and to hand down the
unspotted name of the Pelhams. He was long at the head of
the Ecclesiastical Commission; presided over the Quarter
Sessions of East Sussex with much judicial ability; and,
since 1860, has filled the highest office in his native county
—that of Lord Lieutenant. In many ways he has approved

the soundness of his breeding; he has always upheld civil
and religious liberty, and been a true friend of the English
Establishment as a Protestant Church.   By his late Countess
(a daughter of the 6th Earl of Cardigan) he has four sons—
the eldest of whom, Lord Pelham, has sat in Parliament for
Lewes—and three daughters, the latter all married, so that
neither in its direct line nor collateral branches is the great
Sussex House of Pelham likely to come to an end.

The story of the Pelham House has been a long one; it
has extended over between 800 and 900 years.   But it is one
worth telling and studying. We doubt if it can be matched—
most certainly it cannot be surpassed—by that of any family
in Europe; for it presents an unbroken line of brave men
and virtuous women, able and willing to do the work of their
days—in war and in peace—in the battle-field and at the
Council-board—in public and in private life, without flinching
from their post; loyal to their Princes, true to the people,
and without even the eye of envy being able to espy a spot
to dim the brightness of their escutcheon.

The Percies in Sussex.

WHEN we think of the Percies, it is generally in connection with the North and the West of England—the borders of Scotland or the Marches of Wales. They are the antagonists or the allies of the Douglases or the Glendowers—now meeting them with varying success at Otterborne and at Halidon Hill—now fighting side by side with them at Shrewsbury. Yet from a very early period, up to the extinction of the family, the Percies were closely connected with Sussex, and some of their most interesting monuments and family relics are still to be found here. Their great deeds of arms were, undoubtedly, performed in the North and in the West. They were Earls of Northumberland, keepers of the Scotch borders, and Lords of the Welsh Marches, the defenders of the kingdom alike against the incursions of the Scot and the Welshman. But they had also *un pied à terre* in the more genial and peaceful South : they were Castellans of Arundel and Barons of Petworth, and the latter title was the distinctive one of the family until 1377.

The Percies, like the Pelhams and the Sackvilles, "came in with the Conqueror." But it is not the lineal descendants of this friend and follower of William the Bastard who are the famous Percies of English history and of Shakspeare's tragedy—or, at least, only on the female side. The original Percies failed in the male line at the third in descent; he died at Jerusalem in the first and only successful Crusade, when the Holy City was captured by Godefroi de Bouillon, with whom William de Perci (surnamed Algernon, or, in modern French, *aux moustaches*, from the magnitude of those

C

manly appendages), was, doubtless, a companion in arms. He left two daughters, the youngest of whom, Agnes, married Joceline of Lovaine, a younger son of Godfrey, Duke of Brabant, and brother of Queen Adeliza, the relict of Henry the First. It was no light acknowledgment of the high standing of the Percies that the son of a foreign Potentate (for the Dukes of Brabant at that time were no less), and the brother of an English Queen assumed the family name and title. Joceline of Lovaine was Lord of Petworth, and held, under William of Albini, Queen Adeliza's second husband, the office of Castellan of Arundel Castle. He inherited the vast estates of the Percies—in Sussex alone, 16½ knights' fees, or about 10,200 acres; and from him and his wife Agnes descended that famous race of Percies, Earls of Northumberland, whose name stands so high both in English history and poetry.

It was not, indeed, until several generations after the union of Agnes Percy, the representative of the original family, with Joceline de Lovaine that the great northern Earldom of Northumberland was conferred upon the Percies. The father of Hotspur was the first Percy, Earl of Northumberland. His mother was a Plantagenet, and he himself was the chief prop of his cousin, Bolingbroke, when that son of John of Gaunt aspired to the throne. It is he whom Shakspeare makes fill so large a space in the historical play of Henry the Fourth, and who laments the death of his gallant son in language as terrible in its expression of grief and despair as ever fell from mortal lips :—

> " Now let not Nature's hand
>   Keep the wild flood confin'd; let order die !
>   And let this world no longer be a stage
>   To feed contention in a lingering act ;
>   But let one spirit of the first-born Cain
>   Reign in all bosoms, that, each heart being set
>   On bloody courses, the rude scene may end,
>   And darkness be the burier of the dead."

This great nobleman was, in all probability, of Sussex birth. Up to his time the chief residence of the Percies had been at Petworth, from which they took their title as Peers of the Realm. There is no doubt that from the earliest period there was a lordly mansion of the Percies at Petworth; but it was that Henri de Perci, first Baron of Alnwick, who lived in the second Edward's reign, and who had married Lady Eleanor Fitz-Allan, the daughter of the then Earl of Arundel, who received (in 1309) a royal license to "fortify and crenellate" his "manse" (mansion) at Petworth "for himself and his heirs for ever." Here he and the three succeeding Henries de Perci, we may assume, lived, until the elevation of the third Baron to the Earldom of Northumberland shifted the scene of their domestic life and opened up a new and more extended field for their exploits; investing them, too, with a tragic interest which can never die out.

But even in this tragic interest Sussex is not without a share. The connection of the Percies with Sussex did not close with their translation to the North. They still held their Sussex estates and their fortified mansion at Petworth, and hither it is conjectured that, after the fatal battle of Shrewsbury, Hotspur's noble widow, Elizabeth Mortimer (not Kate, as Shakspeare calls her, though it would be a sin to un-Kate her now) hastened to seek a refuge from her enemies. This, however, is merely conjectural. But it is certain that she left her only son by Hotspur with his grandfather, Earl of Northumberland, then at Warkworth Castle in the north, and that Northumberland fled with him to Scotland, where he was brought up with the Prince of Scotland until recalled by Henry the Fifth, the conqueror of his father, and generously reinstated by him in all the honours and possessions of the Percy family. The influence of his mother doubtless contributed to this. Hotspur's widow, to whatever place she fled after the defeat and death of her gallant husband, was in danger from the Royal power, and had to seek safety in further flight. There is still in existence a warrant issued by Henry IV. ordering one Robert Waterton to arrest her wherever she may be found, and to impress horses for the pursuit, and to spare no expense in capturing

her. She was, it must be borne in mind, not only Harry
Percy's widow, but the sister of that Mortimer whose right
by descent to the Throne of England was better than that of
Bolingbroke. But the Lady Percy had powerful friends at
Court. At least, she knew how to win one such. One of
her Sussex neighbours was Thomas Lord Camoys, of Trotton,
Broadwater, and many other manors in the west of Sussex,
who had served with her husband in the French wars of
Richard II. He had been one of the favourites of that
Sovereign, and, on the accession of Henry IV., found himself
at first "out in the cold." But the fourth and fifth Henries
had the gift, like other great men, of discovering where
merit lay, and Thomas Camoys soon regained favour at
Court. He was appointed a Commissioner with the Bishop
of Winchester to treat with the French, and, when Harry of
Monmouth determined to invade France, Camoys received
an important command, and led the left wing of the English
army at the famous battle of Agincourt. His followers were
chiefly drawn from Sussex, and many of these men were the
terrible bowmen whose boast it was that they carried thirty
Frenchmen's lives in their belts. Some of these Sussex
archers (their names are still preserved in the English
Archives and may be found in the Sussex Archæological
Collections, not omitting that "John Bates" whom Shakspeare has immortalised), it is said, stripped themselves in
order to draw their bows more freely, and by their savage
appearance struck a terror into their enemies, which they
completed by their shafts and battle axes. It was in this
gallant Sussex soldier, who was created a Knight of the
Garter on the day after the battle, that Elizabeth Percy
found a powerful protector and a second husband. Such an
union was a pledge of *her* future loyalty and a safe-guard
from future persecution. As the wife of Lord Camoys, even
the widow of Hotspur might be trusted. It was a remarkable
fate that made one woman the wife of two such men as
Hotspur and Camoys. That she cherished the memory of
the first is proved by the fact that she brought the sword

with which he fought at Shrewsbury, and which he had worn
for many years before, with her to Petworth. And there it is
still to be seen. It is 3-ft. 6½-in. in length, and the blade is
exactly three feet. On the guard is the date "1392." She
had a son by her second husband, but he died in infancy.
Lord Camoys died in 1419, five years after Agincourt (men
did not live long in those days—"old John of Gaunt, time-
honoured Lancaster," did not see sixty), and, as he was
buried at Trotton, we may conclude that he passed the latter
years of his life in Sussex. His wife lies by his side, and
the inscription on the fine "brass" which still remains in the
Parish Church of Trotton runs thus:—"Pray for the souls
of Thomas Camoys and Elizabeth his wife. He was formerly
Lord Camoys. A Baron, and a prudent commander for the
King and realm of England, and a valiant Knight of the
Garter. He commended his life's end to Christ on the 18th
day of March, 1419."

As we have already stated, the son of Hotspur by Elizabeth
Mortimer was restored to his honours and possessions by
Henry V. The generosity of the King was not ill repaid:
the second Percy who was Earl of Northumberland (Hotspur
never bore that title) became a staunch supporter of the
House of Lancaster and died fighting for it against the
Yorkites at the battle of St. Alban's. His son, too, the
third Earl, was a martyr in the same cause. He lost his
life at the battle of Towton, in which he commanded the
Lancastrian forces. By his marriage with the heiress of the
last Baron of Poynings he became still more closely connected
with Sussex, and, before he succeeded to the Earldom of
Northumberland, was summoned to Parliament as Baron of
Poynings. This manor, however, he bequeathed to his
youngest son, Josceline, on the condition that he "shall be
of loving and lowly (lauly) disposition towards Henri, his
eldest brother, and give him his allegiance: and that I charge
him to do and to be, upon my blessing, and as he will answer
before God."

Some injunction of this kind was not unnecessary in an

age which had seen sons and fathers fighting against each other, and brother murdered by brother. Whether Josceline obeyed his father's behest we do not know : but he died early, and the Poynings property again reverted to the elder branch, until sold by the sixth Earl. This sixth Henri Percy was the disappointed lover of Anna Boleyn, and he was involved in the ruin of that unfortunate Queen. He sold the Poynings property for the use of the Crown (compulsorily, no doubt), and it was granted to Sir Anthony Browne, the first Viscount Montague, and the builder, or rather restorer, of Cowdray. But Petworth still remained in the possession of the Percies. They had, we have seen, embattled their house there at an early period. But this, probably, had become too small for their wants. The fashion, too, and necessities of the age had changed as respected the dwellings of the nobility. With the close of the Civil Wars fortified houses passed away ; the Tudors discouraged them, and the aristocracy, reduced in power, hastened to please the Sovereign—perhaps themselves —by building a new kind of habitation, adapted for the arts of peace and not of war. Cowdray, Hatfield, and Petworth were specimens of these Tudor buildings. At what period the Percies abandoned the old embattled building (which is supposed to have stood nearer the town) is not known ; but it was the eighth Earl—still a Henri Perci—who enlarged, between 1576 and 1582, the house to which they removed, and which stood on the same site as the present, though this latter has been wholly reconstructed. The three last Percies, Earls of Northumberland, lived in the olden house, "in great splendor," but with a total loss of that almost sovereign power which belonged to the older Earls. The sword and the axe, long imprisonment, and confiscation and fines had abated their pride and reduced their power. For sixteen years the ninth Earl was held captive in the Tower on suspicion of being an abettor of Popery. When released, he was fined £30,000 by the Star Chamber, and this tremendous imposition prevented his carrying out his plans for re-building Petworth House. His son Algernon had the same intent, but was equally unable to execute it. His plan is still preserved among the muniments of Petworth House. The last of the Percies, Earls of Northumberland—the eleventh of the line—died in the old Tudor Mansion, and it was by a Seymour—the "proud Duke of Somerset," as he was called, who married the heiress of the Percies, Elizabeth—that the existing house, or, at all events, the main body of it, was erected. The architect is said to have been a Frenchman, M. Pouget, the builder of Montague House in London. But English workmen and artists were employed on it, and one of the glories of the house is the exquisite wood carving of Grinling Gibbons and Jonathan Ritson.

We have now arrived at the last dying gleams of the Percies. As they rose from Sussex—shining with a tempestuous glory in the North—so they sank here. The Earls were already extinct. Elizabeth, Baroness Percy, after being twice married and twice a widow before she was sixteen, became the wife of the sixth Duke of Somerset. She died in 1722, leaving an only son by the Duke, and who himself became the seventh Duke of Somerset, thus uniting the Percies and the Seymours in one representative. But it was a short-lived union. He died without male issue in 1749-50, and his only daughter became the wife of a London physician, Sir Hugh Smithson! What would "the proud Duke" have said to this? By a family arrangement, the Petworth and other Percy estates went, not to the daughter of the last Duke of Somerset (of the Seymour line), but to his nephew, the eldest son of Sir William Wyndham, the famous statesman, by Catherine Seymour, the Duke's sister. This nephew also became Earl of Egremont by succession from his uncle, the Duke, who bore that title, and it is his son, Charles O'Bryen Wyndham, Earl of Egremont, who is still remembered in Brighton as one of its earliest patrons and most munificent supporters of its charitable institutions, and whose portrait adorns the walls of the Pavilion. This nobleman's descendants, the Earls Leconfield, still reside at Petworth House, the seat of the Percies, whose monuments fill the family Chapel. But their name is heard there no more, and even their memories and associations are not strong in the seat of their Sussex greatness. As we said at the outset, it is always with the North or the West — with Halidon Hill, Otterbourne, Chevy Chase, or Shrewsbury—Northumberland or Scotland—that we connect the name of the Percies, and not with Sussex or Petworth. Yet they rose and sank in Sussex; it is in Sussex that the remains of Harry Percy's widow, Shakspeare's Kate, lie at Trotton; and if any one wishes to see the weapon which Hotspur's dying hand clasped in his last fight at Shrewsbury, he must go to Petworth to find it.

The Shirleys, of Wiston.

HE Shirleys, who, up to 1678, were the possessors of the Wiston estate, also take us back to one of the families who came into Sussex with the Conqueror. After the defeat of Harold at Hastings, William de Braose, who contributed to the victory, received, as his share of the spoil, the Rape of Bramber, of which Wiston was a portion. Granting it, as was the custom of the times, to one of his followers, Ralph, Lord of Wiston, as he dubbed himself, the estate passed to the De Bavents, until, singularly enough, the last female representative of this family married, in the 14th century, another William de Braose, descended from a junior branch of the Lords of Bramber, and so it continued in the possession of the de Braoses until it devolved upon another lady, the sole sister and heiress of the last Braose of Wiston, namely, Beatrix de Braose; and this lady married a Shirley and brought the Shirleys into Sussex from their native county of Warwick, where they had been settled immediately after, if not anterior to, the Conquest.

Sir Hugh de Shirley, the husband of Beatrice de Braose, was, like the Pelhams, a follower of John of Gaunt and attended him in his not over-fortunate expedition into Guienne. He also, like the Pelhams, adhered to the fortunes of John of Gaunt's son, Bolingbroke, when he snatched at the Crown, and he followed him and his gallant son to the field against Harry Hotspur and fell in the famous battle of Shrewsbury, in which he was "one of those four knights, who, clad in the Royal armour, successively encountered and fell under the victorious arm of the Earl of Douglas in single combat."

It is to this valiant Shirley that Shakspeare makes Prince
Henry refer when the Prince in his turn meets with the
Scotch champion and makes him seek safety in flight :—

> " Hold up thy head, vile Scot, or thou art like
> Never to hold it up again ! The spirits
> Of valiant *Shirley*, Stafford, Blount are in my arms.
> It is the Prince of Wales that threatens thee,
> Who never promiseth but he means to pay."

The son of this first of the Sussex Shirleys was named
Ralph. He was only thirteen years of age at the death of
his father ; but he lived to emulate his sire's deeds and even
go beyond them. He was amongst those gallant spirits who
accompanied the fifth Harry to France ; was with him at the
siege of Honfleur ; held a high command at Agincourt ; and
took a leading part in the succeeding events of that stirring
time, up to the death of the conqueror—assisting, too, at the
coronation of his infant son at Paris. It was this Shirley's
fate, like so many of the heroes of Agincourt, to die abroad ;
but his body was brought to England and interred at Newark.

To these fighting Shirleys succeeds for a time a more
peaceable race, Ralph following Ralph, not " as Amurath an
Amurath," but as Harry, Harry—that is, in quiet succession
and engaging in quiet rural pursuits. The one who served
the office of Sheriff in the eighteenth year of the seventh
Harry's reign left to his son Richard no less than 91 head of
cattle, 4 horses, and 800 sheep—clear indications of the
direction in which *his* tastes lay ; and the said Richard
followed in the steps of his sire and looked to the main
chance at home, instead of trying, like his earlier ancestors,
to win *chateaux en Espagne*, or, what was still worse, because
more difficult to keep, castles in Normandy ! From the
second son of this Richard Shirley sprang the Westgrinstead
Shirleys, but who eventually gave way to the Carylls. as the
Carylls did to the present owners of the Westgrinstead estate,
the Burrells.

But the Wiston Shirleys were reserved for a longer career and
higher destinies. They sent out branches, indeed, to Preston,

Chiddingly, and Wivelsfield, in the last of which their residence, Ote-hall, still stands, though in dilapidated condition. One of them, Sir Thomas Shirley, re-built the fine old house at Wiston as it now stands, or partly stands; was knighted by Elizabeth at the same time that one of the Pelhams was; and it was in this Sir Thomas Shirley's three sons that all the adventurous and warlike tastes of the race seemed to revive and spring up in one last bright flame. They carried the fame of the name farther, if not higher, than it had ever been carried before; and it may be doubted if three brothers of any English family ever displayed a more remarkable genius for adventure or carried it out, on the whole, with more success. The Marco Polos, father and son, come nearest to them in the field and character of their exploits; but they, as Venetians, stood, as it were, on the threshold of adventure, and were at the portals of that then mysterious and almost closed land to Europeans, the East; whilst the Shirleys of Wiston, the natives of an obscure Sussex village, must have been impelled by more than the usual restlessness of mortality to strike out so far and so boldly as they did to the lands of the rising sun.

The names of the "three Shirleys" were Thomas, Anthony, and Robert. Only one year separated the birth of the two first. Robert was much younger. The same spirit inspired all three. But Anthony takes precedence by the magnitude of his exploits. These, in his earlier years, were of a military nature. Having married a cousin of Essex, though he did not live happily with her—and perhaps that incited him to a roving life—he followed the fortunes of the ill-fated favourite of Elizabeth; and, after serving under him in France and receiving from Henry IV. of France the order of St. Michael for his services, he accompanied Essex when he went as Lord Lieutenant to Ireland. There, too, he was knighted. But Ireland did not afford a field wide enough for his adventurous spirit. The Turks at this time threatened Europe, and Anthony Shirley had an idea that the Shah of Persia might be induced to join the Christian Powers against their common enemy, and that, at the same time, a trading intercourse might be opened between Persia and the West. Accompanied by his younger brother, Robert, and twenty-three others, he set sail from Venice in an *argosie* bound for Scanderoon, determined, according to his own statement, "to do some extraordinary thing before he returned back again."

Of this expedition several contemporary accounts are preserved. After a tedious journey by sea and land the party reached Aleppo, where they endured much indignity from the Turks, and on their route by way of Babylon to Persia they fell into the hands of a horde of Arabs, who robbed Sir Anthony of the rich jewels which he had purchased in order to propitiate the Persian monarch. At length they reached Kazveen, where the king, or "Shah," Abbas, was then resident. Here Sir Anthony's reception was all that the most dignified ambassador could have desired; he was welcomed with gorgeous ceremonials, and received into the confidence of the monarch, who, in a subsequent allusion to their friendly intercourse, said of him: "We have eaten together of one dish and drunk of one cup like brethren." Sir Anthony explained to the Shah the nature of our fortifications, and, in conjunction with his brother Robert, introduced the use of our artillery in the army of the Eastern Potentate, so that ere long he had five hundred pieces of brass cannon and sixty thousand musqueteers in his army. In return, Shah Abbas created him a Mirza, or prince—the first instance of a Christian receiving an oriental title. But his good-will did not stop here: he appointed Sir Anthony his ambassador to the courts of Europe, and at his departure from Ispahan, in bidding him farewell, kissed him three or four times and gave him a seal of gold, saying: "Brother, whatsoever thou dost seal unto, be it the worth of my kingdom, I will see it paid."

Under such favourable auspices Sir Anthony returned to Europe. His first point was the court of Russia, where, after a journey of six months, he arrived in 1599. His reception by the Czar Boris was very cool and unpromising, and, after a few months' stay in Russia, he took his departure for Germany. Meanwhile the suspicious temper of Queen Elizabeth was unfavourable to his designs; yet still this did not prevent his being well received by the Emperor Rodolph at Prague in 1600. He next proceeded by way of Nuremburg, Munich, Innspruck, and Trent to Rome. Here he avowed himself a Roman Catholic; but from some cause which can hardly be explained he left the Pontifical Court in disgrace, and repaired once more to Venice. All his negociations with the various Courts seem to have failed of any useful result.

Soon after this we find Sir Anthony paying a second visit to his patron, the Emperor Rodolph, at Prague, by whom he was despatched on an embassy to the King of Morocco, to stir him up to hostilities against the Grand Seignior, or, as we call him, Sultan of Turkey. At Morocco he lived in a magnificent style and exercised a princely hospitality, making use at the same time of his influence with this barbarous Court for the release of many Portuguese subjects who were held in slavery. Soon afterwards he accepted a commission from the King of Spain, by whom he was created a knight of St. Jago, and made General of the Mediterranean Seas. It was at this time that Sir Anthony's humanity met with a most base and ungrateful return. He had procured freedom from a Turkish prison for three Spaniards, two of whom on their return home promptly paid the money he had advanced for their ransom, but the third, in order to avoid the payment of his share, administered poison to him, causing him to lose his nails and hair, and almost his life. At this period he was suspected of disloyalty to his own sovereign, a suspicion which received some support from the fact of his having presented the Spanish monarch with a hundred pieces of cannon. "How he came by them," says Captain Alex. Hepburn (a Scotchman in the pay of Spain), "I know not, but this is true by God in heaven." The reader will have little difficulty in tracing the source of this artillery, when he recollects the anxiety of the Spanish king to obtain, through Gondomar, his ambassador, permission to import our Sussex cannon, and remembers that Sir Thomas Shirley, Sir Anthony's father, was an extensive manufacturer of Sussex iron. Acts of Parliament were frequently passed prohibiting the export of Sussex-made artillery.

In 1608 Sir Anthony again visited Italy, but returned the same year to Spain. A year later he was in Sicily for the purpose of molesting the Turkish ships. He made an attack upon Mitylene in the Archipelago, but proving rather unsuccessful was deprived of his command. Still, however, he received a pension of 3,000 ducats a year from the Spanish government —a sufficient income indeed ; but such had been his expensive and improvident course of life that he was deeply involved in debt, and nearly the whole of his allowance was devoted to the discharge of his liabilities. Indeed, we are assured that this gallant knight, who had occupied a diplomatic position in nearly every court of Europe, was sometimes actually on the verge of starvation ! The latter part of his life was passed in comparative obscurity. In 1627 we find him still in Spain, as intent as ever upon schemes and negociations, "and daily exhibiting new projects to the Council." He died, according to Grainger, in 1630.

Robert, the second of the three Shirley Brothers, had, like Anthony, accompanied his father to the wars in the Low Countries ; he also saw service afterwards in Italy, and was, as we have seen, the companion of his brother Anthony in his Persian expedition. When, too, Anthony resolved to return to Europe, Robert remained behind at the Court of Shah Abbas, and, notwithstanding the failure of his brother's embassy to the Princes of Europe, retained the favour of the Persian monarch, and availed himself of this to procure liberty of conscience for all Christians throughout the Persian Empire. He showed his own freedom from prejudice by marrying an Eastern lady, Teresia, daughter of a Circassian chief named Ismail Khan, and by her he had two children. In 1608 Shah Abbas despatched him on an embassy to the Christian Powers, giving him a special letter to King James of England, signed " King Abbas, the servant of the King of Kings." Shirley went by way of Poland, and was entertained at Cracow by Sigismund III. The following year he received the honour of knighthood from the Emperor Rodolph, and was created a Count-Palatine of the Empire. He next proceeded to Rome with a suite of eighteen persons, eight of whom were Persians. He wore the Persian costume; but, to show his orthodoxy, crowned his turban by a crucifix. He had a grand reception from Pope Paul V. and twelve Cardinals, and was loaded with empty honours. Thence he proceeded in succession to Milan, Barcelona, and Madrid. At the Spanish Court he was well received, and during his sojourn there was joined by the Lady Teresia, his wife. In 1611 they came to England, and in August of that year were at Wiston, where he found the family affairs in a very disordered state. His father, in fact, had for some time lost the favor of the Court; had been deposed from his office of Treasurer of War in the Low Countries; and, in order to meet his liabilities to the Crown, had been compelled to sell all the family property in Sussex and elsewhere, with the exception of Wiston. This was saved, for a time, by being settled upon his wife, a member of the Kemp family, by whom he had twelve children. The year after his son's return Sir Thomas Shirley died and was buried in Wiston Church. This event did not detain Robert Shirley at home. After a sojourn of eighteen months in England, during which he and his Circassian wife were favorably received at the Court of James the First, he again, at the beginning of 1613, set out for Persia, spending nearly nine months on that dangerous journey, and taking India in his route. Here he paid a passing visit to the Great Mogul. At Ispahan he remained about a year, returning to Europe in 1615, on another embassy. He was successively at Goa, at Lisbon, and at Madrid. His allowance at the Spanish Court was fifteen hundred ducats a month, with house and equipage. Here he resided till 1622, when he again visited Rome, and there

it was that Vandyke painted the fine portraits of Sir Robert
and the Lady Teresia now preserved in the Petworth
collection. In 1624 he was again at the English Court,
where his position was much damaged by the intrigues of the
East India Company, who were jealous of the commercial
policy he was striving to establish. They even represented
his Embassy as an imposture and his credentials as forgeries.
He ultimately returned to Persia, where, overcome by anxiety,
disappointment, aud fatigue, he died at the age of about
fifty, at Kazveen, and was buried there, beneath the threshold
of his own residence, in 1628. The Lady Teresia ended her
singular career by becoming a nun at Rome.

A more "strange, eventful history" than this it is not
easy to conceive. In the extent of its range, and the
boldness of its aims, it seems to image forth the after-deeds
of Englishmen in the East and to "take seisin," as it were
by anticipation, of that great Eastern Empire now governed
by Englishmen. In this respect the Sussex Shirleys stand to
Clive, Warren Hastings, and the other founders of our Indian
Empire in the same relation that Xenophon did to Alexander
the Great. They opened the way to those sunny lands and
showed how Englishmen could make their way through the
greatest perils and the highest paths of adventure to the
topmost heights of Empire.

The third and eldest Shirley, Thomas, yet remains to be
spoken of. Compared with his brothers', his career was
undistinguished. But still, like their's, it was full of action,
though not in an Oriental field. Like Anthony, after a
military education in the Netherlands (where, as we have
seen, the father held a high post), he went to Ireland, and,
like Anthony, was knighted there. Making a clandestine
marriage with a daughter of Sir Thomas Vavasour, he was
punished by Elizabeth (as was Raleigh for a similar offence
with the fair Throckmorton) by an imprisonment of fourteen
weeks. He then again saw service in the Low Countries—
the favourite field of action for enterprising English youth in
Elizabeth's day, but where little was to be won beyond hard

blows. Getting tired of these, and the family fortunes being very low (his father's goods at Wiston had been seized by the Sheriff), Thomas Shirley turned to the sea, and fitting out two vessels as privateers, joined in those buccaneering attacks on the Spaniards which Drake and Hawkins had made so popular. In his first voyage he was pretty successful, capturing four vessels and also sacking some villages; but, transferring his operations to the Mediterranean, he had the ill-luck to be captured by the Turks, and was taken, after an imprisonment in the island of Zoa, to Constantinople. It seemed to be destined that all the Shirleys should be brought in connection with the East. Here he remained in captivity for two years, and then, regaining his liberty by the intercession of James I., after some wanderings in Italy and Germany, he returned to England in 1606, a poorer man than he had left it.

Nor did he ever light on more prosperous days. In his attempts to open the Levant trade, he was in advance of his age and came in contact with parties who got him imprisoned in the Tower on a charge of interfering with their privileges, and he issued from it so broken by debts and misfortunes that he was driven to sell Wiston, and retired to the Isle of Wight, where he died (the date of his death is uncertain) a ruined and disappointed man.

So closed the connection of the Shirleys with Sussex. A grandson of the last owner of Wiston, who attained to some celebrity as a physician, attempted to recover the estate by questioning the power of his grandfather to alienate it; but the purchaser, Sir John Fagg, proved too much for him, and the suit hastened the death of the last Shirley of Wiston. The house still stands, a noble monument of Tudor architecture (the hall is the finest in Sussex), and here the Sussex Archæological Society met in 1851; but it is the residence of a branch of the Goring family, who have held their ground in Sussex better than the Shirleys. The Shirleys still exist as an English family, their head being Earl Ferrers, but in Sussex we no longer know them except as part of the past.

D

The Ancestor of the Sussex Shelleys.

THERE was a period in English history when the Englishman was by no means an insular being—when he belonged to the Continent as much as to England, and when no small part of the Continent belonged to him. What the ocean and the countries beyond the Atlantic became to Englishmen after the loss of the French Provinces—that is, a " field of fame " —the Continent was previously—not only France, but Spain and Italy; and the number of distinguished warriors who at that time closed their careers in foreign lands, either on battle-fields or in adopted homes, was, perhaps, greater than it is now, when, as a rule, Englishmen, however far they may roam for fame or wealth, return " home " to die.

Amongst those whose bones repose on foreign soil—beneath a monument erected to him by the gratitude of the citizens of Florence in the Cathedral of that city—is Sir John Hawkwood, the famous Condottiere chief, whose descendants, the Shelleys, of Lewes and Maresfield, still keep their position in the county. It was by the marriage of Hawkwood's daughter and heiress, Beatrix, with a Shelley that the wealth accumulated by the Chief, and brought by his widow and daughter into England, passed into that family and enabled them to extend their possessions in Sussex.

The origin of Hawkwood was a humble, and, if we regard popular prejudice, an ignoble one. He was, by trade, a tailor, and he was a native of " famous London town." At what age he exchanged the shears and needle for the sword and lance we do not know—most likely at an early one. He gained distinction in France, under such chiefs as the Black

Prince, Chandos, and Sir Walter Manny, and he must have given early proof of higher qualities than mere personal courage, for when the Peace of Brittany was concluded between the French and English Monarchs, and the main body of the combatants were disbanded, Hawkwood was chosen as the leader of one of those bands of adventurers who made war on their own account or let out their services to such princes or cities as might be in want of them and could pay them best. France had been pretty well exhausted by the terrible campaigns of Edward the Third and the Black Prince, and, besides, was no longer so easy a prey as she had been before Duguesclin came upon the scene. But Italy was full of wealth, and was at this time split into a multitude of small States—Republics and otherwise—which carried on perpetual wars with each other, and were only too ready to avail themselves of the courage and skill which the English were renowned for in that age above all the other nations of Europe.

The band of adventurers who had placed themselves under the leadership of Hawkwood were known as the White or English Company—for what reason Sismondi (whom we follow in his History of the Italian Republics of the Middle Ages) does not tell us—perhaps from the colour of their armour, which shone like a mirror—perhaps from their fair complexion. On their first arrival in Italy they numbered 2,500 horse and 2,000 foot, and one of their first exploits, on their road from France to Italy, was one which, however it might scandalise good Catholics in those days, will not be judged·very severely by later ages of Englishmen. They approached within ten leagues of Avignon—then the seat of the Popes—under the pretence of protecting it from another band, composed of Bretons, but, in reality, to draw a contribution from the Pope, who paid a sum of 100,000 florins in order to induce the White Company to proceed on its road to Italy, and enter the service of the Marquis of Montferrat. From Piedmont the Company passed into Lombardy—then, as now, one of the most fertile districts of Italy, bearing with them the scourge of disease as well as that of war; for the Pest, or Black Death, was then devastating Europe; it had broken out in France, and it was introduced by the English Company into Italy.

On the 18th of July, 1363, the English Company arrived at Pisa, then at war with Florence, and was hired by that Republic for a short period. Under the Pisan General, they entered the valley of the upper Arno and took possession of Figline without resistance from the Florentine General. Then surprising and taking his camp they approached and ravaged the neighbourhood of Florence, throwing the inhabitants of that city into the greatest alarm; for, though inferior in numbers to the Florentine forces, the English Company was held in awe by the Italians alike for their courage and skill. They were, says Sismondi, the first to introduce into Italy the custom of counting cavalry by " lances." That name signified three horsemen, acting together, and whose horses only served to carry their heavy armour to the field of battle, where, for the most part, they fought on foot. They wore coats of mail, and their cuisses and boots were of iron. At their side hung a heavy sword and a dagger. Two men held the same lance, which they lowered, and then slowly advanced, closely linked in phalanxes and uttering loud shouts. Every horseman was followed by one or two pages, whole sole occupation was to clean his armour, so that it shone like a mirror.

It was, proceeds Sismondi, the first time that men-at-arms had been seen to dismount in order to fight on foot. To the impenetrable armour of the knight was thus joined the solidity of the foot-soldier, and it was almost impossible to break their phalanx. The English despised the utmost rigour of an Italian winter; continuing their operations during all seasons. They displayed not less dexterity in surprises and *coups de main* than valour in pitched battles. They carried with them ladders divided into three sections, which fitted into each other, by which they could scale the highest towers, and which, not rising higher than the wall, furnished no hold to those above to throw it down.

All parties in Italy—the Popes, aiming at the recovery of what they called their patrimony—the Seigneurs or tyrants of States, like the Visconti, aiming at independence or conquest —the Republics, warring with each other or torn by factions —all were eager to secure the services of these foreign allies, who, on their part, only cared for the pay or plunder they could carry off, and passed from one to the other with the greatest indifference.

The Pisans, as we have seen, were the first to secure the White Company. "They had," says Sismondi, "at their head an adventurer who became subsequently famous in the wars of Italy, and who had already served with distinction in the English wars in France. This was John Hawkwood, called by the Italians Acuto or Auguto, and whose name (he adds in a note) has been disfigured in a thousand ways in the Italian chronicles; but its translation, by a writer of the age, as 'Falcon in a wood,' leaves no doubt as to the identity of its bearer." This leader, he proceeds to tell us, traversed the valley of Nievole in the middle of April, and entered, without resistance, the territory of Pistoai and of Prato, passed before the gates of Florence, and advanced as far as the Mugello, carrying off a large booty from these rich districts. In returning from this expedition at the end of April, the English again drew near to Florence. Some entrenchments had been erected by the Florentines before the gates of their city; but the English attacked and carried them by assault, killing a large number of their defenders. Several of the conquerors received knighthood on the field of battle, and during the ensuing night the Company celebrated the fête of their knighthood; the citizens from their walls beholding the foreign warriors dancing in a round with flambeaux in their hands, and repeating in their orgies the sacred names employed by the heads of the Republic in their solemn deliberations.

After pillaging for two days the fertile fields of Florence, Hawkwood led his forces back to Pisa, having carried desolation into nearly all the Provinces of the Florentine territory.

It would weary the reader to follow the English Condottiere in all his various enterprises. From the Pisan service he passed into that of Galeaz Visconti, the Lord of Milan, whose daughter Violante had married the English King's son, Lionel, Duke of Clarence, and, though opposed to a very superior force of 50,000 Hungarians, Bohemians, &c., led by the German Emperor, Charles IV., into Italy in order to free the Italians from the tyranny of the Visconti, Hawkwood so impeded their progress and harassed their march that they had eventually to quit Italy without performing any exploit.

But the death of the Duke of Clarence broke the tie between Hawkwood and the Visconti; and these latter, says Sismondi, had the imprudence to dismiss John Hawkwood, the ablest of the Captains who then made war in Lombardy. He passed into the service of the Pope's Legates—for Popes had armies then, and made wars—and turned the tide of fortune, attacking and defeating the Milanese army on the 8th May, 1373, and making prisoners nearly all its chiefs. Again, at the head of the Army of the Church, Hawkwood attacked the Florentines, though, to save appearances (for Florence had long been a faithful friend to the Popes), he was disowned by the Legate of Gregory XI. The Legate's secret orders to Hawkwood were to offer to spare the harvests of the Florentines for a certain ransom, but to demand so exorbitant a sum that its non-payment would give a pretext for breaking off the negotiation. The sum demanded by Hawkwood was 130,000 florins, and the Florentines paid it. The Legate wrote to him to break off the bargain; but the English leader spurned such a shameful act and led off his forces, levying, however, large sums on the Siennese and the Pisans as he marched through Tuscany. He then took service with another Papal Legate, and it was whilst in this service that one of the most terrible acts of his life was committed. The city of Bologna had thrown off the yoke of the Pope and driven out the Legate and his forces, including a portion of the English Company, and even taking prisoners Hawkwood's two sons. Hawkwood himself, however, and the bulk of his forces were at a distance, and the English leader hearing of the revolt of Bologna, and suspecting that Faenza was about to follow the example, suddenly entered that city, and giving it up to his soldiers, 4,000 of its population were massacred and the greatest enormities committed. Hawkwood was still at Faenza when he was summoned by the Cardinal of Geneva to join with the Breton Company in punishing another city, Cesene, for having also attempted to revolt from the Pope. Hawkwood hesitated to take part in this crime, on which the Cardinal exclaimed, "I will have blood, blood;" and when the massacre began, he was heard frequently to exclaim, "Kill all." Nobody, indeed, was spared. The Bretons seized infants at the breast by the feet and dashed their brains out against the walls. Priests, nuns—even the virgins consecrated to the Altar—were slain, and 5,000 perished in the butchery. Such was the way in which "Mother Church" treated her disobedient children in the Middle Ages!

This dreadful act of Ecclesiastical vengeance was the last in which Hawkwood took part in the service of the Pope. He now passed, with the English Company, into the service of the Republic of Florence, at that time under the popular and patriotic government of "the Eight," and from this moment we can follow the steps of the English Captain with some feeling of pride and satisfaction; for he was fighting for the cause of liberty and independence against tyranny, oppression, and fraud. Fidelity was not a virtue of the age, and, of all men, the Condottiere could lay the smallest claim to it. But Hawkwood was faithful to the Florentine Republic. It put trust in him, and he gave signal proofs that he was worthy of that trust. Galeaz Visconti, the Duke of Milan, then aiming at the subjugation of all Italy, made war by fraud, falsehood, and treachery. Personally timid, and shutting himself up in his fortified Palace in Pavia, where he took precautions against the very guards by whom he surrounded himself, he was yet a daring as well as unscrupulous politician, and was incessantly attacking his neighbours— now by open force, now by corruption and assassination; his favourite mode of attack being to disarm them by professions of friendship, and then, when they were off their guard, seizing an opportunity of attack. If discovered, he disowned his instruments, and commenced a fresh web of deceit; for he never lost his temper — never abandoned his designs—never gave up the hope of deluding his victims. To this despicable but dangerous man, the Republic of Florence was the only Power in Italy that offered real defiance—that refused to believe in his professions, and that did not fall a victim to his arts. And Hawkwood was the General whom the Republic opposed to the numerous chiefs that Galeaz had in his pay, and by whom, and his own forces, he was continually attacking Florence and its allies. One by one, these latter fell before him. Sienna and Pisa— recently Republics—Verona, Vicenza—where the Della Scalas had reigned—and Padua, the seat of the Carraras, were subjugated by his arms or seduced by his gold. Florence alone was proof against both. The Pope was his ally and Venice shrank from open war with him, only covertly giving assistance to his enemies. Amongst these was one man who was fit to co-operate with Hawkwood, the General of the Florentines, in defence of Italy. This was Francis of Carrara, who, after being stripped of his possessions by Galeaz, had escaped with his wife (then near her confinement) from Italy into Germany under circumstances of danger and suffering for wife and husband that have made them a favourite subject for poets and painters. Carrara now determined, with the aid of Florence, to recover his possessions. In this he was signally successful. The citizens of Padua received him with open arms; the Milanese garrison was driven out; and the Florentines were now in a position to attack the Duke of Milan instead of being attacked by him. With this view they entered into an engagement with another Condottiere Chief, a Frenchman, the Count d'Armagnac, who was to march with his Company of Bretons into Lombardy on the one side whilst Hawkwood advanced with his English and Florentines on the other, effecting a junction under the walls of Milan. Hawkwood faithfully performed his part of the plan. He marched to Padua, was there joined by the contingents of that State and of Bologna, and then, on the 15th of May, 1391, he advanced on Milan, by Vicenza and Verona, with a force of 6,600 cuirassiers, 1,200 musketeers, and a large body of infantry. Passing the Mincio and the Oglio, he arrived within fifteen miles of Milan, and celebrated, on the banks of the Adda, by which river alone he was separated from the capital of Galeaz Visconti, the fête of St. John, the Patron Saint of Florence. Here he awaited the arrival of the Count D'Armagnac, who had received strict injunctions from the envoys of Florence to avoid any engagement until he had passed the Po and joined Hawkwood. Instead of which, although a veteran warrior of eighty years, he suffered himself to be drawn by his impetuosity into a battle with Galeaz's General, Jacques del Verme, in which his whole force was either cut to pieces or made prisoners ; he himself being so badly wounded that he died shortly afterwards in the hands of his enemies, not without suspicion that his end was hastened by poison.

Hawkwood now found himself in a position of the greatest danger. He was far advanced in an enemy's country, with several deep rivers between him and Florence, and was about to be attacked by superior forces. The head-quarters of Jacques del Verme, in fact, were only separated by a little stream and a distance of a mile and a half from Hawkwood's camp. Hawkwood shut himself up in this, with every appearance of fear, allowing the enemy's men-at-arms to approach his entrenchments and utter all kinds of insults. For four days he presented this aspect to the foe, and then, on the fifth, when the Milanese troops were advancing in greater number, as though to storm his camp, he threw open the gates and suddenly fell upon them with such fury as to put them to the rout and to capture above a thousand horse.

Upon a smaller scale, this reminds one of the fury with

which Hannibal broke through the Roman lines on their first attempt to besiege Capua, and of the similar feat of Napoleon, when, throwing open the gates of Dresden, he drove back the armies of Europe, assembled before that city. But as, on each of these occasions, the routed armies closed upon their prey, so did the forces of the Visconti re-assemble and follow upon the traces of Hawkwood, who, passing the Oglio and the Mincio without interruption, found, on arriving on the banks of the much swifter Adda, that its dykes had been fortified against him, and some of these dykes having been broken by Jacques del Verme, the plain in which Hawkwood's army now found itself was suddenly inundated, and his camp became the centre of a lake which hourly grew deeper and threatened soon to cover the ground on which his soldiers stood. So convinced was the Milanese General that he had caught his opponent in a trap that he wrote to Galeaz to ask how he would have his enemies sent to him, and he sent to Hawkwood, by a trumpeter, a cage with a live fox in it! The English General (remarks the Italian historian who tells the story), on receiving the significant present, enjoined its bearer to tell his General that the fox did not seem to be very sad, and that, doubtless, it knew by what door it could get out of the trap!

No other General but Hawkwood (says Sismondi) would have known or dared to venture upon such an issue; but that old warrior, who joined great prudence to great courage, had inspired his soldiers with such confidence that they never hesitated to follow him wherever he led. Hawkwood left his tents all standing and his flags flying on the ground where he had planted them, and, at break of day, he boldly entered the submerged plain, himself leading his army towards those dykes of the Arno which lie seven or eight miles below Lignogo. In this way he marched all the day and a part of the following night, with his horses up to their bellies in water. His march was impeded by the mud, in which his soldiers frequently embedded themselves, and by the canals, which could not be distinguished from the water which covered them. Thus they traversed the whole Veronese valley until they arrived opposite Castle Baldo, upon the dyke of the Adige, the bed of which was dry. At this Castle, which belonged to the Lord of Padua, Francis Carrara, Hawkwood refreshed his troops. The weakest horses and some of the foot soldiers had perished in so fatiguing and dangerous a march ; but the army of Florence and of its allies was saved ; for Jacques del Verme never thought of following up the pursuit by such a track !

The Milanese General, finding that the English fox had found a door to escape by, now attempted to reach Florence before him. But Hawkwood was quickly on his footsteps, checked his ravages, and cut off his scattered soldiers, so that at last the Milanese General feared to be caught in his turn, and, indeed, only escaped by abandoning his camp in the middle of the night and flying across the Apennines with the loss of a portion of his infantry.

So the English General came off victorious at last. He had won many battles; but this was, perhaps, his greatest feat of generalship. It was also his last; for peace was now concluded between the two belligerents, both exhausted by their efforts, and, before hostilities broke out again, and at the very moment, says Sismondi, when a great captain was more than ever needful to the Florentine Republic, she lost that one to whom she owed her success in the late war. John Hawkwood died on the 16th of March, 1394, of disease (the greater number of men in those days perished by the sword, by the executioner, or by poison), upon an estate which he had bought near Florence. The Government of the Republic caused him to be interred with the greatest honours in the Cathedral of the city; and, adds the historian of the Italian Republics, his tomb is still to be seen there, surmounted by an equestrian statue.

We have seen that Hawkwood had two sons old enough to take part with him in the dangers of war; but whether they survived their father, and, if so, their after-fortunes, we

do not learn from Sismondi. They certainly did not equal
him in the art of war, or we should hear of them in the
subsequent wars that devastated Italy. We know, however,
that his wife and his daughter returned to England, and that
the latter became the wife of one of the Sussex Shelleys, in
whose veins, therefore, the blood of John Hawkwood, the
renowned Condottiere Chief and the General of the Republic
of Florence, still flows.

Sussex Families: Their Ups and Downs.

ENGLAND ought to be a country of old families, for it has not been disturbed by the presence of an invader for these 800 years, and for the last 200 of them its Government has been a settled one. Of all English counties, too, Sussex ought to be the Eden of old families, for, whilst it is near enough to the metropolis to share in the protection thrown around the heart of the nation, it is, or rather was, distant enough from London to make it a pleasant retreat from the turmoil of a great city. Great cities of its own it never had until within this last half-century; but it was dotted over with small towns and villages which nestled under the Castles, Halls, and Mansions of Dukes, Earls, and Baronets, Knights and Squires: places within fifty or sixty miles of London, and yet so secluded in themselves—so remote from the din of war and the conflicts of parties, so fenced about by villainous roads and dense woods, that it is the well-weighed opinion of Mr. Lower that a battle like that of Naseby might have been fought in England and the news of it never have reached the inhabitants of many of these Sussex hamlets!

A county like this must have been, one would think, prolific in old families, and we should expect to find them abounding in all the luxuriance of tropical growth.

But what is the fact? Sussex can boast of very few really old families. The process of family disintegration and dispersion seems to have been as rapid in Sussex as in any other English county, if not more so. If the county itself was a very Eden of repose, there was a spirit of restlessness in its occupants which drove them, like Adam and Eve of old, out of their Paradise, in search of that good and evil they were so anxious to know upon a wider stage. Where are the Poynings, the Pierrepoints, the Brownes, the Poyntzs, the Lunfords, the Culpeppers (with whom both Sussex and Kent swarmed in the time of the Charles's), the Lewknors, the De la Bordes, the Challoners, the Coverts, the Carylls (Pope's friends), the Castedells, the Combes, the Farnfolds, the Bisshopps, the Wells's (of Buxted), the Shirleys (of Eastern renown), the Wharbletons, and many other noble and knightly families who were once as "plentiful as blackberries" in Sussex, and held, at one time or another, the larger part of its broad acres in their hands? May we not reply, in the smooth and sadly humorous lines of Praed, " they are forgotten—

> —"as old debts,
> By persons who are used to borrow;
> Forgotten,—as the sun that sets,
> When shines a new one on the morrow;
> Forgotten—like the luscious peach
>   That blessed the schoolboy last September;
> Forgotten—like a maiden speech,
>   Which all men praise, but none remember."

Saxon, Norman, Anglo-Saxon, Anglo-Norman, Cavalier and Puritan, Protestant and Catholic, Whig and Tory—they have either voluntarily vacated their seats or been pushed from them by new men, who are as little remembered as they; for, in this county, new families soon become old; if we have, like Bolingbroke, a genius to rise, we have also, like Falstaff, "a kind of alacrity in sinking," or else the present roll of county families would not be so meagre in names that were once in every Sussex mouth.

But it is not our intention to write an essay on this theme, or to go to past generations for examples of the proposition, that families, if they spring up quickly, do not strike deeply into Sussex soil. We prefer to take a modern instance which meets us on our very threshold and lives in the memories of men not yet very old; that is, it *would* live in their memories

but for the rapid rush of modern events, which, with their
lightning-like speed and obtrusive force, crowd out everything
that is older than yesterday. But some Brightonians will,
perhaps, see the force of our illustration of the vanity of
family pride when we put the simple question: " Is there a
Wigney in the town of Brighton at the present moment ?"

Of course, the Wigneys of Brighton were mushrooms.
So were the Howards and Cavendishes once upon a time.
That only strengthens our position. They *were* mushrooms—
springing up no one knew how or whence. But, mushroom-
like, they throve and spread, until they filled a large space
in men's eyes; and if wealth, magisterial dignity, political
power, and fashionable position could give consequence,
they possessed it in Brighton fifty years ago.

No family, indeed, in the history of this town ever rose
so rapidly or so high as the Wigneys, and none ever fell more
quickly or completely.

The founder of it, old William Wigney, was, according
to the voice of rumour, which dogs the heels of prosperous
men, originally a pedlar, and made his money by bringing
over franc-pieces from France and passing them as shillings.
There was doubtless a spice of truth in the report. He came
from the north of England at the close of the last century,
set up as a draper in North Street, and married the daughter
of a captain of one of the vessels running between Brighton
and Dieppe. Very likely he dabbled a little in smuggling—
as who on the Sussex coast that had the chance did not ?—
and was not found out! At all events, he made money
enough to start a bank at a time when it needed more
confidence than cash to do so; and when the panic of 1825
came which gave the *coup de grace* to so many mushroom
bankers, he had so consolidated his position as to breast
the storm boldly and to outlive it. Whilst other and older
establishments in the town went down, we have heard those
who remembered that terrible time, when all credit seemed
to have perished, say that the stern-looking handsome old

man took his station each day at his counter, from the opening to the closing hour, with heavy bags of gold at his elbow, ready to pay in cash all demands. That of itself was enough to stop a "run." Wigney's was soon voted "as safe as the Bank of England;" and the bank came out of the ordeal stronger than ever. From that day not a suspicion was raised of its solvency until—but we are anticipating.

Many a proud day was given to the Wigneys before they had to answer to the Nemesis that waits upon success. They were prosperous in more ways than one, and they sent out many shoots, and, to all appearance, sturdy ones. There was George, the brewer, a solid, steady-going man, who kept to his beer-making and beer-selling; and there was his son, young George, a dashing young fellow, brimful of spirits; and there was Robert Wigney, " Gipsy Bob," a brother of the old man, and a man of talent and energy. And there was Clement, a young man of pleasing appearance and popular manners. But, above all, there was Isaac Newton Wigney, the third and favourite son of the old banker—the heir to his prosperity—on whom all his dreams of ambition rested.

And were they not realised? Did he not live to see this favourite son the first Member returned to Parliament by enfranchised Brighton? Did he not see him take his seat on the Brighton Bench as a Magistrate of the County? Did he not see him marry a beautiful woman, of good family, and assume with her a position in fashionable society, which, whatever envy it might excite, could not be challenged? For Isaac Newton—or, as he preferred to be called, Newton Wigney—had the look and manners of a gentleman, and, though he might lack that ease which time or Nature only gives, yet he was admitted into the best society of Brighton and of London. His success in this direction was, indeed, fatal to him in the end. Not only did it excite envy, but, in the sequel, it gave rise to suspicion. It provoked political hostility; for the Wigneys had sprung from the people within the memory of all. Isaac Newton was, on first coming forward, supported by the Radicals as well as Whigs of the town as a people's man, and when he began, as he soon did, to cool to his Radical colleague (George Faithfull) and place his chief reliance on the Whigs; when he was known to frequent fashionable circles, to affect fashionable manners, and to "scorn the base degrees by which he did ascend" the ladder of Fortune, then the wrath of the Brighton Radicals (roused by the defeat of their man in the second contest for the Borough, in 1835) burst out against the upstart—the *parvenu*—and, in a moment of necessity, when the Tories pressed hard upon the Liberals, some half-dozen men played traitor to the cause, split with Dalrymple, and "turned out the Banker."

It was a severe blow to the Wigney family; but the motives of those who dealt it were so petty that the public sympathy was with the ejected Member, and the Radical party, which sacrificed a seat to gratify personal animosity, fell into disrepute, and did not for many years recover its position. At the next election (in 1841) Isaac Newton Wigney was re-seated as Member for Brighton, and at this period he seemed to stand as high as ever, if not higher, on Fortune's wheel. But, in point of fact, several things had occurred which tended to undermine his position. His father had died, and the old man's property was distributed among several members of his family instead of being consolidated in one focus—the Bank. Then the will of the old man, which was published, showed that his wealth was not so great as it had been supposed to be. Still, the proportion left to the son, who succeeded to the bank, Isaac Newton Wigney, was sufficient to secure its credit, if the same caution and judgment which its founder had displayed had been still brought to its management. But the position of the son was very different from that of the father. There were claims upon the former, in respect both to his political position and his character as a man of fashion, which the old man had known nothing of. A portion of the year had necessarily to be spent in London, and, as was now made known, in the dissipations

E

of London life ; for among the witnesses who were called to give evidence in the famous De Ros trial, the card-cheating case, which threw such discredit on the highest circles, was Isaac Newton Wigney; and this fact did more to damage his credit with sober-thinking men of business than anything else.   At this time many accounts were withdrawn from Wigney's, and though the bank still went on, the head of it was struggling with his fate.   At this time such as knew Isaac Newton Wigney could but be struck by the care-worn lines on his face, and the quickness with which he seemed to age. He must, indeed, have suffered for some years all the tortures of Damocles: the sword was suspended by a thread above his head, and he knew that it was only a question of time when it should fall.   His efforts to rescue himself only involved him in deeper ruin.   He entered into speculations of the nature of which he knew nothing, and which turned out to be failures, and at length he was unable to meet his engagements, and the long-suspended blow fell.   It was not the loss of public confidence; the character won for the bank by its founder served it well up to the last.   Nor was it a " run " or a " panic."   It was the exhaustion of all the funds of the establishment in disastrous speculations, and the refusal of its London agents to make more advances, to meet inevitable demands, that obliged it to close its doors.   Business was carried on at it in the usual way up to the closing hour on Thursday, March 3, 1842, and though rumours were current in the town that night (traced, it was said, to the too frank disclosures of a younger member of the family who was dining at the officers' mess) as to the event of the morrow, it was not until the day and the hour—ten o'clock of Friday, the 4th of March, 1842—arrived that the certainty of the catastrophe was made known by " the handwriting on the wall."   On the closed shutters of the Bank in East-street was posted the fatal notice:—

" Messrs. Wigney & Co. deeply regret the painful
necessity of suspending their payments."

" *March* 4, 1842."

So the edifice which had been reared up by a life of care and frugality was tumbled down in a few years by the opposite qualities, and yet more by the pride and vanity which had over-weighted the original foundation. For this Newton Wigney was not altogether to blame—his father was the original sinner; but the son had to pay the penalty. And a terrible one it was. Immediate death would have been a lighter punishment. What remained to him of life was a prolonged agony. He was not of that hard texture which can outface shame or brave misfortune; on the contrary, he was of a delicate and susceptible organisation, rather inclining to the effeminate. And yet the ordeal he had to pass through would have tried the most iron nerves. He was made a bankrupt, and, by the Bankruptcy Laws of that day, the examinations were conducted in the towns where the bankrupt's business had been carried on. Thus, Isaac Newton Wigney, for years the foremost man in his native town—the first Member it had sent to Parliament—the favourite son of the rich old banker—but now Member and Banker and Magistrate—had to appear almost as a criminal in a Court held in the Town Hall of Brighton, presided over by a Barrister of Brighton, crowded by people who had known him in his prosperity, and had to undergo the questioning of a local attorney who certainly could not be complimented for the delicacy of his feelings or the refinement of his language. Some of the questions put to Isaac Newton Wigney by Sidney Walsingham Bennett, touching his wife's expenses and property, were such as would hardly be tolerated at the present day, and would not have been permitted even then, but that men's feelings were steeled against pity, or even decency, by recent losses, and by a desire of vengeance against the unfortunate man who was held to be responsible for those losses. To him these questions must have been like the stabs of a dagger, or rather like the blows of a hatchet in the hands of a butcher. How he held up against the torture is marvellous: how, day after day, he came up to the table—the stake—and narrated the

tale of his ill-starred attempts to retrieve his position by
engaging in speculations of which he knew nothing—could
explain nothing—is one of those things which, when we
consider the physical and moral weakness of the man and the
demand it made on his brain and heart and nerve, is a thing
that baffles one.   But the fact was, he was drawing on his life
resources; he was concentrating in a few agonising days the
strength that would, under happier circumstances, have been
diffused over long years.   He was, in popular phrase, being
killed by inches.   He passed through the ordeal, as men do
pass through such things, and, coming out of it alive, very
little if any pity was given to him.   The pity, naturally enough,
was bestowed on those—and there were many—who were
ruined or impoverished or embarrassed by his imprudencies.
But, looking back at the scene as it still lives in the memory
of those who were eye-witnesses of it—looking back upon
that scene, and recalling that pale, haggard, scared, but once
handsome, if weak, face—knowing that his nature was a kind
and gentle one—knowing that he loved and was proud of his
wife and doted on his son—remembering that he had been,
during the whole of his life, petted by his father, and looked up
to by every Wigney as the pride of the family—remembering
all this, and what he had to endure as he stood there to explain
and justify acts which could not be explained or justified, and
that his questioner was the legal bully of Brighton—we can
but feel pity for the man, and think that, if the punishment
inflicted on him be measured by that which others worse than
he have since met with in the same position, he was hardly
dealt by.

But he came out of the torture-room alive, and pity was
dead, at least for a time.   We do not know, indeed, that it
ever came—certainly not in his life-time.   He did not long
survive his disgrace and ruin; and the family dispersed—sank
out of sight much more rapidly than it had sprung up.   Such
of the elder members as remained in the town died quickly;
the younger ones went to Australia, India, Scotland, London,
and were lost in the vast throng of life.   At the present

moment there is not, so far as we know, a remnant of the Wigney family left in Brighton.

But this local instance of the rise and fall of families has nothing but its recent occurrence to distinguish it from the many other instances which might be cited of the rapidity with which families spring up to wealth and position in this England of ours, and then sink again into their original insignificance. For it is not to be supposed that in every case, or even in the majority of cases, the family dies out—root and branch. It has been conjectured that even the blood of the Plantagenets may still flow in very humble veins. And men who had Pierrepoints and Lewknors, Culpepers and Challoners, Carylls and Coverts for their ancestors, may be plodding as labourers over the broad acres which their forefathers owned, and have no higher ambition than to earn their 16s. or 18s. a week! If this be so in the staid and sedate country—as most certainly it is—how much more so is it the case in modern towns, where every decade changes the face of society, and makes the lines in which Homer described the mortality of men applicable to their fortunes :—

> Like leaves on trees the race of man is found ;
> Now green in youth, now withering on the ground.
> Another race the following Spring supplies,
> They fall successive, and successive rise.
> So generations in their course decay ;
> *So flourish these when those have passed away.*

The warning is some 3,000 or 4,000 years old. And yet but little heed is taken of it ; and the pride of family—a pride that dates from yesterday and will die out to-morrow—is still one of the strongest and most disagreeable ingredients of modern society !

The Sussex Martyrs.

IN the sharp agony of three years which England underwent for conscience' sake in the reign of Queen Mary, the county of Sussex bore a large part. Thirty-three men and women, married and single, perished at the stake in different parts of Sussex from 1555 to 1557, and as Hume estimates the total number of victims in that persecution to have been 277, it is obvious that Sussex furnished more than its due proportion to " the noble Army of Martyrs."

It is not improbable that it owed this honorable distinction in part to its adjacency to the Metropolis, which brought it under the eyes of the Ministers of the Queen ; also to the circumstance of the diocese being put, in the latter years of her reign, under the rule of a man, Dr. Christopherson, who stood forth as a champion of the Romish Church. But, after taking into account these reasons for sharper persecution in Sussex, we may claim something for the character of the Sussex husbandman and artisan, from whose ranks the majority of the victims were taken. To those who have any knowledge of the Sussex farmer, even in these days, when men are no longer called upon to seal their faith with their blood, the stoutness, or, if you will, the stubbornness with which they maintain their opinions must be quite familiar, and no less the independence with which they exercise their cherished right of private judgment. We have often been astonished at the freedom of speculation, and the wide range it takes, in a Sussex farmhouse, and as we listened to the theological opinions of men of this class we have ceased to wonder at the zeal and fortitude with which they defended the doctrines of the Reformers in the terrible days of Queen Mary, or at the readiness with which they responded to the call of the great champions of English liberty in the succeeding century. Whether as Protestants or as Puritans, it is certain that the yeomen of Sussex had turned to good account the opportunity which was given them in the Eighth Harry's time, to "search the Scriptures." From the translating of the Bible into English in that reign, and from the teaching of children to read in the following one of Edward VI., it is pretty evident that this spirit of independent thought in matters of religion sprang. In Sussex the seed fell on a soil ripe and ready for it, and in the lonely homestead, or in the humble village workshop, that attention was bestowed on the Sacred Writings that brought forth its fruit in such men as Derick Carver and Richard Woodman.

To the former of these two men belongs the honor of having been the first to suffer as a Sussex Martyr. Derick Carver was an inhabitant of Brighthelmston, and had been so for eight or nine years when the storm of religious persecution burst upon him. By birth he was a Fleming—by business a brewer; and to him is attributed the introduction of "true beer"—that is, beer brewed from hops—into this part of the country. From the days of Von Arteveldt brewers have, as a rule, ranged themselves on the side of freedom, and Derick Carver approved himself no unworthy follower of the art. Coming into England, with many other natives of the Low Countries, in the favorable times of Edward VI., when foreigners were even allowed to form their own religious communuties independently of the State Church, Carver had been in the habit of collecting a little congregation of men of his own way of thinking at his house in Brighthelmston, and it was, doubtless, this invasion of the rights of the clergy, as they deemed it, that drew down on him, on the accession of Mary to the throne, the vengeance of the newly-restored priests. Towards the close of October, 1554, Carver being then 40 years of age, he and twelve of his flock—of whom only three, Thomas Iveson, William Veisy, and John Launder, are named

—were apprehended as they were at prayer in Carver's house, using the service of Edward VI.'s time, by Mr. Edward Gage, of Firle, a magistrate of the county, and sent up to the Queen's Council in London. As only the four whose names are given are afterwards referred to in Foxe's narrative, we must conclude that the other eight were discharged. Carver, Iveson, Veisy, and Launder were subjected to a preliminary examination and then committed to Newgate, where they lay above seven months before it suited the convenience of Bonner, Bishop of London, to question them more strictly as to their religious doctrines. On the 8th of June, 1555, they were brought from Newgate to the Bishop's house in London, and here, in his chamber, questioned by Bonner himself, and, as the result of this oral examination, they made, and signed, certain "confessions," as they were called in that day, or declarations of faith, upon which a capital charge of heresy was founded against them. It being demanded of them, at the close of the examination, if they "would stand to their answers?" Launder replied, "I will never go from these answers so long as I live," and the three others making a similar declaration, they were remanded to Newgate until the 10th of the same month (June), and then again brought before Bonner, who sat on this occasion at the Bishop's Consistory at St. Paul's. Their "confessions" and their answers to the "articles," or charges, previously objected to them by the Bishop, were now read over to them in the order usually adopted by Bonner at the condemnation of (so-called) heretics, and the Bishop first put it to Carver if he would stand to the same? To which (writes Foxe, in his "Acts and Monuments") "the sayd Diricke answered, that he would, ' for your doctrine (quoth he) is poyson and sorcery. If Christ were here, you would put Him to a worse death than He was put to before. You say that you can make a God; ye can make a pudding as well. Your ceremonyes in the Church be beggary and poyson. And farther, I say that auricular confession is contrary to God's word, and very poyson ; ' with divers other such words."

Whereupon, proceeds Foxe, the Bishop, "seeing this

constancy, and that neyther his accustomed flatteries, nor yct his cruel threatenings, could once move this good man to enclyne to their idolatry, pronounced his usuall and generall blessing, as well towards this Diricke as also upon the sayd John Launder," and then handed them over to the secular authorities, the Sheriffs, for the execution of the Church's sentence.

In the case of Carver, this took place at Lewes, then the chief town in the eastern part of the county, and the inhabitants of which, it is obvious, inclined to the Reformed faith, for, proceeds Foxe, in his graphic and touching chronicle of Carver's last moments—

"At his comming into the town of Lewes to be burned, the people called upon hym, beseechyng God to strengthen him in the faith of JESUS CHRIST. He thanked them, and prayed unto God, that of hys mercy he would strengthen them in the lyke faith. And when hee came to the signe of the Starre, the people drew neare unto him, where the Sheriffe sayd that he had found him a faithfull man in al his aunswers. And as he came to the stake, he kneled downe and made his prayers, and the Sheriffe made hast. Then hys booke was throwen into the barrel, and when hee had strypt him selfe (as a joyfull member of God) he went into the barrel him selfe. And as soone as ever he came in, he tooke up the booke and threw it among the people, and then the Sheriffe commaunded in the Kyng and Queenes name, in paine of death, to throw in the booke againe. And immediately, that faithfull member spake with a joyfull voyce, saying:

"'Deare brethren and sistern, wytnes to you all that I am come to seale with my bloud CHRISTES Gospell, for because I knowe that it is true; it is not unknowen unto al you, but that it hath bene truly preached here in Lewes, and in all places in England, and now it is not. And for because that I wyll not denye here Gods Gospell, and be obedient to mans lawes, I am condemned to dye. Deare brethren and sistern, as many of you as do beleve upon the father, the sonne, and the holye ghost, unto everlasting lyfe, see you doe the workes appertaining to the same. And as many of you as do beleve upon the Pope of Rome, or any of hys lawes, which he sets forth in these daies, you do beleve to your utter condemnation, and except the great mercy of God, you shall burne in hell perpetually.'

"Immediately the Sheriffe spake unto him, and sayd: 'If thou doest not beleve on the Pope thou art damned body and soule.' And farther the Sheriffe sayd unto him; 'speake to thy God, that he may deliver thee now, or els to strike me down to the example of this people;' but this faithfull member said, 'the Lorde forgive you your sayings.' And then spake hee againe to all the people there present, with a loude voice, saying, 'deare brethren, and all you whom I have offended in wordes or in dede, I aske you for the Lordes sake to forgeve me, and I hartly forgeve all you, which have offended me in thought, word, or deede.' And he sayd further in his prayer, 'Oh Lorde my God, thou hast written; *He that will not forsake wife, children, house, and all that ever he hath, and take up thy crosse and folow thee, is not worthy of thee.* But thou, Lorde, knowest that I have forsaken all, to come unto thee; Lorde, have mercy uppon me, for unto thee I commend my spirit; and my soule doth rejoyce in thee.' These were the last wordes of that faithfull member of CHRIST, before the fire was put to him. And afterward that the fire came to him, he cried; 'Oh Lord have mercy upon me,' and sprong up in the fire, callyng upon the name of JESUS, and so ended."

The heroism and steadfastness with which the Brighton brewer maintained his religious opinions and underwent his terrible fate are impressed upon us the more strongly by the fact that he was a husband and a father, and also, as Foxe remarks, "a man whom the Lord had blessed as well with temporal riches as with his spiritual treasures." His business as a brewer was a prosperous one, and it was carried on prosperously by his son after his father's death. This is deducible from the will of the martyr's grandson—also a Derick Carver, and a "beere brewer" of Brighthelmston—which was found by the late Mr. M. A. Lower in the Lewes Registry, under the date of December 6th, 1628. That the Christian name of the martyr was held in high respect by his descendants is shown not only by the grandson bearing it, but also by his giving it to his eldest son, then a minor, but whom, in his will, he directs to dwell with his mother, " Helping forward her business of bruinge." Mr. Lower adds that down to a late period the Christian name Derick was found among Brighton families; and there is still a tradition that the Bible which figured so prominently in the martyrdom of Carver was in existence and in the possession of a Lewes family. But this would scarcely agree with the inference to be drawn from Foxe's narrative that after being thrown by Carver out of the fire it was, at the command of the Sheriff, thrown in again.

But, if the book perished, the memory of its owner lived, and his family, it is clear, flourished in Brighton "unto the third and fourth generation."

Two at least of the three men who shared Carver's imprisonment followed in his footsteps to " the bitter end." But not at the same place. The policy of Bonner doubtless was to strike a general fear into the people of Sussex, and with that view the scenes of martyrdom were assigned to three different places. Thomas Iveson was burnt at the stake in Chichester, and John Launder at Steyning. They were both natives of Godstone, in Surrey—Launder being described in his "confession" as a husbandman and 25 years of age ; and Iveson as a carpenter. Launder had already displayed his steadfastness to his faith in his reply to Bonner, and Iveson was not less firm. Being " earnestly travailed " to recant, he exclaimed, " I would not recant and forsake my opinion and belief for all the goodes in London. I do appeale to God's mercy, and wil be none of your Church, nor submit myself to the same ; and that I have sayd I will say agayne. And if there came an Anngell from Heaven to teach me any other doctrine than which I am in now I would not beleve him."

No details are given of these two men's last moments ; but, with such sentiments, who can doubt that they bore faithful testimony to the last ?

As Foxe is silent in respect to the fourth man sent up to London for examination—William Veisy—we must conclude that he escaped the fate of his companions.

These, the first executions in Sussex in the reign of Mary, took place in the July of 1555, and it was probably expected that such terrible examples would have the effect of turning the people back from the reformed faith and of making them conform to the will of the Queen and her Ministers. At all events, it was nearly a year later before any fresh victims were sent to the stake in Sussex, and then the town of Lewes again saw the fire of religious persecution lighted in her High Street, and four martyrs perished in it, namely, Thomas Harland, carpenter, of Woodmancote ; John Oswald, husbandman, of the same place ; Thomas Avyngton, turner, of Ardingly ; and Thomas Read. They had all lain for a long time in the Queen's Bench, and persisted in their rejection of the Mass. One of the chief reasons for arresting them was, that they did not come to church, and of one of them (Read) the story is handed down by Foxe that, previous to his arrest, he had resolved to go to church ; but, the night following, he saw, in a vision, "a company of tall young men in white, very pleasant to behold, to whom he would have joined himself; but it would not be. Then he looked on himself and he was full of spots, and therewith waked, and took hold and stood to the truth."

As these four martyrs suffered at Lewes on the 6th of June, 1556, two other victims to the same cause trod the same path a few days afterwards (about the 20th) at the same place. These were Thomas Whoode, minister, and Thomas Mylles, the former supposed to have been the minister of one of the seven parishes of Lewes, to whom Derick Carver alluded at the stake, when he said, "Christ's gospel hath been truly preached here in Lewes;" and the native place of Mylles being supposed by the late Mr. M. A. Lower to be Hellingly, from the fact of a John Mylles, "of Hellingly," having subsequently suffered in the same cause.

The persecution was now at its height. The constancy of the sufferers, or, as their judges called it, their obstinacy, and the compassion which this excited in the lookers-on, raised the worst passions of the human heart in the men who had set themselves to change the religion of the English people, and the growing work having been devolved by Gardiner on Bonner,—a man, says Hume, "of profligate manners and of a brutal character, who seemed to rejoice in the torments of the unhappy sufferers,"—it went on with accelerated pace.

In Sussex the ground of persecution was now extended. At Eastgrinstead two men, Thomas Dungate and John Forman, and a woman, Ann Tree—more familiarly known as "Mother Tree"—were sent to the stake on the 18th June, 1556, "paciently abidying," says Foxe, "what the furious rage of man could say or work agaynst them;" and on the 24th September, in the same year, four men suffered at Mayfield, in the eastern extremity of the county, of whom the names of two only—John Hart and Thomas Ravensdale—have come down to us.

It was in the following year, 1557, the third of the persecution, and when the calamitous reign of Mary was approaching
its close (she died in the autumn of 1558), that the most
terrible holocaust was offered up at the shrine of bigotry; no
less than ten victims, four of them women, being burnt
in one fire at Lewes on the 22nd of June. The character,
too, of one of the sufferers, and the circumstances preceding
and accompanying his arrest, serve to invest this wholesale
act of slaughter with unusual interest. If Derick Carver is
entitled to head the roll of Sussex Martyrs by priority of
suffering, Richard Woodman may claim to be the most eminent
by his social position, his learning, and his intellect. He was
one of those Sussex ironmasters who, by their skill and industry,
had added so much to the wealth and importance of their
county, and he was descended from a family of considerable
antiquity in Sussex. Besides his iron-works at Warbleton,
where he lived, he was an agriculturist, and possessed manorial
property in the shape, to use his own words, of "a lordship and
a honour and half a honour," worth the net sum of £56 per
annum, equal to nearly £500 at the present day. He employed
no less than a hundred men, and was, consequently, a man
of influence in his parish. At the time when the storm of
persecution burst upon him he was 30 years of age, and having
married early, and, as after-facts showed, a woman worthy of
him, he was the happy father of several children. The change
which followed the accession of Mary was, to such a son of
the Reformation as Woodman, a most trying one; but it is
evident, by what followed, that he had not neglected the
opportunities which the seven years' reign of Edward the
Sixth had given him. The Bible had not been translated into
English in vain for him, and he had studied and mastered those
points of doctrine on which the Reformers and the Romanists
took such deadly issue. When, therefore, the Rector of
Warbleton, one George Fayrebank, a married priest, who had
been accustomed to teach and defend the doctrines of the
Reformation in the days of Edward VI., saw fit, to use the
homely but forcible language of Foxe, to " turn head to tail

and preach clean contrary to that which he had before taught,"
Woodman stood forth and admonished him for his inconstancy:
" Now before-tyme he had taught them one thing, and now
another," and desired him to teach them the truth.   As was
to be expected from such a reproof, addressed to such a man
at such a time, Woodman was quickly called to account for
his words ; he was apprehended and brought before four
Justices of the Peace for the county of Sussex : Mr. John
Ashburnham, Mr. Tofton, Mr. Culpeper, and Mr. Robertes,
by whom he was committed to the Queen's Bench prison.
This was in June, 1553, so that Woodman was really the first
person called to account for his opinions in Sussex, and he
continued in this prison for nearly a year and a half, and was
then transferred by Dr. Story to a place of confinement for
Protestants, popularly called " Bonner's tollhouse."   He
remained in this place for two months, and during that time,
according to his own written statement, preserved by Foxe,
was called several times before Bonner, having previously, whilst
in the Queen's Bench, been twice before the then Bishop of
Chichester—Day—and five times before the Queen's Commissioners.   In these early days of Queen Mary's reign there was
some hesitation in the career of persecution, afterwards so
headlong ; and Gardiner had not yet handed over the work
to Bonner.   So, on this occasion, Woodman escaped with a
long imprisonment.   He and four others were set at liberty
on the 18th of December, 1555—the very day on which John
Philpot, a zealous Reformer, was burnt at the stake in another
part of the kingdom.

The subsequent trials of Woodman ; his frequent hidings
and escapes ; his betrayal by his own father and brother ; his
flight from his house at Warbleton, and his ultimate capture—
these are narrated in so graphic and touching a manner by
Woodman himself that we cannot do better than copy thus
much of his own statement from Foxe's book :—

" After (he says) I was delivered, the papistes sayd that I had consented
to them, wherof they made themselves glad : the which was the least part
of my thought (I prayse God therfore) as they well perceaved, and knew

the contrary within a while. For I went from parish to parish, and talked with them to the number of 13 or 14, and that of the chieftest in all the countrey: and I angred them so, that they with the Commissioners complayned on me to my Lorde Chamberlaine that was then to the Queene, Syr Iohn Gage, shewing him that I baptised children, and maryed folkes, with many such lyes, to bring me into theyr handes agayne. Then the Commissioners sent out certayne citations to bring me to the Court. My Lorde Chamberlayne had directed out 4 or 5 warrantes for me, that if I had come there, I should have bene attached and sent to prison straightway. Which was not God's will; for I had warning of theyr laying awayt for me, and came not there, but sent my deputy, and he brought me word that the Bailiffes wayted for me there: but they mist of theyr pray for that time; wherupon they were displeased.

"Then within 3 daies after, my Lord sent 3 of his men to take me, whose names were, Deane, Jeffrey, and Fraunces. I being at plow with my folkes, right in the way as they were comming to my house, least mistrusting them of all other, came to them and spake to them, asking them how they did. And they sayd, they arested me in the King and Queenes name, and that I must go with them to theyr master the Lord Chamberlayne. Which wordes made my flesh to tremble and quake because of that sodein. But I answered them that I would go with them. Yet I desired them that they would go to my house with me, that I might breake my fast and put on some other gere. And they said I should. Then I remembered my selfe, saying in my hart: why am I thus affrayd; they can lay no evill to my charge. If they kill me for well doing, I may thincke myselfe happy. I remembred how I was contented gladly before to dye in that quarrell and so had continued ever since: and should I now feare to dye? Godforbid that I should, for then were all my labor in vaine.

"So by and by I was persuaded, I praise God, consideryng it was but the frailtie of my flesh which was loth to forgo my wife and children and goods; for I saw nothing but present death before mine eyes. And as soone I was persuaded in my mind to die, I had no regard of nothing in this world, but was as mery and glad, and joyfull, I praise God, as ever I was. This battel lasted not a quarter of an hower, but it was sharper than death it selfe for the time, I dare say.

"So, when I had my breakfast, I desired them to show me their warrant, thinking therby I should have seene wherefore I was arested; to the intent that I myght the better aunswere for my selfe when I came before their maister. And one of them answered, they had not theyr warrant there. Which words made me astonied; and it was put in my minde by God, that I nede not to goe with them unles they had their warrant. Then sayd I to them, that is marvayle, that you will come to take a man without a warrant. It seemeth to me that you come of your owne mynde to get thanke of your maister, for indeede I heard say (sayd I) that there was 4 or 5 warrantes out for me, but they were called in agayne, because I had certified my Lord and the Commissary by a letter that I sent to the Commissaryes court, that I was not faulty in that they layed to my charge, which was for baptising of children, and marying of folkes; the which I never did, for I was never minister appointed to do any such thing. Wherefore set your hartes at rest; I will not goe with you (said I) unlesse you will cary me by force. And if you will do so at your own adventures. And so I rose from the borde and stepped into my chamber, meaning to go from them if I coulde possibly, seing God had made the way so open for me. I ment to play Peters part wyth them, but God would not it shoulde bee so, but sent a feare amongest them, that as sone as I was gone into my chamber, ere ever I coulde come out agayne, they were gone out of my house.

"When I saw that, I knew it was Gods doing to set me at libertie once agayne. Yet I was compelled to speake to them and sayd: if you have a warrant, I desire you for Gods sake shew it me, and I will goe with you wyth all my hart : if not, I desire you to depart in Gods peace and the kingses : for surely I will not goe with you without the order of the law: for I have bene too simple in such things already. For before I was sent to prison first, I went to the justices to two sessions, without any warrant or commaundement, but had word by one of theyr men, and I went gently to them, and they sent me to prison, and kept me there almost a yeare and iii. quarters without all right or equity, as it is openly knowen, not hearing my cause justly debated. And it seemeth to me that I should bee thus evill handled, and therefore I wyll not goe to none of them all henceforth, wythout the extremitie of the law.

" Then one of them answered me and sayd ; we have not the warrant here, but it is at home at my house ; the worst is you can but make us fetch it. Then I sayd, fetch it if you will, but if you come in my house before you have it, at your owne adventure. So I shutte the dore and went my way out of the other dore. So they got helpe to watch my house, while one of them fet the Constable and many more, thinking to have had me in my house, and to have taken me in my house, and carried me away wyth a licence ; but I was gone before, as God would have it. Notwithstanding they sought every corner of my house, but could not prevayle. I mistrusted they would search it agayne that nyght, and kept me abroade, and indeede there came seven of hys men and the Constable and searched my house. And when they saw that they could not meete with me, they were ready to rent their coates that I had scaped them so, knowing they should have such a checke of their maister. When I heard that they had sought so for me again, I perceiving that they were greedy of their pray, came home, and my wife tolde me all thinges.

" Then I supposed that they would lay all the Countrey for me, and the sea coaste, because I should not goe over, and then I thought they would not mistrust that I would dare be nigh home. So I tolde my wife that I would make my lodging in a wood not past a flight shot from my house, as I did indeede, even under a tree, and there had my Bible, my penne and myne incke, and other necessaries, and there continued a vi. or vii. weekes, my wyfe bringing me meat dayly, as I had neede. Yea I thought my selfe blessed of God, that I was counted worthy to lye in the woods for the name of Christ. Then there came word into the Countrey that I was seene and spoken to in Flaunders ; whereupon they left laying a wayte for me, for they had layd all the countrey for me, and the sea coast from Portesmouth to Dover, even as God put in my mynde they would.

" So when all was husht, I went abroad among our frendes and brethren, and at length I went beyond the sea, both into Flaunders and in Fraunce : but I thought every day vii yeare or ever I were at home agayne. So I came home againe as soone as it was possible. I was there but 3 weekes, but as soone as I was come home, and it once known among Bales Priests, they could not abide it, but procured out warrantes agaynst me, causing my house to be searched sometymes twise in a weeke. This continued from S. James tyde to the first Sonday in Lent. Otherwhile I went prively, otherwhile openly, otherwhile I went from home a fortnight or iii weekes, otherwhile I was at home a moneth or five weekes together, living there most commonly and openly, doyng such workes as I had to do : and yet all myne enemyes could lay no hands on me, till the hour was full come : and then by the voyce of the Countrey, and by manifest proofes, myne owne brother as concerning the fleshe, delivered me into their hands by that he knew that I was at home.

"For my father and he had as much of my goodes in their handes as I might have lvi. £. for by the yeare cleare, and therunto prayed.   It was a Lordshyp and a honnor and halfe a honnor, that I had delivered into their handes, to pay my debtes, and the rest to remaine to my wife and children. But they had reported that it would not pay my debtes : which greved me sore.   For it was ii hundreth poundes better than the debtes came to. Which caused me to speake to some of my frendes, that they would speake to them to come to some reckenyng with me, and to take all such money agayne of me, as they were charged with and to deliver me such, writynges and writtes, as they had of myne agayne, or to whom I would appointe them.

" So it was agreed betwixt my father and me, that I should have it agayne, and the day was appointed, that the reckening should be made and sent to me that same day that I was taken, my brother, supposing that I should have put him out of most of all hys occupying, that he was in : for it was all mine in a manner that he occupyed, as all the country can, and do well know.   Whereon (as it is reported) he told one Gardillar my next neighbour, and he told some of M. Gages men, or to M. Gage him selfe : and so he sent to his brother, and his brother sent xii of his men (he beyng Sheriffe) in the night before I was taken, and lay in the bushes not farre from my house, till about ix of the clocke, even the hour that was appointed amongest them selves : for about the same tyme they thought to have had me within my house.

"They had taken a man of mine, and ii of my children that were abroad in the land : and kept them with them, till theyr hour was appointed to come in, and then a little girle, one of my children, saw them come together, and came runnyng in and cryed : 'mother, mother, yonder cometh xx. men.'   I sittyng in my bed and makyng of shooe thonges, heard the words, and suspecting straight way that I was betrayd.   I stirred out of my bed and whipt on my hose, thinkyng to have gone out of the doores or ever they had bene come.   My wife being amased at the childes wordes, looked out of the doore, and they were hard by.   Then she clapped to the doore and barred it fast, even as I came out of my chamber into the Hall, and so barred the other : so the house was beset round straight way, and they bad open the doores, or els they would breake them in peeces.   Then I had no shift, but eyther I must shew my selfe openly, or make some other remedie.

" So there was a place in my house that was never found, which was at the least, I dare say, xx. tymes and sometymes almost of xx. men searched at once, both by night and day, into which place I went : And as soone as I was in, my wife opened the doore : wher by incontinent they came, and asked for me and she sayd I was not at home.   Then they asked her wherefore she shut the door if I were not at home.   She sayd because she had bene made afraid divers times, with such as came to search us, and therfore she shut the doore.   For it is reported (sayth she) that

F

whosoever can take my husband, shall hang hym or burne hym straight way: and therfore I doubt they will serve me or my children so: for I thinke they may do so unto us as well as to him, she said. Well, sayd they, we know he is in the house, and we must search it, for we be the Shrives* men, let us have a candle. It is told us, there be many secret places in your house. So she lighted a candle, and they sought up and downe in every corner that they could find, and had geven over, and many of them were gone out of my house into the Churchyarde, and were talkyng with my father, and with some that he had brought with hym.

"Now, when they could not find me, one of them went to him that gave them word that I was at home, and sayd, we cannot find him. Then he asked them whether they had sought over a wyndow that was in the Hall (as it was knowne afterward) for that same place I had told hym of myself. For many tymes when I came home, I would send for hym to beare me company; yet as it chaunced I had not told hym the way into it. Then they began to search anew. One looked up over the window and spyed a little loft, with iii. or iv. chestes, and the way went in betwixt ii. of the chestes, but there could no man perceave it. Then he asked my wife, which was the way into it. Here is a place that we have not sought yet. Then she thought they would see it by one means or other. She sayd the way was into it out of a chamber they were in even now. So she sent them up and cried away, away! Then I knew there was no remedy, but make the best shift for myself that I could. The place was boarded over, and fast nailed, and if I had come out that way that I went in, I must needes come amongst them all in the hall. Then I had no shift, but set my shoulders to the bourdes that were nayled to the rafters to keepe out the raine, and brake them in peeces, which made a great noyse, and they that were in the other chamber, seekyng for the way into it, heard the noyse, and looked out of a window, and spyed me and made an outcry. But yet I got out and leaped downe, having no shoes on.

"So I tooke downe a lane that was full of sharpe sinders, and they came runnyng after, with a great cry, with their swordes drawen, crying strike hym, strike hym. Which wordes made me looke backe, and there was never a one nigh me by an hundred foote; and that was but one, for all the rest were a great way behynd. And I turned about hastely to go my way, and stepped upon a sharpe sinder with one foote, and savyng of it I stepped in a great miery hole, and fell down withall, and ere ever I could arise and get away, he was come in with me. His name is Parker *the wild*, as he is counted in al Sussex. But if I had had on my shoes, they had bene lyke to have gone away arrandles if there had bene v. C. more, if I had caught the playne grounde once, to the which I had not a stones cast; but it was not Gods will; for if it had, I should have scaped from them all, if there had bene ten thousand of them.

"Then they tooke me and led me home agayne to put on my shooes and such gere as I had neede of. Then sayd John Fauconer; 'Now your master hath deceaved you. You said you were an Angell, and if you had ben an Angell, why did you not fly away from us?' 'Then' said I, 'what be they that ever heard me say that I was an Angell? It is not the first lye by a thousand that they have made of me. Angells were never begotten of men, nor borne of women; but if they had said, that they had heard me say, that I do trust I am a saint, they had not sayd amisse.

---

* Sheriff's.

'What? doo you thinke to be a saint?' 'Yea that I doo, and am already, in Gods sight. I trust in God; for he that is not a saint in Gods sight already is a devill. Therefore he that thinketh skorne to be a sainte, let him be a devill.' And with that worde they had brought me to mine owne doore; where met with me my father, and willed me to remember my selfe.

"'To whom I aunswered; 'I prayse God, I am well remembred whereabout I go. This way was appointed of God for me to be delivered into the handes of mine enemies, but woe unto hym by whom I am betrayed. It had ben good for that man, that he had never bene borne if he repent not with speede. The Scriptures are now fulfilled on me : *For the father shall be agaynst the sonne, and the brother shall deliver the brother to death,* as it is this day come to passe.' Then sayd one; 'he doth accuse hys father; a good child in deede.' I accuse hym not, but say my minde; for there was no man knew me at home but my father, my brother, and one more, the which I dare say would not hurt me for all the good in this town.'

" There was one George Bechyng that maried one of my sisters, and he thought that I had ment hym, that he had betrayed me, and he sayd; 'Brother I would you should not thinke that I was the cause of your takyng.' To whom I aunswered that I ment hym not ; I ment one that was nerer of my bloud than he was. Then sayd one of Lewes, that had been a Gospeller, and stoode from them, when I was brought to a Sessions to Lewes, and he sayd, I thought you would have bene an honest man when you were at Lewes, and I offred Hussey the Sheriffe to be bound for you that you should go home to your wife and come to him agayn.' Then I remembred what he was, and said; 'Be you the Pewterer'? And he sayd, 'yea.' Then sayd I: 'It is happened to you according to the true Proverbe, as sayth S. Peter; *The dogge is turned to his vomit agayne, and the sowe that is washed to wallow in the mire,* and the end of all such wil be worse then the begynnyng.' Then his mouth was stopped so that he had nothing to say.

" All this while I stode at my doore without; for they would not let me go in. So I put on my shoes and my clothes, and then they put on an harnes about myne armes made of a dogs slippe; which rejoised my hart that I was counted worthy to be bound for the name of God. So I tooke my leave of my wife and children, my father, and other of my frendes, never thinking to see them more in this world. For it was so thought of all the countrey, that I should not lyve vi. dayes after my takyng; for they had so reported. But yet I knew it was not as they would, unlesse God would graunt it. I know what God can do; but what he will do I know not; but I am sure he will worke all thinges for the best, for them that love and feare hym. So we dranke and went our way, and came to Firle about iii. of the clocke."

Richard Woodman had now entered on a new phase of his trials. He had been brought to bay by his persecutors, and it was, doubtless, thought that it would be an easy matter for such skilled casuists and such learned Doctors of the Roman Church to put him down. In this, however, they found themselves sorely mistaken, and the fight maintained by this Sussex farmer and ironmaster against such men as Gardiner, Christopherson, Dr. Story, and others, is one of the most remarkable to be found in the pages of Foxe, so rich in these conflicts.

It should be stated that Dr. Christopherson, whom Foxe characterises as a "Bonner, junior," had lately succeeded Bishop Day (who died in 1556) in the diocese of Chichester. He had himself suffered from religious persecution in Edward's reign at the hands of the Reformers, and was now returned from exile to become the confessor of the Queen, and, in November, 1557, Bishop of Chichester. In this latter capacity it fell to him to examine Woodman, at Blackfriars, London ; and he appears to have done so at first with some degree of moderation, and even commiseration, if not admiration, for the spirit and learning displayed by Woodman. We might almost be tempted to think, by some of the Bishop's words and acts, that he could have said, with Agrippa when speaking to Paul, "Almost thou persuadest me to be a 'Protestant.'" Thus, to quote from Woodman's statement :—

Chichester : You said you doo not disallow the true catholicke church.

Wood.: No, that I doo not.

Chiches.: Why do you not then go to the church ? You come not there, it is enformed me.

Wood.: I trust I am in the true church every day. But to tell you truth, I come not at the church where the most doo resorte. For if I should, I should offende, and be offended. For the last time that I was there, I offended many, and was offended my selfe. Wherefore for conscience sake I would not come there. For I was sent to prison for my comming there, and now I am sent to you for biding thence. So they will not be pleased any way with me, for they seeke my life. Wherfore looke you to it, for I am now in your handes, and you ought to be a house of defence agaynst mine enemies. For if you suffer them to kill me, my bloud shall be required at your handes. If you can finde any just cause in me worthy of death by Gods worde, you may condemne me your selfe, and not offend God; wherefore looke to it. The matter is weighty; deliver me not into theyr handes, and thinke so to be discharged.

Chiches.: I tell you truth, I can do litle in the matter. For I have not full authority, as yet, of myne office; but I will send for you and talke with you, if I wist I shuld do you any good.

Wood.: I would be glad to talke with you and to shew you my minde in any thyng that you shall demaund of me, now or at any other tyme.

"So then he (the Bishop) desired the Sheriffes men to tary dinner with him; that this man (sayd he) may dine with me also; for it is possible that he may have no great store of meate whether he shall go. So we taryed dynner with hym, and had no further talke, neither how to prove where the true church of God is, nor of the Sacramentes, nor of any other thyng pertainyng to me ward, not for the space of two houres or more; but he entred in talke with me, how I understode many Scriptures, and for Byshops and Priestes Mariages, and whether Paule had a wyfe or not. To whom I aunswered; it is a thyng that I have litle to do with, as concernyng Mariages; but I am very well content to talke with you in the matter as far as my poore learnyng wil serve. So when he had talked with me of divers Scriptures, he lyked my talke well. He asked me how I said by Paul, whether he were maryed or not. To whom I aunswered; I prove by the Scriptures that he was never maryed."

After a close dispute upon this point, and upon the marriage of Priests, the Bishop exclaimed—

"Marry, I am glad that you have sayd as you have done. Many doo affirme boldly that Paul had a wife, and yet can not prove whether he had or had not, by the Scriptures; but you have sayd very well. I am glad that ye are contented to be ruled by Gods word. And if you wil be contented likewise in other matters, no doubt you shall doo well; therefore gentle goodman Woodman be ruled. God hath geven you a good wit. I protest before God, I would you should do as well as myne owne soule and body, and so would (I dare say) all the worshypful men in the countrey, as they have reported to me."

And to Woodman's remark that "there be as many unlearned Priests in your Diocese as in any one Diocese in England," Christopherson (himself a man of learning) replied:—

"I promise you I do much lament it my selfe; for I heare say no lesse, but it is true that you say. I would I could remedy it, but I can not; but I will do the best that I can when I come into the countrey, and I will be glad to talke with you some other tyme, when I am somewhat better at ease. You see I am very tender now, as I have bene this halfe yeare and more. Come to dynner; our dynner is ready. I caused you not to tary for any great chere that you shall have, nor I would you shoulde not thinke that I goe about to wynne you with my meate. But you be welcome with all my hart. Come, sit down."

"I thanked him," continued Woodman, "and went to dinner; and there dyned with hym a Marchaunt man, one of the Sheriffes men, and I, and no mo, and we had good chere, God bee praysed therfore. We had no talke of the Scriptures al the dynner while; but when dynner was done, the Bishop sayd; Now cal M. Stories man. For the Commissioners have committed you to prison; but I will send for you or ever it be long, and I pray God I may do you good. I would be very glad of it."

"If it please you to send for me," said Woodman, "I would be very glad to talke with you, for I lyke your talke well. And then if it please your Lordshyp to examine me upon any particular matter, I will shew you my mynd therein, by Gods grace, without dissimulation."

It would almost seem, by the tone of this and other passages of the Bishop, that, if Dr. Christopherson had been free to take his own course, he would not only have let Woodman

go, but have followed in his path.   But he stood so committed
to a course, and was so coupled with other men in it, that little
liberty of thought or action was left to him.

Woodman was now taken from the Bishop's to the custody,
first, of Dr. Story, and then of Dr. Cooke, two of Bonner's
worthy instruments, and by them was delivered to the Sheriff's
prison in Southwark ; and his next examination, on the 27th
April, was at Dr. Story's house, "besides St. Nicholas'
Shambles." It was opened by the Bishop of Chichester in
the same amicable tone which had marked the close of the
preceding one. "You be welcome," said the Bishop, "How
do you now?" "Well, I praise God," replied Woodman,
"thanking your Lordship for the gentle talk that you had with
me at my last departing from you."

This beginning promised well.   But it is not easy to keep
cool in theological discussions, and Woodman having reminded
the Bishop of his pledge to give Scripture authority for the
seven Sacraments of the Romish Church, and the Bishop,
heated by opposition, having, we may presume, indulged in
strong language, Woodman reproved him for swearing,
"which," he went on to say, "is a great fault in Bishops, of
all others, that should be an example to the flock."

This was putting the match to the train.   "Then,"
proceeds Woodman, "he (the Bishop) and his prelates were
in a great rage with me." "What," exclaimed the Bishop,
"I perceive this man is worse than he was the last day.
What! he taketh upon him to teach me to speak, as though
I could not tell what I had to do," and, a little later, he told
him to "follow your vocation ; you have little learning," and,
still later, after a very lively discussion upon the meaning of
altar and the true nature of the Lord's Supper, the Bishop
exclaimed, "I see it is but folly to talk with you ; it is but lost
labour ;" and Woodman having dared them to "talk with
me by the Scriptures," then they made a great laughing, and
said, "This is a heretic indeed ; it is time he were burned."
"Which," Woodman goes on to say, "moved my spirit," and

I said to them, " Judge not, least you be judged, for as you judge you shall be judged yourself."

To this exhortation Dr. Story responded, "What! be you a preaching? You shall preach at a stake shortly with your fellows." And' then, addressing the Bishop, " My lord, trouble yourself no more with him."

"With these words," proceeds Woodman, " one brought word that the Abbot of Westminster was come to dyne with the Byshop, and many other gentlemen and women. Then there was rushyng away with speede to meete hym." Then sayd Dr. Story to my keeper, "Cary him to the Marshalsee againe, and let him be kept close, and let no body come to speake to hym." And so they departed. Then one of the Priests begon to flatter with me, and sayd : " For Gods sake remember your selfe. God hath geven you a good witte ; you have read the Scriptures well, and have borne them well in memory ; it were great pitie you should do amisse." To which Woodman responded, " What a flatterer be you, to say my witte is good, and that I have read the Scriptures well ; and but even now you sayd I was an hereticke, and despised me. If I be an hereticke I can have no good witte, as you have confessed. But I thinke your own conscience doth accuse you. God geve you grace to repent, if it be his will."

Priest : I call it a good witte, because you are expert in all questions.

Wood.: You may call it a wicked witte, if it agree not with Gods word. Then one cried, "Away, away; here commeth straungers." So we departed, and I came agayne to the Marshalsee with my keper.

Three further examinations took place, in which the Archbishop of Canterbury, the Bishops of Chichester, Winchester, and Rochester, Dr. Langdale, rector of Buxted (Woodman's native place), and others took part, and in which the Sussex ironmaster held his ground against all the assaults of his antagonists. The last of these conflicts, on the 15th of June, 1557, closed as follows :—

Bishop of Winchester: He is the naughtiest verlet hereticke, that ever I knew. I will reade the sentence agaynst hym.

Then they spake all at once ; and I aunswered them as fast as I could. But I can not remember it all, the wordes came out so thicke, and that I spared them not (I prayse God therefore) ; for I spake freely. Then they that stoode by, rebuked me, and sayd ; "you cannot tell to whom you speake, I thinke."

Wood.: No? thinke you so? they be but men. I am sure I have spoken to as good as they be, and better than they will ever be, for any thing that I can see, if they repent not with speede.

Winc.: Geve eare; for I will reade sentence agaynst you.

Wood.: Will you so? wherefore will you? you have no just cause to excommunicate me ; and therefore if you doe condemne me you will bee condemned in hell, if you repent not; and I prayse God, I am not afrayde to die for Gods sake, if I had a hundred lives.

Winc.: For Gods sake? nay for the devilles sake. Thou sayest thou art not afrayde to die; No more was *Judas* that hanged himselfe, as thou wilt kill thy selfe wilfully, because thou wilt not be ruled.

Wood.: Nay, I defye the devill, *Judas* and all theyr members. And *Judas* flesh was not afrayd, but his spirite and conscience was afrayd, and therefore dispayred and hong him selfe. But I prayse God, I fele lothsomnes in my flesh to die, but a joyfull conscience and a willing minde therto. Wherfore my flesh is subdued to it, I prayse God; and therefore I am not afrayd of death.

Chich.: *Woodman*, for Gods sake be ruled. You know what you sayd to me at my house. I could say more if I would.

Wood.: Say what you can; the most fault that you found in me was, because I praysed the living God, and because I said, I praise God, and the Lord; which you ought to be ashamed of, if you have any grace, for I told you where the wordes were written.

Winchest.: Well; how say you? will you confesse that *Judas* receaved the body of Christ unworthely? tell me playnely.

Wood.: My Lord, if you, or any of you all can prove before all this audience, in all the Bible, that any man ever eate the body of Christ unworthely, then I will be with you in all thinges that you will demaund of me; of the which matter I desire all this people to be witnes.

Priest: Will you so? then we shall agree well inough. Saint Paul sayth so.

Wood.: I pray you where sayth he so? rehearse the wordes.

Priest: In the xi. of the first of the Corinthians, he saith; *who so eateth of this bread, and drinketh of this cuppe unworthely, eateth and drinketh his owne damnation, because he maketh no difference of the Lordes body.*

Wood.: Doth these wordes prove that Judas eate the body of Christ unworthely? I pray you let me see them. They were contented. Then said I; these be the wordes even that you sayd. Good people, herken well to them: *Who so eateth of this bread, and drinketh of this cup unworthely.* He saith not, who so eateth of this body unworthely or drinketh of this bloud unworthely. But he sayth: *who so eateth of this bread, and drinketh of this cup unworthely* (which is the sacrament) *eateth and drinketh his own damnation,* because he maketh no difference of the sacrament which representeth the Lords body, and other bread and drinke. Here good people, you may all see they are not able to prove theyr sayinges true. Wherfore I cannot believe them in any thing that they doo.

Winchest.: Thou art a ranke hereticke in deede. Art thou an expounder? Now I will read sentence agaynst thee.

Wood.: Judge not least you be judged. For as you have judged me, you be your selfe. Then hee red the sentence. Why, sayd I? will you read the sentence agaynst me, and cannot tell wherfore?

Winchest.: Thou art an hereticke, and therfore thou shall. be excommunicated.

Wood.: I am no hereticke. I take heaven and earth to witnes, I defie al heretickes; and if you condemn me, you will be damned, if you repent it not. But God geve you grace to repent all, if it be his will.

THE BURNING OF RICHARD WOODMAN AND NINE OTHER PROTESTANT MARTYRS

And so he red foorth the sentence in Latin, but what he sayd, God knoweth, and not I. God be judge betwene them and me. When he had done, I would have talked my minde to them, but they cried, away! away with him! So I was carried to the Marshalsea agayne, where I am, and shall be as long as it shal please God; and I praise God most hartely, that ever he hath elected and predestinated me to come to so high dignity, as to beare rebuke for his names sake; his name be praysed therfore, for ever and ever, Amen.

Woodman's fate was now sealed. He had shown too bold a face to his adversaries, and displayed too much knowledge and skill as a controversialist, to be allowed to escape a second time. He was condemned as a heretic and handed over to the secular power to be burnt at the stake. Nine more victims were swept together from different parts of Sussex, in haste, as it would seem, and without form of law, for eight of them had only been apprehended two or three days previously, to perish with him. Lewes was again chosen as the place of execution, and here, in front of the Star Inn—in the vault of which, still in existence, Woodman is supposed to have been confined—was enacted the last dreadful scene of the tragedy. It took place on the 22nd of June, 1557. No detailed description has been preserved, as in Derick Carver's case, of Richard Woodman's last moments; but we may be assured that he displayed the same constancy in this ordeal as he had shown in his long conflicts with his adversaries, and that his death, as his life, was worthy of the cause he had taken up. His name and memory are still held in veneration in his native county.*

This was, in all probability, the last martyrdom in Sussex. But the names of six other martyrs have yet to be added to the list already given, though there is no record of the places where they suffered. These were John Warner, of Eastbourne; Christian Grover, of Lewes; Thomas Atholl, priest; John Mills (or Mylles), of Hellingly; Nicholas Helden, of Withyham, and John Asshedon, of Rotherfield.

It will be remarked that in these, as in all the other

---

* For permission to use the illustration to this paper, "The Burning of the Martyrs at Lewes," I am indebted to the designer of it, Mr. Frederic Colvin, a very clever artist of Lewes.

instances, the martyrs were natives of the Eastern parts of Sussex.   Here, it is clear, the doctrines of the Reformation had taken the strongest hold.   In the West of Sussex the Howards, Dukes of Norfolk; the Brownes, Earls of Montague; the Carylls, the Shirleys, and other Catholic families had kept back the stream, and to the present day there are localities in West Sussex, as Arundel and Slindon, where a large proportion of the population adheres to the old faith.

The total number of martyrdoms in Sussex in the reign of Mary was 33; and few other counties (putting aside the Metropolitan ones) can show so large a list of witnesses to the truth of their doctrines.   We may hope that the roll is closed for ever.

The late Mr. M. A. Lower, in the biography of Richard Woodman in his " Worthies of Sussex," gives some topographical facts as to Woodman's house at Warbleton and his places of concealment and confinement, which will still be read with interest :—

"The wood to which Woodman retired for concealment, the lane full of sharp 'cinders' (the scoriæ of his own iron-works), down which he ran to escape his pursuers, the site of his dwelling-house, and several other particulars, are as fondly remembered by the simple folk of Warbleton as are the homes and haunts of Shakspeare by the people of Stratford.   As to his house, there is little difficulty in proving that it was close to the church-yard of that interesting village, although there may be some want of evidence as to the precise spot.   .   .   . The lane down which poor Woodman ran is less questionable. It is still traceable for about a mile, in what is now a thicket running from a point not far from the village hostelry, known by the punning sign of the 'War-bill-in-tun,' to the farm called Cralle, erst the residence of the De Cralles, and now the property of John Day, Esq.   It was evidently the 'coach-road' to the parish church.   But the most interesting memento of Woodman is a portion of the church tower, the second or middle story of which is said to have been his temporary prison. That it was a prison is clearly proved by its heavy oak door. The apartment is about 11 feet square, and is reached by the usual newel or winding staircase of stone. The walls, of Sussex sandstone, several feet in thickness, are pierced with two small window openings for light and air, and the door, two inches in thickness, is clad on the outside with iron plates secured with five massive horizontal bars of the same metal strongly riveted. The inside of the door has some remains of iron fittings which I could not understand, but which appear to corroborate the village tradition that they were devised for purposes of bodily confinement. There, assuming the tradition of Woodman's temporary incarceration to be true—which I see no reason to dispute—he would have been within ear-shot of the wailings of his faithful wife and her little ones, and the iron doubtless entered his manful and unflinching soul!"

The Quakers in Sussex.

F, as Lucretius tells us, it is a pleasant thing to look in safety from the shore on the terrors and dangers of the sea, it is still more satisfactory to contemplate, in a day of freedom and toleration, the persecutions of a bygone age. Few bodies of men, perhaps, can claim to indulge in this innocent enjoyment more than the members of that Society who, in popular phraseology, are called Quakers—a term which once had much significance, but which now carries little or no meaning with it; for we do not see in the present day that the Quakers quake, or have reason to quake, spiritually or civilly, more than their neighbours! But few religious bodies can look back upon the past with greater satisfaction than the representatives of this community, for they carried out to the letter the direction of their great Master, and, if reviled, they reviled not again, and for the cruel usage they underwent in their early days, all the return they have made is to heap coals upon the heads of their persecutors in the shape of benefits. They have ever steadily laboured for the extension to others of the freedom of thought and of worship which were so long denied to them; and at the present moment they may look around and exclaim, as they gaze upon the universal religious tolerance which prevails, not only in England, but throughout Europe, " Behold, this is the work for which *we* laboured and suffered."

Like other victors, however, the Quakers are in danger of being merged in the mass of those whom they have overcome. There is now little or no difference, in speech or dress, manners or morals, between Quakers and other religious bodies, such as the Independents and Presbyterians, by whom

at one time they were regarded with the greatest aversion,
but with whom they now appear on the same platforms and
contend for the same political, social, and moral objects—
from whom, indeed, it is now difficult to distinguish them.
It is not easy for us at the present day to conceive how such
violent prejudices could have existed against a body of men so
inoffensive as the Quakers, and it may not be without its use
to be. reminded that the chief persecutors of Fox, Roberts,
Latey, Story, and other early Quakers, were not Churchmen
or Roman Catholics, but Independents and Presbyterians—
men who themselves had only just escaped from persecution,
and who were fated again to endure it.   Not the less did they,
in their day of triumph, indulge in that intolerance towards
others—and especially towards the Quakers—which goes to
show how dangerous it is to place political and spiritual
power in the same hands, be they what men and professing
what principles they may.

Of all the towns in Sussex in which the Quakers seem to
have suffered most, Lewes stands out with a very unenviable
pre-eminence.   The late William Figg, F.S.A., of Lewes,
collected with great industry the records of the sufferings
endured by the Quakers of Lewes at the hands of their fellow-
townsmen, and, if not quite so terrible as the barbarities
inflicted (and in the same town) by Roman Catholics upon
Protestants, they were still sufficiently severe to make us
appreciate the tolerant days in which we live.   " Scorn and
derision, with beatings, buffetings, stonings, pinchings, kick-
ings, dirtings, pumpings, and all manner of abuses "—with
" spoiling of goods, stockings, whippings, imprisonments, and
banishments, and even death itself "—such is the list drawn
up by Joseph Besse, in chronicling the sufferings of his people
in the days of the Commonwealth, and of the succeeding
Stuart Kings, until William III. came to them, and, indeed,
to all England, as a Deliverer.

Sussex generally seems, about the year 1655, to have been
ready for the seed which George Fox and his contemporaries

came to sow in it. In Chichester, Arundel, Horsham, and in
smaller places, such as Walberton, Ifield, &c.—but especially
in Lewes—the visit of a few men—at first John Slee, Thomas
Lawson, and Thomas Lawcock, but subsequently George, or,
to follow the spelling of the times, Georg Fox and Alexander
Parker—was sufficient to wake up in the middle classes that
deep religious feeling—that sense of personal responsibility—
which followed, as light follows the sun, the translation of the
Scriptures in the preceding century. A perusal of the
biographies of the first Quakers—men like John Roberts and
Gilbert Latey—leaves no doubt as to the standard which they
set up, and the example they tried to follow. They appealed
continually to the words and actions of the Founder of
Christianity as their rule of life in the 17th century. It was a
reaction from the utter ignoring alike of the letter and spirit
of Christianity in the Middle Ages, and the substitution for it,
in the Papal system, of something utterly different from anything taught by Christ. With the Quakers, the pendulum
swung to the other extreme, and for the most intricate and
artificial system of religion ever organised—in which the
individual man was reduced to nothing in the face of Pope,
Councils, Synods, and all the machinery of a huge Hierarchy—
was substituted the text of the Bible, but chiefly that of the
Gospels, as interpreted by those who read it. With these
weapons the Quakers—the real primitive Christians of the
Reformation—went forth into the towns and villages of
England, and played much the same part, active and suffering,
which the early propagators of Christianity did in the East.
The spirit was the same—so, too, was the doctrine—and, in
the belief of some of the "Confessors," so were the gifts and
powers vouchsafed to them. But the results were very
different, because the conditions were not the same. If the
Quakers had been the missionaries of Christianity among a
heathen people, we can conceive that they might have effected
conversions like the early Christians, or, even if they had been
the earliest assailants of a corrupt Church like Rome, they
might have done what Luther and Calvin did before them.

But they had a harder work even than this to do, and that was, to use their own words, " to testify against prophaness (*sic in orig.*) and immorality on the one hand, and superstition and will-worship on the other "—to give a " testimony levelled against the darling vices of the laiety and the forced maintenance of the clergy." And for this work the only authority they had was that which might, indeed, suffice for their individual justification, but to which any other men might equally appeal in support of a totally different line of conduct. In fact, they claimed no authority for themselves beyond other men—only they sought to put an end to all spiritual authority over and above that which any man or woman with the necessary " lights " might feel he or she had a right to exercise; an impossible task, and which we see at the present day to be impossible, when the Quakers enjoy all the liberty they could wish for, and yet there is as much " superstition and will-worship "—to say nothing of "vices " and " forced maintenance of the clergy"—as ever.

But we are digressing from our purpose, which was to show what the Quakers of Sussex generally, and of Lewes especially, had to endure in the 17th century. The chief offence given by them was, it seems, in their meeting in their own houses to pray ! A singular cause of offence certainly to Christians ! But not so singular if the ancient custom of meeting in churches be considered. Not so to meet was an offence at law (it was so up to a very recent period), and it was also a cause of suspicion to the more ignorant and prejudiced classes. So, we are told, in 1658, that " for these two yeares " " there hath been fire throwen in among friends severall times to the danger of fireing the house, some friends receiving much wrong by the fire, and they allso have throwen in water, dirt, and cowdung upon friends in their meeting, and have broke the glass windows very much, and have beaten friends as they have passed to their meetings."

The Independents were the ruling power in England in 1658, and were, it would seem, as ready to persecute those who differed from themselves in religious opinion or practice as the Romanists, the High Churchmen, and the Presbyterians had all been before them.

These cases of interruptions of meetings, of commitments to prison, finings for non-attendance at Church and non-payment of tithes, &c., are innumerable, and become tedious by their sameness; so, after the fashion of Sterne, we will take an individual case by way of example, and it shall be a domestic one, and the sufferer a woman, and a wife to boot.

In this year (1659), says the very quaint old chronicle quoted by Mr. Figg, Mary Akehurst, the wife of Ralph Akehurst, of the Cliff, neare Lewis, beeing moved to goe to St. Michals' Steeplehouse (soe called), where an Independent priest was speaking, she, for asking him a question, was by people haled out, and then sent for her aforesaid husband, who, after shee came home, did so hunch and pincht her, that she could not lift her armes to her head. The said Ralph again, on the seaventeenth day of the third month of this present yeare, bound the hands and feet of his said wife and pinioned her, and then covered her very hot with bed-cloaths, and soe kept her for the space of foure or five houres; this it seems he did because she tooke occasion to reprove a hircling priest for belying her.

Againe, upon the twenty-fifth day of the eighth month of this present yeare 1659, the aforesaid Ralph did sorely abuse his wife, on which the following lines were sent unto two Justices of the Peace (soe called), to complain of and to declare the same, that she might not perish in private, but to lay it home to them, then in authority, viz. :—

"Whereas complaint hath beene made unto two of those who are in place to doe justice, as, namely, Richard Boughton and Nathaniel Studly, of cruel persecution inflicted upon the body of a woman in the Clift, neare Lewis, by the hands of a wicked tirant, who is called her husband; his name is Ralph Akehurst, he hath chained his wife in a close back chamber in his house, between two high bead-steads, with a great chain much like a timber chain, containing thirty-five links, and a staple and a lock, soe that this woman cannot move aboute the roome, or lye in the bed without this chaine, soe that with waits of itt it hath done much wrong to her legg, besides blows and bruses that he hath given her in executing his cruelty in putting on of this chaine, soe that thereby her body is much weakened at present, and murther may ensue if the Lord by his providence doth not some way for her deliverance ; or if this man hath promised that he will never unlock the chaine from off her, soe that in all likelyhood his heart is bent to destroy the body of this woman someway, for he hath attempted her life, as she hath said, by endeavouring to throatle her."

No redress or relief was, it seems, expected for this unfortunate woman from her brutal husband; the above declaration being only made by the parties signing it (three women and a man) with a view to absolve themselves, "Soe that if inocent blood be shead we shall be cleare, and the guilt shall remaine upon the heads which suffer such things to be done."

Of the ultimate fate of Mary Akehurst, of Lewes, there is no record. But Quaker-ladies may congratulate themselves in 1882 that they live in more tolerant days than 1659, and under less tyrannical rule than that of the Independents.

More grievous acts than these pinchings and pinionings and chainings were, however, done, and by men in authority. Thus, in 1655, the Mayor of Arundel—one Thomas Ballard —sends his constables to the house of Nicholas Rickman (the progenitor of a long line of Rickmans, including our old friend, Clio), and under the pretence of taking-up of idle wandering persons for the voyage to Jamaica (in other words, to sell into slavery), seizes that "just man and servant of the Lord, Joseph Fuce;" and, notwithstanding that every information was given as to his place of abode, relations, and employment, "judged in plain words that he was not a Person fitt to Live in the Comonweale, but a vagabond, and so fitt to be sent away, which was according put in Execution, he being put into company with a vile crue and soe sent to Portsmouth to be shiped to Jamaica."

A judicial murder, this, if ever one was committed. But by no means uncommon in this and the following age. As a participator in acts like this, such a man as Judge Jefferies appears in his proper place; and it is on record that at a Quarter Session at Steyning in 1681 he presided as Chairman when "eleven persons were indicted for three weeks' absence from the church. They were fined 3s. each, and, refusing to pay the same, were committed to prison." In this instance, however, Jefferies went beyond his instructions. James, his master, was favourable to the Quakers as supporters of passive resistance and upholders of the principle of universal toleration in religion which suited *his* policy as a Roman Catholic—Penn was one of his supporters, and accordingly the above act was quickly revoked and a letter sent to the gaoler of Horsham Gaol by Henry Goring, one of the

G

Justices, instructing him that the prisoners " might have all lawful favour that could be showed. Therefore, my desire to you is, to give them what liberty you can without danger to yourself."

A most cautious and politic Justice this Henry Goring!

We might go on quoting by the page the barbarities and injustices committed at Lewes and elsewhere in Sussex on these poor people for worshipping God after their own fashion; and on which Mr. Figg remarks " the Quakers in Lewes, and, indeed, in Sussex generally, bore the persecutions and revilings heaped upon them with Christian meekness and forbearance, and with a great amount of endurance, although with much sacrifice of personal comfort and worldly goods." Not, however, as Mr. Figg remarks, without, in some instances, bestowing upon their persecutors a few of those odd nicknames for which the age was famous. Thus one Fisher addressed the celebrated Dr. John Owen, Dean of Christ Church, in the following style:—"Thou fiery Fighter and green-headed Trumpeter; thou Hedgehog and Grinning Dog; thou Bastard that tumbled out of the mouth of the Babylonish bawd; thou Mole; thou Tinker; thou Lizard; thou Bell of no mettle, but the tone of a Kettle; thou Wheelbarrow; thou Whirligig; O thou Firebrand; thou Adder and Scorpion; thou Louse; thou Cow-dung; thou Moon-calf; thou ragged Tatterdemallian; thou Judas; thou livest in philosophy and logic which are of the Devil."

After this the title of Thomas Lawson's, book in reply to the Priest of Clayton, "An Answer to a Dawber with Untempered Morter," and Joseph Fuce's answer to a Baptist, "The Ould Botle's Mouth Stopped," are mild and temperate! But, after all, these were only word-buffettings, and broke no bones. The Quakers' opponents fought with different weapons!

With the coming-in of William of Orange the sufferings of the Quakers ceased, or were reduced to the seizure and sale (often a mere fiction) of a little furniture or plate, for tithe or Church-rate. But with the persecution ended the proselytisings of the Quakers. From this time they turned their attention more to the making of money than the making of converts, and the discipline which was gained in the first process has not been turned to bad effect in the latter.

So the main design of the Quakers failed; they never became a numerous body, and may now be said to be, for anything that distinguishes them from their brother-Christians, an obsolete and almost extinct one. But it was a noble attempt—a glorious failure, which has left precious legacies to succeeding ages. The influence of the early Quakers upon the 17th century—the effect of their teachings and sufferings—can scarcely be duly appreciated now, when we have passed beyond both. But there is instruction, and also some amusement, in the lesson, as it has been handed down to us in certain biographies, kindly placed at our disposal by a friend, and we shall make no excuse for laying a few passages from these before our readers. The biography most to our taste is not that of a Sussex man—we wish it had been—but of John Roberts, of Siddington, near Cirencester, in Gloucestershire, by his son Daniel. Roberts was in early life a soldier under Cromwell, and was connected by marriage with Chief Justice Hale, one of the greatest men of England. As in most conversions to Quakerism (though not yet so named), his "call" was sudden, and dated from the visit of "two women-friends, out of the North, to Cirencester," at whose instance he had a religious meeting in his house; and religious meetings in those days were illegal. But, once converted, the work was done, and to the close of his life John Roberts was "testifying" against what he regarded as "superstition and will-worship"—"the darling vices of the laity and the forced maintenance of the Clergy." The Parish Church was to him a "steeple-house," of no more sanctity than any other structure, and the Parson, or "hireling Priest," was to be judged by what he taught in the pulpit, and, if necessary, confuted and reproved for it. When John Roberts goes to church (which, by the bye, the law called on him to do, and it was his duty to obey the law) he keeps his hat on and waits patiently until the sermon is over, but then he calls in question the false doctrine of the Preacher, whereupon he is forcibly put out, and taken before the Justice, or, perhaps to the Bishop himself. And in this particular piece of biography we can but admire the Bishop of Gloucester of that day. We are inclined to think that, of the two, he had the spirit of Christian charity quite as strong in him as John Roberts had, if not stronger. The most pleasing parts of this biography are the dialogues between the Quaker and the Bishop. There is one scene in which the Bishop, on his road to a Visitation, calls, with all his clerical following, at Roberts's house, and drinks some of his beer, which (we mean the scene, not the beer), to use an old saying, is "as good as a play:"—

Some time after this, the Bishop and the Chancellor in their carriages, accompanied with Thomas Masters, Esq., in his coach, and about twenty clergymen on horseback, made my father's house in their way to the visitation, which was to be at Tedbury the next day. They stopt at the gate, and George Evans, the Bishop's kinsman, rode into the yard, to call my father; who, coming to the Bishop's coach-side, he put out his hand, which my father respectfully took, saying, "I could not well go out of the county without seeing you." "That's very kind," said my father; "wilt thou please to alight and come in, with those who are along with thee?"

Bishop: "I thank you, John; we are going to Tedbury, and time will not admit of it now; but I will drink with you, if you please."

My father went in and ordered some drink to be brought, and then returned to the coach-side.

Geo. Evans: "John, is your house free to entertain such men as we are?"

J. Roberts: "Yes, George; I entertain honest men, and sometimes others."

Geo. Evans (to the Bishop): "My lord, John's friends are the honest men, and we are the others."

J. Roberts: "That's not fair, George, for thee to put thy construction upon my words; thou shouldest have given me leave to do that."

'Squire Masters came out of his coach, and stood by the bishop's coach-side; and the chancellor, in a diverting humour, said to my father, "My lord and these gentlemen have been to see your burying-ground, and we think you keep it very decent. (This piece of ground my father had given to friends for that purpose; it lay at the lower end of the orchard.) My father answered, "Yes; tho' we are against pride, we think it commendable to be decent."

Chancellor: "But there is one thing among you, which I did not expect to see; I think it looks a little superstitious; I mean those grave-stones which are placed at the head and feet of your graves."

J. Roberts: "That I confess is what I cannot much plead for; but it was permitted, to gratify some who had their relations there interred. We, notwithstanding, propose to have them taken up ere long, and converted to some better use. But I desire thee to take notice, we had it from among you; and I have observed in many things wherein we have taken you for our pattern you have led us wrong; and, therefore, we are now resolved, with the help of God, not to follow you one step further."

At this the Bishop smiled, and said, "John, I think your beer is long a coming."

J. Roberts: "I suppose my wife is willing thou shouldst have the best, and therefore stays to broach a fresh vessel."

Bishop: "Nay, if it be for the best, we'll stay."

Presently my mother brought the drink, and when the Bishop had drank, he said, "I commend you, John, you keep a cup of good beer in your house; I have not drank any that has pleased me better since I came from home."

The Chancellor drank next, and the cup coming round again to my father's hand, the 'Squire Masters said to him, "Now, old school-fellow, I hope you'll drink to me."

J. Roberts: "Thou knowest it is not my practice to drink to any man; if it was, I would as soon drink to thee as another, as being my old acquaintance and school-fellow; but if thou art pleased to drink, thou art very welcome."

The 'Squire then taking the cup into his hand, said, "Now, John, before my lord and all these gentlemen, tell me what ceremony or compliment do you Quakers use when you drink to one another?"

J. Roberts: "None at all; for me to drink to another, and drink the liquor, is at best but a compliment, and that borders much on a lye."

'Squire Masters: "What do you do then?"

J. Roberts: "Why, if I have a mind to drink, I take the cup and drink; and if my friend pleases, he does the same; if not, he may let it alone."

'Squire Masters: "Honest John, give me thy hand, here's to thee with all my heart; and, according to thy own compliment, if thou wilt drink thou mayst; if not, thou mayst let it alone."

My father then offering the cup to priest Bull, he refused it, saying, "It is full of hops and heresy." To which my father replied, "As for hops I cannot say much, not being at the brewing of it; but as for heresy, I do assure thee, neighbour Bull, there is none in my beer; and if thou pleasest to drink, thou art welcome; but if not, I desire thee to take notice, as good as thou will, and those who are as well able to judge of heresy. Here, thy lord Bishop hath drank of it, and commends it; he finds no heresy in the cup."

Bishop (leaning over the coach-door, and whispering to my father), said: "John, I advise you to take care you don't offend against the higher powers. I have heard great complaints against you, that you are the ringleader of the Quakers in this country; and that if you are not suppressed, all will signify nothing. Therefore, pray, John, take care for the future, you don't offend any more."

J. Roberts: "I like thy counsel very well, and intend to take it. But thou knowest God is the highest power; and you mortal men, however advanced in this world, are but the lower power; and it is only because I endeavour to be obedient to the will of the higher powers, that the lower powers are angry with me. But I hope, with the assistance of God, to take thy counsel, and be subject to the higher powers, let the lower powers do with me as it may please God to suffer them."

And here is one other little passage between the Bishop and John, *à propos* of certain stories which had reached the Bishop's ears as to a power possessed by Roberts of discovering lost property:—

Bishop: "I remember another story Mr. Bull told me, about a parcel of sheep a neighbour had lost, and you told him where to find them."

J. Roberts: "The truth of the story is this—A neighbour of mine, one John Curtis, at that time a domestic of George Bull's, kept some sheep of his own; and it so fell out, that he lost them for some days; but happening to see me, and knowing I went pretty much abroad, he desired me, if I should see them any where in my travels, to let him know it. It happened the next day, as I was riding towards my own field, my dogs being with me, put up a hare, and seeing they were likely to kill her, I rode up to take them off, that she might escape; and by mere accident, I espied John Curtis's sheep in one corner of the field, in a thick briary part of the hedge wherein they stood as secure as if they had been in a pound. I suppose they had been driven thither by the hounds. When I came home I sent him word of it. And though this is no more than a common accident, I find George Bull hath endeavoured to improve it to my disadvantage."

Bishop: "I remember one story more he told me about a horse."

J. Roberts: "If I shan't tire thy patience, I'll acquaint thee how that was; one Edward Symmonds came from London, to see his parents at Siddington. They put his horse to grass in some ground, with their own, beyond a part of mine, called the Fursen Leases, through which they went with the horse; and when they wanted to take him from grass, they could not find him. After he had been lost some time, and they cried him at several market-towns, somebody, who, 'tis likely, might have heard the former stories told, as thou might'st hear them, directed this Edward Symmonds to me: who telling me the case, I asked him, which way they had the horse to grass: he answered, through the Fursen Leases. I told him, the horse being a stranger to the place, it was very likely he might endeavour to bend homewards, and lose himself in the Fursen Leases: for there are a great many acres belonging to me and others, under that name, which are so overgrown with furze bushes, that a horse may lie there concealed a long time. I therefore advised him to get a good deal of company, and search the places diligently, as if they were beating for a hare; which if he did, I told him I was of the mind he would find him. The man did take my advice, and found him. And where is the cunning of all this? 'tis no more than their own reason might have directed them to, had they properly considered the case."

Bishop: "I wanted to hear these stories from your own mouth: though I did not, nor should have credited them, in the sense Mr. Bull related them:

but I believe you, John. And now, Mr. Barnet, we'll ask John some serious questions. I can compare him to nothing but a good ring of bells. You know, Mr. Barnet, a ring of bells may be made of as good metal as can be put into bells ; but they may be out of tune : so we may say of John ; he is a man of as good metal as ever I met with ; but he's quite out of tune."

J. Roberts : "Thou mayst well say so ; for I can't tune after thy pipe."

Bishop : "Well, John, I remember to have read, at the preaching of the apostle the heart of Lydia was opened. Can you tell us what it was that opened Lydia's heart ?"

J. Roberts : "I believe I can."

Bishop : "I thought so. I desire you to do it."

J. Roberts : "It was nothing but the key of David."

Bishop : "Nay, now John, I think you are going wrong."

J. Roberts : "If thou pleasest to speak, I'll hear thee ; but if thou wouldst have me speak, I desire thee to hear me."

Bishop : "Come, Mr. Barnet, we'll hear John."

J. Roberts : "It is written, Thou hast the key of David, which opens, and none can shut ; and if thou shuttest, none can open. And that is no other but the Spirit of our Lord Jesus Christ. It was the same spiritual key that opened the heart of Moses, the first penman of the scripture, and gave him a sight of things from the beginning. It was the same spiritual key that opened the hearts of all the holy patriarchs, prophets, and apostles, in ages past, who left their experience of the things of God upon record, which if they had not done, you bishops and priests would not have had any thing to make a trade of ; for it is by telling the experiences of these holy men that you get your great bishopricks and parsonages ; and the same spiritual key hath, blessed be God, opened the hearts of thousands in this age ; and the same spiritual key hath, in a measure, opened my heart, and given me to distinguish things that differ. And it must be the same that must open thy heart, if ever thou comest to have it truly opened."

Bishop : "It is the truth, the very truth. I never heard it so defined before. John, I have done you much wrong : I desire you to forgive me ; and I'll never wrong you more."

J. Roberts : "I do heartily forgive thee, as far as it is in my power ; and I truly pray the Father of mercies may forgive thee, and make thee his. As to the latter part, that thou wilt never wrong me more, I am of the same mind with thee ; for it is in my heart to tell thee, I shall never see thy face any more."

Bishop : "I have heard you once told the jailor of Gloucester so, and it proved true."

Seeing the hard words that the Quaker sometimes applied to Bishops and Priests, and the odd things he did, stopping little short of claiming a power to predict people's death, and actually predicting that of the poor old Bishop to his face, we think the Bishop of Gloucester comes out remarkably well in this piece of biography ; and so do some of the Justices and gaolers under whose hands John Roberts came.   There is, in fact, a degree of kindness and toleration shown to him which is creditable to the age.   He evidently had that power of exciting sympathy and respect which is often a personal gift, and which, perhaps, might lead him to the belief that he was endowed with something more than a natural power. Other Quakers, however, have had this gift of persuasion as well as Roberts.   Illustrations of it occur again and again in Quaker biographies.   These men, with their protests against "steeple-houses" and "hireling Priests" and "prophaneness," were often, like the Jews of old, in favour in high places. Such was the case with Penn and Gilbert Latey, John Roberts, and others in those days, and we have seen the same phenomenon in our own.   A curious interview is described in the biography of Gilbert Latey, between him and some other friends and Charles II.   The object was to present a petition to the King in favour of the Society, which had been undergoing much persecution.   Here it is:—

They proceeded on towards Hampton Court, and, having gone about something more than half way up the park, saw a concourse of people near the canal; and, drawing a little nearer, perceived the King was there, upon which they drew towards him, and being come pretty near the King, some of his nobles took notice of them, and said, the Quakers were coming towards his Majesty.   The King then looking towards the friends, said he thought he knew them; upon which they spake, and prayed the King that he would be pleased to hear them a few words, they being come on purpose from London to attend the King. Upon this the King was pleased to make a little stop, and George delivered to the King the suffering case of our friends, and laid before him the severities and hardships they underwent, and that it was contrary to law; upon which the King was pleased to say he would search into the matter; adding, "I will not have them over-charged contrary to law by any means, but will have my laws observed;" and, after his thus speaking, was very pleasant, and asked the friends several questions, as why they could not as well say, Aye and No, as Yea and Nay?   To which they answered, that it was equal to our friends, either to say Aye or No, or Yea or Nay, that which was most proper they could make use of.   "But," said the King, "You will say Thee and Thou, and what is your reason for that?"   To which Gilbert made answer, "The same reason expressed in the 26th of the Acts of the Apostles, the second and third verses, give we now to the King, where the Apostle Paul, speaking to King Agrippa, says, I think myself happy, O King Agrippa, that I shall answer for myself before thee, especially because I know thou art expert in all customs, &c.   Also, verse 27, ' King Agrippa, believest thou the prophets?'   And, verse 29, ' Would to God not only thou, but also all that hear me this day, were both almost and altogether such as I am, except these bonds.'" Upon this the King made a little pause, and seemed to question whether these passages were truly translated, yet said, the translators might have translated You, as well as Thou, from the Greek; upon which George answered, " Then the translators were as simple as we Quakers;" then the King replied, " But you will not pull off your hats, and what have you to say for that?" To which Gilbert answered, " If to any mortal, then to the King in the first place;" but that it was a matter of conscience, and " we only do it when we approach the Lord in prayer." " But," said the King, " for all this, there are some among you that have not done well;" to which Gilbert answered, " They have no more pleased us than the King;" whereupon some of the nobles said, " May it please your Majesty, your Majesty says some among these people have not done well; must they be charged with that? It may be possible that some of your Majesty's own servants may not have done well, shall we therefore be blamed for that?" " No," said the King, " God forbid;" upon this some of the nobles replied, " Pray, your Majesty, hear these men, for they speak well, and they look well on your Majesty." Said the King, " I protest so they do, I admire to see such wise men Quakers." Then Gilbert asked if they might speak freely, for that they were in great hazard in approaching the King's presence; upon which the King stretched out his hand, and said, " Let no man molest or meddle with them, but let them come to me when they have occasion;" upon which Gilbert replied, " We thank God we have had the favour of seeing the King's face this day, and wish the King health, prosperity, and length of days; and all you nobles that attend the King this day, the Lord reward you for your moderation towards us."

Not only with Charles II., but with James II.—a much severer King in points of religion—did the Quakers find favour; whilst Cromwell showed them little grace. This seems singular. But some of the principles of the Friends, and especially that of passive resistance and acquiescence in " the Powers that be," took off the edge of royal displeasure against them, as, in the present day, we have seen their peace principles win them the favour of the Czar. There was, indeed, a strange contradiction between their religious and their political principles, or rather the former were supreme with them, and took little account of the absolute power of Cæsar so that it did not call upon them to go to Church, and hear " false doctrine," or to pay tithe or Church rates. And yet in this assertion of the spiritual freedom of man there was without doubt a soul of freedom that was very dangerous to tyranny, and it was the nature of Quakerism to develop into liberty, civil and political, as well as religious. Such it has done in these latter days, when the Friends take their side, as a matter of course, in the Liberal ranks, and are as active in politics as they used to be in religion. Whether, in so doing, they keep strictly to the tenets of their forefathers —whether George Fox or John Roberts would have approved of the conduct of John Bright, may well be doubted. But, as a religious body, the Friends may be regarded as extinct. The fire—divine, they believed it to be—with which they burnt in the 17th century, and which enabled them—simple, uneducated men, as they often were—to stand up against Bishops and Priests, and testify against the superstition and vices of the age, burns no longer; or, at least, if it burn, is so well regulated that the flame is never perceived. If any one want to know what the genuine Quaker was, and the mission he aspired to, let him get the memoirs of John Roberts, Gilbert Latey, and Christopher Story, and others of the worthies of the 17th century. They will be struck by the power, and amused by the simplicity, of the men; their command of Scripture, and their curious deductions from it; by the depth and width of some of their principles, and the childishness of some of their practices. They will, indeed, recognise in them the strength and weakness to be found in all ages in men who think there is only one road to human excellence and Divine favour, and that they have found it. For a time the force of this belief will hold them up as with a supernatural strength, and they will touch a high point, if not the point they aspire to; and then, either by their falling off, or by the improvement of others, the space between them and their fellow-men will become less and less, until they are merged in the mass from which they had issued: a mass leavened, doubtless, by their efforts and sacrifices, but still far —very far—from perfection.

Hermits in Sussex.

NE of the most popular and poetical appendages of the Roman Catholic religion was the hermit's cell. As such a mode of retirement from the world doubtless existed before its adoption by Rome—for much more ancient religions recognise such self-seclusion as a merit—some may still think it might have been allowed to survive the Roman system in England without much harm to society. And it did linger on, in one form and another, for some time, though not with that religious sanction and strictness which made it so imposing in the eyes of our forefathers. We ourselves can remember a kind of hermit who made himself a home under the walls of the late Mr. Colbatch's grounds, overlooking Ireland's Gardens (now Park Crescent), in Brighton, some half-century ago, and who, having seen service as a marine under Nelson in his younger days, amused himself and eked out a living by cutting out lines of fortifications and batteries and ships in the chalk, after the fashion of Uncle Toby and Corpl. Trim, on which, and on the maimed form of the old hermit, we have often looked with childish admiration. The end of Corporal Staines—that was his name—was a proof how the age of hermits, like that of chivalry, has passed away. A rumour that the poor old man had laid up a little store of wealth caused some scoundrels to attack his castle one night and to maltreat him in a very brutal manner. The consequence was, that he was transferred to the Brighton Workhouse; and there the last Sussex semblance of a hermit ended his days.

But, *à la* Tristram Shandy, we are wandering from our subject before we have entered upon it! To find the real hermit or anchorite in Sussex we must go back some hundreds of years, and the most authentic case that has come down to us is in connection with that Aldrington Church which has since been raised from its ruins and restored to its position among Sussex parish churches.   In the year 1402, according to the archives of the Diocese of Chichester, the Rector of Aldrington, one William Bolle, who is also entitled a chaplain, petitioned the Bishop of Chichester for a license to construct a cell near the parish church, in which he might pass the rest of his life in solitude, and devote himself to poverty and to prayer for the honor and glory of the Holy Trinity, our Blessed Virgin Mary, St. Richard (the Patron Saint of Chichester), and all other Saints.   William Bolle's petition was supported by the Dean and Chapter of the Cathedral, and granted by the Bishop.   So the cell was built by the side of the Church, against the chancel wall, and in it, doubtless, William Bolle lived, died, and was buried.   But here our source of information fails us, and, to form an idea of what, in all probability, the habitation and mode of life of the Aldrington hermit were, we must go to other channels.

The original life and *habitat* of a genuine hermit were very different from the picture which poets and romance-writers have since drawn of them.   Invested as these recluses and their habitations have been with much of that ease and quiet and the charms of country life which in the present day we look upon with rather desiring eyes, we see little in the life of the hermit to be admired for its abstinence, and are rather inclined to associate the hermit's cell with the good things of this life which the Clerk of Copmanhurst, *videlicet,* " Friar Tuck," set before the Black Knight in the Forest of Sherwood, or with such love-lays as that of Edwin and Angelina, than with the real privations that a recluse had to endure.   But, whatever the later hermit may have become—and, doubtless, he shared in the corruption which brought on the dissolution of the religious establishments in England—it is certain that when men and women first took to immuring themselves in cells and abjuring the society of their fellows, it was a severe ordeal and called for no slight amount of physical and mental fortitude. There was always, it would appear, a distinction between the hermit and the anchorite. The hermit, whilst avoiding the abodes of men, might wander about freely from place to place; the anchorite shut himself in a cell and never left it. This cell was generally in the neighbourhood of a monastery, or, if the recluse was a female, which was frequently the case, of a nunnery, or of a Church, as in the Aldrington instance; and was placed in such a position as to enable the recluse to see the altar and hear the service when it was performed. So completely was it looked upon as an act of self-immurement that extreme unction was first administered, and then a part of the funeral service was read, during which the anchorite was admitted into his cell, and then the door was closed upon him for ever, the presiding Bishop putting his seal upon it, if, indeed, it was not walled up. It was a living tomb, and was often so spoken of. In some instances the cells were built up like a tower; the only means of communication from without being by a kind of garret-window, through which food or the holy elements were passed.

From the end of the 12th to the commencement of the 16th century the churches of the principal English towns, like Norwich, Coventry, Northampton, &c., not only had one but many anchorages (as they were called) attached to them, either built on to the fabric or erected in the adjoining church-yard. It was not everybody that was allowed to undertake such a life. Even for a monk a year or two's confinement in a cell in a monastery was often imposed as a probation, and by a non-religious candidate two years' probation had to be undergone, and two years' notice had to be given to the Bishop, who then, if he were satisfied, might grant his license of inclusion. Thus it was no light matter to become an anchorite.

Towards the end of the 9th century the stringency of these rules was relaxed. It was no longer required that cells should be a part of the fabric of the Church, and the recluse was no longer confined to his cell, but might have a garden to labour in for his health and profit, and, if a Priest, might add a small oratory. Another important rule, too, was broken through. Several anchorites might dwell together in one common enclosure, and, though not permitted to associate, and though each had to provide for his own daily sustenance, yet they might communicate with each other, if necessary to do so, by means of a window. Disciples also were sometimes entrusted to their care, though not allowed to dwell in the same cell, and these, after they had passed a certain novitiate, were obliged to become anchorites themselves. The usual dress for lay hermits was a frock; if Priests, they wore a cope.

That this life of seclusion was not altogether prejudicial to health is shown by the longevity of many of the recluses. Some inhabited their cells forty or fifty—others sixty or seventy years ; and one is recorded to have lived in seclusion ninety-seven years.

Besides the anchorite at Aldrington, mention is made in the archives of Chichester of Friar Humphrey, the recluse of Pagham; the female recluses of Houghton and Stopham; the recluse of Hardham (all in the western division of Sussex); and a female recluse of the Blessed Mary of Westoute (now St. Anne's, Lewes). All these Sussex anchorites were bequeathed sums of money varying from 5s. to 40s. each by the canonised Bishop of Chichester, St. Richard (1242). The earliest Sussex anchorite, however, of whom any traces have come down to us is a Lewes one—called Magnus—a man of Danish race and royal descent. How he came to take up his abode in an English town, and in the little church under the Castle—"Saint John-sub-Castro"—at Lewes, is now only matter for speculation. But of the fact of his having done so there is no doubt. The presence within the church of a memorial of the fact was noted by Camden 250 years ago. It ran (in Latin) as follows: "Here is immured a soldier of the Royal family of Denmark, whose name, Magnus, indicates his distinguished lineage. Relinquishing his greatness, he assumes the deportment of a lamb, and exchanges for a life of ambition that of a humble anchorite."

The late Mark Antony Lower held that this inscription was written by the anchorite himself. It is to be regretted that he did not add the date, by which he would have saved much unprofitable speculation; for it has been asserted that the Danish Magnus was identical with Magnus, the youngest son of Harold, who, after his father's defeat at Hastings, underwent many vicissitudes of fortune, and at length, two or three years after the Conquest, became the anchorite of St. John's-sub-Castro : a story which Mr. Lower tracks to an equally absurd one of Harold himself escaping to Chester, and there ending his days as a recluse near the Church of St. John in that place; the son being substituted for the father, and St. John-sub-Castro for St. John *in Cestria!* Mr. Lower, like a true archæologist, disposes of this story by the authority of the inscription itself (which, by-the-bye, he saved from demolition when the old church was pulled down in 1839, causing it to be removed to the present edifice), "which," he says, "does not appear to be older than the 13th century."

There is no doubt that Sussex boasted of a great many more anchorites and hermits than those few whose names or the localities of whose cells have come down to us. The temptations to a life of seclusion were much greater in the early ages of the world than they are now. Life itself was harder, coarser, and more repulsive. There was little other choice for the mass of the population than that between the life of a soldier and of a peasant—that is, a life of violence and a life of sordid labour and penury. The only escape from these in the Dark Ages was the life of a monk. If a man was inclined to study or contemplation, how could he indulge in it in an age when nearly all life was out of doors or subject to the constant intrusion of coarse and ignorant persons?—when there were no books except in abbeys, monasteries, or palaces, and few opportunities of study or privacy out of religious society, and not many in that! It was rough work, we may be sure, to push through life in the Middle Ages, and no wonder some got weary-hearted with the toil and strife, and sought to escape even into such tomb-like quiet as that of the anchorite's cell. The line between secular and religious life was more marked than it is now; the latter was the only haven of rest in this world and seemed to be the surest approach to heaven. So the meek-spirited, and the disappointed, and the weary-hearted sought the only asylum open to them, and almost every religious institution had its adjacent cell, filled by a holy man or woman, often a former member of their own society. As the world encroached upon the monastic orders, and they themselves were won to it and its ways, and the boundary line between secular and spiritual became less marked, the life of the anchorite became more antagonistic and anomalous with all about it. It was not wanted as an example to others, nor did it present those advantages of quiet which were its original attraction. Men found that they could live quietly in the midst of the world, and study and think to more advantage in it than out of it. So the life of the hermit became a life of idleness and ignorance, often of dirt and vice, only suited to a lower race of men than the active student of the world. And so it was swept away; and to attempt to restore it would be almost like trying to bring back the underground habitations of our Celtic ancestors: very well adapted, no doubt, to the wants of their day, but utterly out of date now and serving no good or useful purpose.

Race-Tracks in Sussex.

THERE is an air of great wisdom in the maxim which directs us to "begin at the beginning." But how if there be no beginning? Such is really the case with respect to those venerable, and, in their way, doubtless, respectable individuals, our ancestors. Of course, they had a beginning, like every thing else in this world— even the world itself. But we cannot get at it. The search after it takes us into caves and pits and all kinds of queer places and strange companionship—bears and hyenas, and wolves and elephants. But *this* was not the beginning. Beneath these depths there was a deeper depth, into the abysses of which we will not venture to look. Science may peer, or attempt to peer, into these gloomy recesses of the human race. History only takes up the strange tale at a period when men, having established their dominion over the lower races of animals, had begun to contend with each other for the spoil, and to fight for the fairest and most fertile spots of the earth. How often this little island of ours has been fought for—won, and lost—how many races of men it has seen enter, inhabit it, and then driven out of it, or slaughtered— perhaps eaten—in it, it is impossible to say. Our ideas on these points are continually extending. As there were great Generals before Agamemnon, so there may have been—nay, judging from the evidence that meets us in such places as Salisbury Plain, there must have been great cities in England before the existence of London, and many a phase of civilisation may have existed here and in the neighbouring land of Gaul—many an abortive attempt may have been made by man to work out a higher destiny, before the path was struck upon on which we have now entered.

H

But it is with that path, and that only, that we are now concerned. We leave science to explore and speculate upon primeval man—the occupant of caves and pits and "pond-barrows"—the companion of beasts not more savage but less sagacious than himself. We leave the poets (like Milton, when he wrote history), or chroniclers scarcely less inventive than poets, to trace the peopling of Britain to Trojan Brutus, and other survivors of Ilium. Our work is much humbler. Our beginning is the men who occupied this Sussex of ours when the great Roman General, Cæsar, having reached the northernmost coast of Gaul and beheld with his own eyes the *Ultima Thule* of the Greeks, resolved to pass over into what was to him a new world,* and subdue it.

Our county cannot claim the honour of having been the first English ground trodden by those Imperial feet. Neither on the first nor the second occasion of Cæsar's incursions into Britain (they were little more) did the Sussex shore see the Roman galleys, or witness the unsuccessful attempts of the natives to beat them back. We must resign that honour to our neighbours, the men of Kent, and also the honourable testimony of Cæsar to their valour and to their comparative civilisation, though his language is scarcely so laudatory as that which Shakspeare puts into the mouth of the unfortunate Lord Saye and Sele :—

> "Kent, in the Commentaries Cæsar writ,
> Is term'd the civil'st place of all this isle;
> Sweet is the country because full of riches;
> The people liberal, valiant, active, wealthy."

The Canti, as Cæsar calls the Celtic tribe who defended their homes against him, had scarcely arrived at so high a point of civilisation as these lines would attribute to them. But they were no longer savages. They had trained the horse to purposes of war; they possessed cattle and cultivated the soil —were very skilful at basket-work, and were mechanics enough to construct cars and to build huts, which were not, perhaps, much inferior to the Irish cabins of the present day. But,

---

* Tacitus so entitles Britain.

though their chief warriors had weapons of bronze, obtained by traffic with the opposite coast, they did not know how to work the iron with which their soil abounded, and their tools were for the most part made of flint and bone. Of letters they had no tincture, or Cæsar would not have omitted to set down such a fact. That they acquired these and other arts— amongst them, how to coin money—in the 90 years that elapsed between the invasion of Cæsar and the arrival of Aulus Plautius, the general of Claudius, there can be no doubt. The process of civilisation had commenced and was going on along the same path it had taken in Gaul when the Romans arrived to give a new impulse and direction to it—it may have been to retard it by arresting its natural development. Let that be as it may, the people who opposed such a fierce and well-nigh effectual resistance to the Roman legions under Didius and Suetonius could not have been such savages as we in our time have had to deal with in North America and in Australia. They were capable of civilisation; they readily acquired all the arts of their conquerors;* they passed over with them from Paganism to Christianity, and for some 400 years they formed a part of that great community which made up the Roman Empire.

It is still a vexed question to what extent we English of the present day owe our descent from these " ancient Britons"— as it was once the fashion to call them, but who no more answered to that Roman appellation than the Red Indians

---

* The artful process by which Agricola reclaimed the natives from their savage freedom is admirably described by Tacitus in his life of that General:—"A fierce and savage people, running wild in woods, would be ever addicted to a life of warfare. To wean them from those habits Agricola held forth the baits of pleasure; encouraging the natives, as well by public assistance as by warm exhortations, to build temples, courts of justice, and commodious dwelling-houses. He bestowed encomiums on such as cheerfully obeyed: the slow and uncomplying were branded with reproach: and thus a spirit of emulation diffused itself, operating like a sense of duty. To establish a plan of education, and give the sons of the leading chiefs a tincture of letters, was part of his policy. By way of encouragement, he praised their talents, and already saw them, by the force of their natural genius, rising superior to the attainments of the Gauls. The consequence was, that they, who had always disdained the Roman language, began to cultivate its beauties. The Roman apparel was seen without prejudice, and the toga became a fashionable part of dress. By degrees the charms of vice gained admission to their hearts: baths, and porticos, and elegant banquets, grew into vogue; and the new manners, which in fact served only to sweeten slavery, were by the unsuspecting Britons called the arts of polished humanity."

answered to that of Americans, or the natives of Australia to that of Australians. They were, in fact, so many tribes of Celts or Cymri. Learned doctors differ on the point. Professor Huxley ridicules the notion that there is any ethnological distinction between the Celts who inhabited this island in Roman days and the natives of the opposite coast of Germany and Scandinavia—Angles, Saxons, Jutes, Danes, and Norsemen—who successively invaded and conquered their land. They were all Aryan descended races—of large frame, with blue eyes and light hair; the only exception being the Silures, who, like the Basques of the Pyrenees, were of a non-Aryan stock. " Is there," he asks, "any evidence to show that there is what may be called a political difference between the Celtic Aryan and the Germanic Aryan ?" And his reply is—"I must say once more that I can find none."

It was, then, by kindred races—only separated from the invaded people by wide intervals of time and space—that this island was assailed after the departure of the Romans; and there is reason to doubt whether, such being the case, the native population was so completely exterminated as has been supposed. No doubt the land was Germanised, if we may be allowed to use the expression, by the Angles, Jutes, Saxons, and Danes, as it was afterwards Gallicised by the Norman conquest ; and there was a greater displacement of population by the former races because they came to win a new home, and not merely, as the Normans did, to acquire new possessions; still retaining their old ones. But it has seldom been the desire of invaders, except where instigated by religious fanaticism, like the Jews or Spaniards, to drive out or destroy a whole population—men, women, and children. The very fact that such emphasis is laid on the wholesale slaughter of the inhabitants of Anderida—a fortified and garrisoned town— leads to the inference that in open and undefended places the natives were *not* destroyed—only reduced to the condition of serfs.

In tracing, then, the existence of the Celts in Sussex we are not seeking for evidence of a race to which we are aliens

in blood, or even, as respects the Romanised Celts, in religion
—for they were Christians—but whom we must regard in a
great degree as our ancestors; not merely as an Aryan-
descended people, but with some of their blood flowing in our
veins, mixed, no doubt, with that of Angles, Jutes, Frisians,
Danes, and Normans, but still as good as theirs, and helping
to make up that very composite being, an Englishman!

What signs, then, are there—and we have now got into the
line of our real theme—what signs are there of our Celtic
ancestors in Sussex?

The answer divides itself into two parts; ante-Roman and
cum-Roman. The evidence of the first period is to be found
in the names of places and in those earthworks which are
more lasting than structures of wood or stone or brick. A
few years ago a writer in the *Brighton Herald*, very learned
in philology, pointed out numerous instances in this locality
—indeed, all over Sussex—in which the names, long supposed to be of Saxon origin, were in reality Celtic, or a
combination of the two, as, in the present day, we are grafting
French and Italian words upon Saxon names of precisely the
same import—for instance, Cliftonville—" ton " and " ville "
both meaning exactly the same thing. What we do in our
day, the Romans first, and then the Angles, did in theirs;
they could not obliterate the names of the spots which they
took possession of—that, of all others, is the most difficult
thing to do—but they often added to them, or, in course of
time, Romanised or Anglicised them. An instance of this
process of transmutation is the change of the Roman Portus
Adurni into Aldrington. According to our correspondent,
the original name of the Adur was Celtic, from " dwr," the
water or river. The Romans came and Latinised it; the Angles
came and Anglicised it, and it bears marks of its triple origin.
Lewes escaped both processes: it is a purely Celtic name, still
pronounced exactly as it must have been 2,000 years ago, viz.,
" Lle Wysg, the river-place, or place on the Wysg or Wisge
—that is, the Ouse, as the river is still called." There is,

adds our authority, the twin name of the Lewes of Sussex in Wales—on the river Wye—Wye being short for Wysg.

Numerous other cases are cited—Brighton being among them; and the honour of naming Beachy Head is snatched from the French and restored to the primitive race. "*Beau Chef,*" exclaims our correspondent, "is a fine etymology to a certainty, but it is not what Beachy Head means. Beachy Head is a Celtic name—Bachiad—and means a bending, turning, or winding, *i.e.*, where the coast bends or trends in a new direction."

Even the Devil's Dyke is taken from His Satanic Majesty, and declared to be a corruption of the Celtic "Dyphwys Dyuchel," significant of a deep pit—an abyss; and "Poynings, at the foot of the Dyke, admits of no doubt whatever as to its Celtic etymology. In Doomsday Book, Poynings is Paninges. Poynings is Panmen gwann ban—a low meadow, a wet or boggy meadow. It is common in Glamorganshire."

Sometimes, without doubt, the Celtic etymon is strained too far. Mounted on his hobby, a Welsh etymologist rides Celtic words very hard indeed! But there is a strong foundation for his theory. When the Angles and Saxons overran England, it had been not merely a populated, but a civilised land, for 400 years, and the names of places—particularly hills and rivers and other natural formations—stick, as our experience in America and Australia proves. Many names in Sussex, utterly meaningless or absurd in their modern shape, become full of significance when Celticised.

Not only in respect to names—but also in respect to works —have our earlier Celtic ancestors left evidence of their dominion. Sussex is full of them. From Heyshott, near Midhurst, on the west, to Birling Gap, on the east, the whole range of Southdown hills is studded with vast earthworks. We have only to quote such familiar names as the Trundle (near Chichester), Chanctonbury, Cissbury, Highdown Hill, Wolstonbury, the Devil's Dyke, Hollingbury and Whitehawk Hill, near Brighton, to call up a range of fortified posts which equal in extent, and in natural and artificial strength, any of which vestiges are to be found in Europe. When the stone and brick fortresses of the Romans and Normans have disappeared, as so many of them have, the "Camps" on the Sussex hills—not of Cæsar, as they used to be called, but of the Celts—will still remain to excite the wonder of the ignorant and the speculations of the learned. These great earthworks used to be attributed to the Romans, and there is no doubt that they occupied many of them. But they must often have found them ready-made to their hands, for the invariable shape of a Roman encampment was a parallelogram, and nearly all these Down camps are circular. There are the remains of many Roman camps in Sussex, as at Hardham, near Pulborough; the Broil, near Chichester; on Ditchling Hill; on Mount Cauburn (above Ringmer), and on the Downs near Falmer; but all these are rectangular. A notable instance of the successive occupation of one point by Celt, Roman, and Saxon, is presented at Cissbury, near Findon. Indubitable proof has been adduced by the explorations of Colonel Lane Fox and Mr. Tyndall that the original works at Cissbury were Celtic; whilst the discovery of Roman coins, pottery, &c., and also the fact of a Roman road running through it, mark it as one of the military posts of that great people; and the name it now bears is Saxon, and has always been attributed, though on doubtful authority, to the same Saxon chief, Cissa, who gave his name to Chichester. In that city, again, the same triple union is traceable; the capital of a Celtic tribe, the Regni (their Celtic name was Caercei) is Latinised into Regnum by its Roman occupants, and then Anglicised into Cissan-Ceaster, or the camp of Cissa, by the new comers from Germany. Supposing that Anderida, the great Roman station at the other extremity of Sussex, had escaped, as Regnum did, complete destruction, we should have had a city with a name of Celtic origin, first Latinised, and then, doubtless, Anglicised. And many a place has passed through this triple transformation or adaptation—Aldrington, for instance, before referred to—which symbolises the mixture of the three races.

But to return to the Celtic works. These, there can be little doubt, did not belong to one age, but date back to and illustrate times when those who erected them were less advanced in civilisation than when Cæsar saw and described them. Such a work, in all probability, is that most remarkable one at Burpham, which has nothing in common with the " camps" along the Downs by which a later people sought to defend themselves from attack. The Burpham earthwork is quite different in character, and harmonises better with the more primitive races who formed and navigated the canoe that was found a few years ago in a ditch at Stoke, a short distance from Burpham. This canoe, hollowed out of a single tree, was the starting-point of the English navy, as its rude, perhaps naked owner, who must have looked upon it as a mighty triumph of skill and industry (and so it was, made with such tools as he possessed) was the starting-point of the great English people!

But, to return to the earthwork at Burpham, we will copy from the columns of the *Brighton Herald* a description written by us some few years back of this singular and rarely-visited Celtic fortification :—

The approach to Burpham from the south, its only assailable point sea-ward, is by a natural causeway; flanked on the west by the Adur and on the east by a stream, which, no doubt, was once a considerable one, at a time when the valley was undrained and when the wooded state of the country caused more rain to fall in these parts. The sides of this causeway may be looked upon as inaccessible—it is no easy task to climb them at the present day, when there are none but natural obstacles. An invading foe, then, must fight his way up from the commencement of the spur, and, as he advanced, he found himself on a narrow and rising piece of ground, flanked by steep sides, with water running at the foot of each. He must for safety's sake fight on, in the hope of coming upon a more open country, and driving the enemy from the hills or the village to which they were retreating. But, at the moment when the ground is at its narrowest and steepest, a new obstacle suddenly rises up—a steep mound, of from 30 to 40 feet in height, stretching right across the causeway, and barring further progress. Behind this is the village. On the summit of the mound, we may imagine, stood the natives of the country, conscious of their advantage, and animated by every feeling of men to defend their homes and families. On ascending the mound—which may now be done with impunity—we look down to the north on the roofs of houses hitherto completely screened from view. Walk to the western end, and the river is flowing at your feet. No boat could pass without being exposed to destruction at the hands of the occupants of the mound. Walk to the other end of the mound, on the east, and you overlook the channel of a stream now almost dry, which, when filled with water, as once it must have been, was equally commanded by this earthwork. The labour that must have been employed in its construction is one of those facts which, like Stonehenge, puzzle the antiquarian who attributes the work to the hands of a barbarous people. From east to west the mound runs for 200 or 250 yards, at a height varying from 20 to 40 or 50 feet, and with a summit broad enough to walk upon. A road into the village now cuts it into nearly two equal pieces; but whether this is the work of modern times, or was part of the original design, we are unable to say. Only in the earliest ages of this country could such a work as this have been of any value. Its object was, doubtless, to defend a small tribe, who had their homes in these hills, and whose flocks sometimes fed in the valley beneath, from any sudden incursion by way of the sea. An approaching enemy could be easily seen from the summit of the mound, and, on the alarm being given, the cattle were driven behind the mound, with the women and children and old people, whilst the warriors either sallied out or awaited the attack on this 'vantage ground. If the enemy attempted to pass up the valley in boats, they were overwhelmed with stones and spears and arrows. If they came up the causeway, they were met by the wall of earth, and, if they could not break through this, they were liable to be driven over the steep sides of the hill up which they had come. The mound is now covered with fine grass, and, when we visited it, the river nets of the villagers were spread upon it to dry—its only use now. The villagers themselves are ignorant that it ever had any other.

The frequent occurrence of Celtic earthworks, not only on the Southdowns, but upon the river-sides (as this at Burpham) and the sandy lowlands of Sussex, is pointed out in a paper in the Sussex Archæological Collections, by Mr. P. J. Martin, a very intelligent Sussex archæologist. He refers to stone and copper axes, found by gravel-diggers upon Commons, and now deposited in the Chichester Museum. Sepulchral barrows, he observes, are not rare in these localities; and he then proceeds to describe two remarkable mounds upon an elevated part of Nutbourne Common, in the parish of Pulborough, one of which (the northern one) was, when it was discovered, some years ago, surrounded by a stone wall, with a doorway to the east four feet wide; and a quarter of a mile to the south of these mounds was a British (or Celtic) settlement, or what he believes to have been such. "It is," he says, "a triangular headland of sandy soil, partly waste and partly arable, now called Winterfield, enclosed on two sides by streams which flow through low meadows, in earlier times unquestionably woody marshes, like the neighbouring unreclaimed peat bogs. On the third it is defended by a broad ditch and vallum, having the perfect character of the Celtic encampment, not improved, as many of them were, by subsequent Roman works. The area of the peninsula thus enclosed may be about six or eight acres. I do not know that any relics of the Celtic or Roman character have been ploughed up in the cultivated part of it, but on the adjoining lands of Hurston and Wiggonholt Roman coins, pottery, and other marks of the habitation of Romanised Britons, have been discovered. This encampment of Winterfield (proceeds Mr. Martin) exactly corresponds in character and situation with the more important one of Burpham, near Arundel, which is in like manner defended by a morass on one side, the river Arun on the other, and at the base of the triangle by a ditch and wall twice the size of the work in question. Arundel itself, the *ad Decimum Lapidem* of the Romans, was originally a British town of the same character, with the river on one side, a marshy and woody ravine on the other, and a fosse and vallum traversing the neck of land between the two, still to be seen, intersected by the London road, just without St. Mary's Gate."

With respect to the walled tumuli near this Celtic encampment, Mr. Martin quotes Sir R. Hoare, the learned historian of Wiltshire, in support of the theory that they were constructed for religious purposes. They also bear a close resemblance to the "Pond Barrows," often found upon the Downs, in which trinkets and articles of domestic use have been often found, and "in looking at which constructions," says Mr. Martin, "I have always been inclined to think that they were the sites of British habitations, perhaps of the superior order. I suppose the shallow excavation to be the area of the hut, and the low circular vallum the basis upon which the superstructure rested, consisting of long rafters meeting at top over the centre of the area, like a pile of hop-poles; and these being strengthened, and closed in with boughs and thatch, formed the habitation—than which we may suppose the noblest Briton, with his flint or copper spear-head, his pottery of unbaked earth, and other rude appliances, 'could boast no better home.' The circular embankment on which the rafters rested would serve to carry off the water as it trickled down the roof, and keep the interior dry and comfortable.

"To this rude cottage was added, in our present instance, a stone wall at the foot of the mound, to defend it from the intrusion of cattle or other injurious animals.

"The supposition of its being the site of a human habitation is strengthened by the discovery of the stones in that part of the crown of the circle which corresponds with the doorway in the wall, and were placed in the entrance of the hut, perhaps, to make the pathway firm ; and also by the discovery of the broken millstone and pottery under the floor of the area.

"To this use I am inclined to assign all the pond barrows, and that is the reason Sir R. Hoare so frequently found trinkets and articles of domestic use in them."

If, as is now generally admitted, the so-called Roman camps in Sussex, such as Chanctonbury, Cissbury, Hollingbury, Wolfstanbury, &c., are of Celtic origin, then the question arises, in what way were they used by that people? As places of abode?—towns? or as military posts? The Romans, there is no doubt, used them merely as military posts; as signal-places from which they could hold communication with each other and carry, by their military *viæ*, aid from one point of their possessions to another. *Their* towns and villas were erected in the plains below, on both sides of the Downs—as at Chichester and Pevensey, Bignor and Hurst, Hardham and Preston. The Romans did not, like the Normans, affect hilly spots for their abode: they had too much confidence in themselves, and had little fear of attack either from the land or the sea-side. The notion that they did not occupy the Weald has been long dispelled; their remains are to be found in many spots in it and their roads pierced through it, from

Aldrington on the coast by Hangleton, St. John's Common, Street, &c., into the great Ermyn-street which led to London, and from London to Dover; and also, in a more easterly direction, to Anderida.   Doubtless the greater part of the plain overlooked by the stations at Chanctonbury, Devil's Dyke, &c., was forest; and the frequent occurrence of " hurst," or wood, in the villages that now dot it shows that it was forest in the days of the Angles.   But to the Romans it must have been a mere hunting-ground, not a hiding-place for enemies; they knew how to drive these out and to subjugate and civilise them.   For 300 or 400 years the native Celts were so civilised, and the Roman villas still at times exhumed, as at Bignor, Preston (near Brighton), and Hurst (Danny), prove that the Roman officers lived here in safety and in luxury, as the English nobility now live in *their* parks and surrounded by *their* ancestral woods.

But it was very different with the Celts anterior to Roman occupation.   They were divided into many tribes and clans, warring with each other, and fortifying their habitations against each other, as, at a later day, the Norman Barons did. It must have been the aim of each of these tribes to secure a defensible place for their families and such rude property as they possessed; and what better spots could they have chosen than these projections—these natural buttresses of the Downs —spots already half fortified by the sharp declivities of the hills to which they were a fringe?   There is scarcely one of these fortresses of Nature which is not " capped " by a Celtic earthwork—occupied, doubtless, by the earlier Celts as permanent habitations, and afterwards utilised by Romans as military stations.

To this latter use, too, doubtless, the Angles turned them when they succeeded the Romans as invaders and conquerors. But they, too, like the Romans—even more so, indeed—were inhabitants of the plain and abandoned many of the hilly camps.   They poured into the forests left by the Romans, made clearings (still denoted by the Anglo-Saxon termination

" lye "), and eschewed fortifications: a circumstance which, unquestionably, facilitated the conquest of the Normans. Had the Saxons built on the Celtic sites some of those stone castles which the Normans soon raised, at Arundel, Pevensey (Anderida), Lewes, Bramber, &c., the task of William would have been much more difficult, if not impossible.

But the Angles cared neither to erect stoneworks nor earthworks; they preferred, as we English—their immediate descendants—do, to live in open towns, villages, and isolated houses, living a rural life and depending on their valour by sea and land for their safety. It failed them once; may it never do so again!

To this circumstance, doubtless—their love of rural life and their contempt of fortifications—is it owing that the Angles and Jutes, whilst giving their names to so many places —whilst fixing the sites of nearly all our modern towns and villages, supply fewer relics to the archæologist than the Celts and Romans who preceded, or the Normans who succeeded, them. To the Celts belong the great earthworks on our hills and such stoneworks as those on Salisbury Plain and at Amesbury; to the Romans or Romanised Celts belong such cities as Chichester, Colchester, and such villas as those at Bignor and Danny; whilst coins and pottery and burial-places, such as that recently discovered at Preston, near Brighton, are found in every direction — on the hills and in the plains. This period of Roman occupation and of Celtic subjugation is becoming more and more illustrated by modern explorations. Pagan Temples and altars, as at Chichester, are found to underlie Christian Churches; our highways, and even our railways, follow the old Roman *viæ;* we are erecting new villas, with the same luxurious appliances of the bath, ventilation, &c., on the sites of the old Roman villas, and find that we have something to learn from them in the arts and conveniences of life! We find the subsoil almost sown with fragments of Roman pottery and Roman coinage, or those of Rome's Celtic subjects, and we even occasionally turn up, as at Mountfield, near Hastings, some few years ago, the golden ornaments of an earlier and free-born Celtic warrior, or, as at Hove, the amber cup, the stone battle-axe, and the bronze dagger (now in the Brighton Museum, thanks to the vigilance of Mr. Barclay Phillips, of Brighton), which were interred with some Celtic chief in the barrow that was raised to mark his grave. Of the stone tools, or weapons, too, with which he worked, or hunted, or fought, there is a rich and apparently inexhaustible supply. What Museum does not overflow with " celts ? "

Of Saxon, or, as we should rather say, English relics, there is a less rich supply. The Celts surpassed them in earthworks; the Romans and Romanised Celts in works of metal and of pottery; and the Normans in buildings of stone. But the Anglo-Saxon had his revenge: he had the bone and muscle and sinew—the indomitable spirit of industry and love of independence which supplied something more precious than all the rest, and which has gradually absorbed them. By his steady endurance, though conquered, he has made all that went before or followed him—Celtic, Roman, Norman—his own, and he now stands surrounded by *their* remains as a part of *his* inheritance. By the vigour of his language, too, he has " taken seisin " of much that did not originally belong to him: camps, towns, hamlets, hills, rivers —spots that once answered to Celtic and Roman names, but have now such apparently pure Saxon appellations as Hollingbury, Chanctonbury, Wolfstonbury, Aldrington, &c.; and the extermination of the Romanised Celts at Anderida was scarcely more complete than has been the extinction of Celtic names by the substitution, or overlaying, of Anglo-Saxon ones. So the English, by the stubbornness of their spirit, the strength of their limbs, and the genius of their tongue, have fashioned the land to the likeness of themselves. It is Angle-land; and all who went before, or even who, like the Normans, came after, are but *disjecta membra.* The living body is English. If we would see the work of the Celts, we must go to the peaks of the Southdowns, or to such spots as

Burpham, and see where they fixed their habitations; if of the Romans, we must follow their military roads, running in lines straight as their own pilum over hill and plain, or we must delve down some ten or twelve feet below the surface till we strike on the tesselated pavements of their villas and temples, or look with wonderment at the gigantic brick walls that once protected their garrison at Anderida, or mark the rectangular lines of their cities and encampments at Chichester and the Broil. If we would know the Norman, and his works, do they not rise up in the stately forms of Cathedral and Castle, still defying the ravages of time and the attack of that swifter destroyer—man? But if the work of the Angle be sought, it is not in any of these directions, or in a lower grade, that we find it: it is in

> "Man, high-minded man,
> That knows his rights, and knowing dares maintain"

it is in free institutions, the outcome of an unconquerable love of independence, and in a literature that, springing from this independence, has, by its inherent vigour, which scarcely acknowledges the rules and trammels of Art, reached to a height that Art never touched—to the utmost bounds of nature and the aspirations of the human soul.

It is the privilege and boast of Sussex that all these successive stages of humanity, by which we have reached the height on which we stand, are to be studied and traced in our county. We are rich in the remains of the Celt, the Roman, the Norman, and in the actual living presence of an English race. From this we would not eliminate the Celtic element, or even, in a minor degree, a tincture of the Roman blood. For did not Constantine wed a Celtic Princess, and must not thousands of the veteran legionaries have settled down as natives of the land they had conquered—taking unto themselves Celtic wives and begetting half-Celtic children? No doubt the Angles and Jutes made sad havoc of this civilised and somewhat emasculated race when they descended on the shores of Sussex—at Pagham and Selsey, it is said—

in the full vigour of savage freedom.   But they did not—could
not—exterminate a whole race—man, woman, and child. They
simply absorbed it, as they afterwards absorbed the Norman
element, and still absorb all the foreign currents of vitality
that pour into us from continental Europe, from Asia, and
even from Africa.   It is this power of absorption—of
assimilation—that makes the race so strong, so rich, so
varied and cosmopolitan—may we not say so Imperial ?—
fitted to go forth in its turn to conquer or to people the
earth: for we carry with us the versatility of the Celt, the
doggedness of the Anglo-Saxon, the shrewdness and tenacity
of purpose of the Norman, the law-making and the law-
abiding attributes of the Roman.   By virtue of the Norse we
are ploughers of the sea; by virtue of the Celt we are
diggers and delvers of the earth; the Angle and the Jute
have given us our love for woods and rural places, made us
growers of corn and rearers of cattle, and land-robbers on
the grandest of scales.   To the Danes, roaming with "hungry
hearts" through the world, to possess and populate it, we owe
something.   Something, too, we have inherited from the
Norman in the rearing up of gorgeous edifices—Castles
and Churches and Palaces, and Mansions equal to Palaces.
From one and all we have taken something with us on our
onward march.   And, to such as deign to turn aside for a
moment and pause to mark the stages of our progress, no
soil can furnish richer opportunities of study—more suggestive
evidence of the Past—than this of our county of Sussex.

Royal Visits to Sussex.

P to the time of the Fourth George, Sussex had no
title to be included in the number of the Royal
Counties—that is, it had no fixed place of residence
like Middlesex, Berks, and Hampshire, for the
Kings of England. Nor is there any record of a lengthened
sojourn in it by any of our Monarchs. From time to time it
was visited by them for the purposes of war or peace—but
not, for the most part, under circumstances calculated to win
their favour, or make them look back upon it with longing
eyes.

To the last of the Saxon Kings—Harold—it was peculiarly
fatal; for it was from a Sussex seaport—Bosham, now a mere
fishing hamlet—that he embarked on that inauspicious voyage
to Normandy, which may be regarded as the first act of the
Conquest of England, involving him, as it did, in an acknowledgment of a promise, or, according to the Normans, an oath,
to support the claim of William as the heir of Edward the
Confessor; and it was to the Sussex coast that he hastened
from his victory in the North over the Danish King, when the
news was brought to him that William and his host had
disembarked in the Bay of Pevensey. It was on Sussex soil
that he gave battle to the invader; here, like a brave man, he
fell, fighting to the last; and here, according to the best
authorities, he lies buried in sight of the coast which, according
to the saying of his successful rival, he had so long guarded.

To the Conqueror the soil of Sussex might be deemed
auspicious and rich in glorious associations; but it is certain
he did not select it as a place of abode, and, after founding
the Abbey at Battle, which he had vowed on the field of battle·

I

to erect in case of victory, he passed onward; and we have no further record of deeds of his on Sussex soil. Yet, as fronting to his native land, and as being the place of residence of his daughter Gundrada (whose remains lie buried at Lewes with those of her husband, William de Warenne), it is not improbable that the Conqueror visited Sussex during his active career, and perhaps traversed the battle-field on which he had won his kingly crown.

Let that be as it may, it is not until the accession of his son, William the Red, that we have evidence of the presence of a King of England on Sussex soil; and it was in order to take possession (in 1097) of Arundel Castle, then and up to the Commonwealth one of the strongholds of the county. It was to besiege, and to take, the same fortress that Rufus's brother and successor, Henry I., entered Sussex in 1102. In the troubled times that succeeded Henry's death, Sussex was visited by both the competitors for the Crown: by Henry's daughter, the Empress Maud, who, with her mother, Queen Adeliza, sought refuge at Arundel in 1139, and by Stephen, his nephew, who besieged both Arundel and Pevensey Castles, and who was, as a deed signed by him testifies, at Lewes between 1148 and 1152.

Of the presence of Henry II., or of his heroic son, Richard Cœur de Lion, on Sussex soil, we have no evidence; but Richard's unworthy successor, John, frequently journeyed through it. It was at Shoreham that he landed (in May, 1199) after taking possession of Normandy on the death of Richard, and in two days after he was crowned in London, so that he must have travelled expeditiously. The next month he was again at Shoreham, on his way to Dieppe with troops, to make good his claims in France. In 1205 he was at Lewes; in 1206 at Battle, Arundel, and other places; and a letter addressed by him in this year to the earls, barons, knights, and freeholders of Sussex, praying them, " for the love of us," to assist us now in carrying our timber to Lewes, " not as a right, but as a favour," is the earliest testimony to the difficulties of land-carriage in the Sussex Weald. In 1208 John was in the west part of the county, at Pagham and Aldingbourne, where there was a royal residence, on his way to Southampton ; and in 1209 he was again at Aldingbourne, Arundel, Bramber, and at Knepp Castle (a residence of the Braose family, whom John treated so barbarously, and now the seat of the Burrells) at West Grinstead, at which place he remained several days both this year and in 1211. In 1212 he was again at Battle and Aldingbourne, and in 1213 at Arundel, Lewes, Battle, Rye, and Winchelsea. In 1224 and 1225 he was at Aldingbourne, and in the latter year at Knepp Castle, directing to the Sheriff of Sussex from Stanstead an order to pay 30s. to Simon Eynulf, " for one cask of wine, which was drunk at our house at Aldingbourne on Sunday, the Feast of the Conversion of St. Paul." In 1226 he was at Seaford, Bramber, and Wool Lavington—places at opposite extremities of the county, and his quick passage from one to the other testifies to that restlessness and rapidity of movement for which John was famous. In one year he changed his residence 150 times, and Matthew of Paris records with wonder the speed with which he travelled by day and night in 1202, in order to rescue his mother when she was besieged in the Castle of Mirabell, in Normandy. Had all his movements been instigated by as good a motive, his subjects would have had reason to love instead of hating him.

John's son and successor, Henry III., we need hardly say, was a visitor to Sussex. It was in the strong and stately Priory of Lewes that he took up his residence with his son Edward, Prince of Wales, and his brother Richard, Duke of Cornwall and King of Rome, when his Barons were in open revolt against him under Simon de Montfort ; it was here he was besieged after the total defeat of his forces on the neighbouring Downs ; and here he was compelled to sign those terms of peace by which the first real English Parliament was called together, and from which the English Constitution may be said to have sprung. By the Battle of Lewes the Battle of Hastings may almost be said to have been avenged ; at all events, it balanced its effects, and put King and people in their right places.

Sussex was visited by the three successive Edwards. Edward I. (whose forced journey from Lewes after the battle to Dover, under the custody of his cousin, Henry de Montfort, was considered so ignominious that the popular ballads of the day speak of him as even deprived of his spurs :—

> "Be the luef, be the loht, Sir Edward,
> Thou shalt ride sporeless o' thy lyard,
> Al the ryghte way to Dovere ward,")

almost met his death at Winchelsea, then the most important sea-port of the southern coast. Whilst riding on the ramparts of the Castle his horse took fright and leaped over the parapet into the road, which, fortunately for its royal rider, had been softened by recent rains. So the animal slipped some twelve feet or more, and yet did not fall, and the King, reining it up, turned it round and rode up to the gate, which he entered unhurt, to the wonder and delight of those who had witnessed the catastrophe.

Edward I. was also a sojourner at Aldingbourne, Chichester, Lewes, Battle, Winchelsea, and Romney, in 1276, and in 1281 he visited Hurst and Chichester, and in 1285 Bramber, Arundel, and Chichester; and Chichester and Midhurst in 1286. At Chichester he made rich presents to the shrine of St. Richard, still to be seen in the Cathedral. In 1295 he was at Winchelsea; in 1297 at Chichester, Arundel, Mayfield, and Lewes; and in 1299, at Mayfield, Uckfield, Bramber, Arundel, Chichester, and Lewes. In 1305 Edward was at Horsham and Midhurst, Cocking, Midhurst, Chichester, Aldingbourne, Arundel, Shoreham, Clayton, Lewes, Buxted, and Mayfield. This was his last journey to Sussex. Both he and Edward de Balliol were sick at Chichester, and his long and glorious reign soon after came to an end.

Sussex is closely connected with Edward II., and a series of letters written by him when Prince of Wales, at Midhurst, Battle, &c., which has been preserved (and published in the Sussex Archæological Collections), relate to a serious difference between himself and his Royal father, and shadow forth his future errors and misfortunes. It was at this period that the young Prince was under the influence of his first favourite, Piers Gaveston, and the King's Chancellor, the Bishop of Chester, having reproved the favourite for misleading the Prince, this latter addressed him in language which called down on him the anger of his Royal father. "On Sunday, the 15th day of June," writes the Prince to Henry de Lacy, Earl of Lincoln, "we came to Midhurst, where we found our lord the King our father, and on the following Monday, on account of certain words which were told him, that had been between us and the Bishop of Chester, he is so angry with us that he has forbidden us, that neither ourselves nor any one of our suite should be so bold as to enter within his household; and he has forbidden all his officers of his household and of the exchequer that they should neither give us nor lend us anything whatever for the sustenance of our household; and we have remained at Midhurst in order to wait for his good pleasure and his pardon, and we will at any rate proceed after him in the best manner that we shall be able, as at ten or twelve leagues from his household, until we may be able to recover his good pleasure, for which we have great desire." For some six months was the Prince thus exiled from Court, and cut off from his usual means of living, and the letters he writes from Midhurst, Chichester, Aldingbourne, Lewes, Hellingly, Battle, &c., are chiefly in order to entreat succour for himself or his attendants. The enmities and the friendships made at this time exercised a baneful influence in the succeeding reign, or rather it was now that the Prince displayed that weakness of character that made his reign so calamitous.

A Royal progress was made through Sussex by Edward II. in 1324, on the eve of his deposition and death. The pretext of the visit southward was to embark at Portsmouth for a military expedition to France. But the King lingered long on the road, and never carried out his design. He arrived at Tunbridge on the 23rd of August, and remained there until the 27th, receiving presents of fish (pike) and fruit from the Archbishop of Canterbury. From Tunbridge he proceeded to Bayham Abbey, thence to Robertsbridge Abbey, and on the 28th of August to Battle Abbey, where numerous presents, including swans, herons, pheasants, pike, oxen, mutton, capons, wine, &c., &c., awaited him. Indeed, it was chiefly at Abbeys and Priories that the Kings of this period took up their abode when on their travels; the accommodation being doubtless very superior to that of secular hosts. On the 30th of August the King was at Pevensey, where he appoints Wardens of Rye and Winchelsea, the large dimensions of the latter port (now a grass field) being specially referred to. Eastbourne was the next stage of the Royal progress, and then Bishopstone, whence he is stated to have proceeded to Thele, which Mr. Lower identifies as Theelands, in Slynfold, a dependency of the Norman Abbey of Fécamp. Stoppages are also made at Shipley, Horsham, Chedworth, Pulborough, and Petworth, numerous presents "in kind" being received at all these places, and the King sometimes making presents of plate in return. Swans and herons often figure in the provisions furnished for the Royal table. Petworth was the last place in Sussex which received the King, who passed thence into Hampshire, but never carried out his intention to proceed to France, where his faithless consort, Isabella, was with her son, Edward, plotting against him. In the following year these intrigues came to a head; the King was deposed; and his cruel murder, in Berkeley Castle, speedily followed. The progress in Sussex was amongst the last acts of his ill-starred reign.

His son, Edward III., made several visits to Sussex, chiefly in connection with his naval expeditions. He visited Rye and Winchelsea in 1350; disembarked at the latter port in 1355, in company with his sons, Lionel and John; and, after sailing to the Isle of Wight, was again driven back to the Sussex port. In 1360 the warlike King landed at Rye, and starting immediately in the evening for London on horseback, arrived at his capital the next morning at nine o'clock: a praiseworthy example of Royal diligence. Once more, in

1372, Edward was at Winchelsea, and prorogued Parliament from it after the defeat of the English fleet at La Rochelle.

There is now a gap in the series of Royal visits. Of the presence of the hapless Richard II. in Sussex we find no trace, nor of the aspiring Bolingbroke's presence, nor of the heroic Fifth Harry, who, we know, sailed from Southampton on his expedition into France. Henry VI. was not an active Monarch, and the battle-scenes of York and Lancaster lay in the Midland and Eastern Counties, not in the South, though the Sussex Howards were the stoutest adherents of Richard III. Edward IV., however, came to Chichester, and there made many Justices of the Peace. The Tudors "took" to the county, and Bluff King Hal came to Rye in 1487, probably to hasten the equipment of shipping for one of his French expeditions. Whether Sussex shared in his many "progresses" is not recorded, but it is likely. His son, Edward VI., made but one Royal progress, and that included Sussex. It was in 1552; and his own journal of it has been preserved. He entered the county from the Surrey side, with some 4,000 horse, which, as the young King himself observes, "ware inough to eat up the country; for ther was little medow nor hay al the way as I went," which showed that the King, youthful as he was, looked about him. Indeed, the Tudors generally did, and sharply too, as one of the noblemen who entertained Henry VII. found out to his cost when he put his labourers into livery to do honour to his Royal guest, that being illegal, and was informed by His Majesty, on his taking leave, that "his Chancellor would reckon with him!"

Petworth, the first halting-place of Edward VI. in his progress, was the southern seat of the Percies, Earls of Northumberland, but, at the time of the King's visit, it was temporarily in the hands of the Crown; and so the charge, which must have been great, fell on Henry, Earl of Arundel, who was master of the game there. The King slept four nights at Petworth. On the 25th of July he was at Cowdray, the splendid seat of the Earls Montague (Browne) and the ruins of which (it was burnt down in 1793) still remain to attest its ancient glories. At Cowdray the King remained until the 27th, and then went eastward to Halnaker, which he describes as "a pretty house beside Chichester." It was at that time the seat of Thomas Lord de la Warre, and had been erected by his father early in the reign of Henry VIII. Scarcely any vestiges of it now remain ; and its grounds are included in the Goodwood estate of the Dukes of Richmond. The Sussex visit seems to have closed with Halnaker, and the Royal invaders (for, to the nobles visited, it was as ruinous as an invasion) turned westward : the next entry referring to Southampton.

Mary does not seem to have honoured (?) Sussex with her presence, and seeing the horrors that her reign brought upon the county, in the martyr-burnings at Lewes and elsewhere, she would hardly have been welcomed. Her Royal and Protestant sister, Elizabeth, made amends. She visited both East and West Sussex. She was at Rye for three days in 1573, and went from thence to Winchelsea, seeing the renewed prosperity of which (it had been destroyed by Edward I. for the assistance its citizens gave to the Barons), she called it a "little London." In 1591 she visited her faithful minister, Sir Anthony Browne, Earl Montague, at his beautiful seat, Cowdray, at Midhurst, and was, as her brother had been, magnificently entertained. The traditions of the visit still hang about the place, and the spot is shown whence the Queen shot a deer with her own Royal hand.

In a contemporary narrative of this visit of Elizabeth to Cowdray some curious details are given, which so closely resemble the account of the doings at Leicester's Castle of Kenilworth, in Scott's novel, that one might almost think the great novelist had seen and made use of them.

As soon, we are told, as the Queen appeared in sight, loud music sounded, which ceased when she arrived on the bridge. A man in armour (standing between two wooden effigies to resemble porters), holding a club in one hand and a golden key in the other, addressed her Majesty, declaring that there was a prophecy, when the first stone was laid, that these walls should shake, and the roof totter, until "the wisest, the fairest, and the most fortunate of all creatures" should arrive. That his fellow-porters gave up all hopes of this beneficial advent, and so fell asleep, but that he would rather have cut off his eyelids than wink till he saw the end. Now that the "miracle of time," "nature's glorie," and "fortune's empresse," had arrived, of course the house was immoveable. He then presented the key, as a crest of his office, at the same time declaring his honourable Lord, the owner of the house, to be second to none in duty and service to her Majesty, and that "his tongue was the keie of his heart, and his heart the locke of his soule."

The Queen then accepted the key, saying she would swear as to the fidelity of the master; and having alighted, she embraced the Lady Montacute and the Lady Dormer her daughter, the former of the two (as if weeping on her bosom) said, "O, happie time! O, joyful day!"

The next day (being Sunday) her Majesty was "most royallie feasted; the proportion of breakfast was three oxen and one hundred and fortie geese."

On Monday morning, at eight o'clock, the Queen rode to the park. A nymph emerged from a delicate bower, and with a sweet song presented Elizabeth with a crossbow, with which she killed three or four deer, placed in a paddock for the occasion, and the Countess of Kildare shot one. After dinner, about six o'clock, the Queen mounted to one of the turrets of Cowdray, and witnessed "sixteen bucks pulled down by greyhounds on a launde," "all having fayre lawe."

The days of the week passed merrily, every day bringing some fresh surprise, planned for the royal guest's amusement. Fulsome orations, delivered by persons in various disguises, a charactertistic pastime of the period, were the order of the day. At one place she was met by a pilgrim, "clad in russet velvet, with skallop shells of cloth of silver," who led the way to an oak, upon which were displayed the Queen's arms, and those of the nobility and gentry of the shire, all "hanged in escutchions most beautifull," and these, the account goes on to state, "shall remain on the oke, and there hang till they cannot hang together, one peece by another."

At another place a "wilde man clad in ivie," started forth and delivered his oration; and at "a goodlie fishpond," an angler did the same.

One day the banquet was spread at Easebourne Priory, and doubtless Elizabeth beheld with interest the tomb, then brilliant with gilt and paint, of her long departed relative, Sir David Owen.

At another time, "the lordes and ladies dined in the walkes, feasting most sumptuously at a table, foure and twentie yardes long." The length of that table was however surpassed by another, laid "in the privie walkes in the garden," which was "fortie-eight yardes long." I believe these feasts took place in the "Close Walkes," still so called, which have been long pointed out as the locality by tradition. Moreover the "goodlie fish-pond," or rather the basin, probably filled with fish for the occasion, is at a convenient distance. These close walks are really most "beautiful to behold." This was on the evening of her last day, and, as a grand finale, "the countrie people" were allowed to present themselves before the Queen, "in a pleasant daunce, with taber and pipe, and the Lord Montague and his lady among them, to the great pleasure of all beholders, and gentle applause of her Majestie."

Her Majesty, it is recorded, slept in the "velvet chamber," on the walls of which had been painted, in fresco, the naval battle fought in the harbour of Brest in her father's reign. The whole of the House was illustrated by the chief events of the Eighth Harry's reign, in which the father of the Queen's host had taken a part. These, too, perished in the fire by which Cowdray was destroyed—in the same year, 1793, and almost on the same day as closed the House of Montague in the death of the last Earl in the Laufenberg Falls on the Rhine. The news of the two events crossed each other from England to Germany and Germany to England.

Elizabeth's successor, James I., did not emulate her activity, and there is nothing to show that he ever favored Sussex with his presence. And the same may be said of Charles I. The great battles of the Civil War were not fought in Sussex. The county itself was pretty equally divided between King and Parliament; the Clergy and most of the nobility taking part with the first; the yeomen and the towns and many of the gentry taking sides with the second. It was against Arundel, where the Howard interest was predominant, and Chichester, in which the Clergy held sway, that Waller led the forces of the Parliament, including in them many Sussex gentlemen, like Colonel Herbert Morley, of Glynde, and member for Lewes; but with the sieges and capture of these places the operations of the war, so far as they affected Sussex, ended. It may well be doubted whether the great Protector ever set foot in it. *His* strength lay in the east. If it had not been for the flight of Charles II. southward, after the battle of Worcester, and his embarcation at Brighthelmstone and escape to France in the vessel of Captain Tattersall, there would be scarcely need to name Sussex in the history of the Commonwealth.

That event—the escape of Charles II.—relieves the otherwise absence of historic interest from our local annals at this period. It was surrounded by a good deal of real romance, and it was naturally invested with still more by the triumphant

Royalists. A very interesting, and, as far as possible, an accurate narrative of the flight of the King through Sussex has been given by Mr. S. Evershed in the Sussex Archæological Society's Collections. In company with the two Gunters, of Racton, near Chichester, he entered Sussex on the morning of the 14th of October, 1651, from Hampshire, at Compton Down, in the disguise of a servant of Colonel Gunter, and kept to the line of hills both for safety and for pleasant travelling. He thus passed Treyford, Didling, Bepton, Midhurst, and Petworth on the left, and, skirting the northern edge of the West Dean woods—then more extensive than they are now—passed over Cocking Warren, crossed the main road from Midhurst to Chichester, rode over Heyshott Down, passing the Dunford farm of the Cobdens at the bottom of the hill on the left, and skirted Singleton Forest, Charlton Forest (the favourite hunting-place in after years of Charles's illegitimate descendants, the Dukes of Richmond), and the Teglease. Still keeping to the hills, the King had a distant view of Chichester spire, the Prelate of which (Juxon) had ministered to his father in his last moments, must have passed over what is now Dale Park and near Slindon, and, overlooking the valley of the Arun, is reported to have exclaimed, with something of a heroic spirit, " *This* is a country worth fighting for!"

In passing through Houghton Forest, which lay at the foot of Arundel, the King's party had a perilous encounter. Suddenly, we are told by Mr. Evershed, honest George Gunter reins in his steed, exclaiming, in an undertone, "We are undone; here is Captain Morley, the Governor of Arundel Castle." "Never mind," quietly replied the King, "move on." And the suspicions of the Governor of Arundel were either not excited, or else he did not choose to undertake so perilous a service as that of arresting the King. However that may be, the interview passed without Charles's disguise being penetrated, and the Royal flight was continued. The night of this perilous day (the 14th of October) was, according to Mr. Evershed, passed at Amberley Castle, once a favourite seat of the Bishops of Chichester, but in Charles's day the residence of the Royalist, Sir John Briscoe, and now a ruin, though there is still a room in it called King Charles's room. But if the journey through Sussex was made in one day, as, according to the narrative of Col. Gunter himself, it was, the night's sojourn at Amberley Castle must be a myth, like many other incidents imported into it by later writers.

Still keeping to the northern side of the Downs, Washington and its desolate common, Parham and its Park, Broadwater, Wiston, Steyning, and Beeding Street were passed, at the latter of which some of the soldiers of our old friend, Col. Herbert Morley, were met, but let the party pass without examination, or, to all appearance, without suspicion. On the Downs, between Steyning and Shoreham, the King and Gunter parted company, the former pursuing his journey with only Lord Wilmot, and Gunter going on through Old Shoreham and Portslade to the George Inn (now King's Head) in West Street, at Brighthelmstone, where he made preparations for the reception of the King and Wilmot. These latter had followed the track over the hills from Beeding to White Lot, and so to Portslade, where, on the west side of the village green—according to tradition, says Mr. Evershed—still stands the cottage, with high-pitched roof visible from the Brighton and Portsmouth railway, at which, in a little chamber, cunningly contrived near the chimney in the roof, the King lay till Tattersall had completed his arrangements for the voyage to Normandy. But the plain fact is, that the King and Wilmot came direct to the George, at Brighton, without molestation, supped and slept the night there, and went on board Tattersall's vessel at two in the morning. But it was eight o'clock before the vessel sailed, and afternoon before it was out of sight; the Royal fugitive landing at Fécamp at ten on the following Wednesday morning, Oct. 15th. According to Gunter, he had "not gone out of the towne of Brighthelmston two houres but soldiers came thither to search for a tall black man 6 foot 4 inches high." It would have been a natural and graceful act in Charles, after

his restoration, to revisit the scenes of his danger and escape
in Sussex; but there is no evidence that he did so.   Tattersall,
it is well known, had to take up his vessel to the Thames
and make a show of it to the Londoners before he could get
his pension, which, indeed, he little deserved, if, as is believed,
he extorted a larger sum from the King, whom he recognised,
than he had bargained for—and, doubtless, Charles dismissed
the recollection of his Sussex wanderings from his mind as
soon as he could.   His only recorded after-visit to Sussex
was when he came to Rye, in 1673, "to see his navy lye in
the bay there, in sight of the town."

There *was*, however, a visit paid to Sussex in Charles's
reign by a quasi-Royal personage which has both a local and
historical interest.   It was by the Duke of Monmouth,
Charles's eldest illegitimate son by Lucy Walters, and who,
had the battle at Sedgmoor had a different result, might have
ascended the throne of England, as William of Orange did
at a later date.   Monmouth was at this time the head of the
Protestant party, threatened by the apostacy of the King and
his brother, the Duke of York, and he put forth his pretensions
in a series of "Progresses" through the country, in which, as
Macaulay tells us, he was "received with not less pomp and
with far more enthusiasm than had been displayed when the
King had made progresses through the realm.   He was
escorted from mansion to mansion by long cavalcades of
armed gentlemen and yeomen.   Cities poured forth their
whole population to receive him."

The visit which Monmouth paid to Chichester on February
7th, 1679, is described in a letter to the Archbishop of Canterbury (Sancroft), from Guy Carlton, Bishop of Chichester, who
was an eye-witness of the scene; but, it is evident, with no
friendly feelings for the hero of the day.   The people who
went out to meet him he calls "a rabble of brutes," "broken
shopkeepers, butchers, carpenters, smiths, and such-like people
—Dissenters and petitioners (for a Parliament), to the number
of fifty or threescore."   But the Bishop is obliged to confess

that, besides this " rabble of brutes," " the great men of our Cathedral welcomed him with belles and bonfires made by wood had from their houses to flare before his lodgings, personal visits made to him, complemented at the lighting from his horse with all that was in their houses proffered to his service, and to be at his disposal."

"The Duke," he writes, " was in a scarlet sute and cloak, which the great men for petitioning for a Parliament call'd the red flagge, to lett see beforehand what oure doome would be ere long." There was a grand Service at the Cathedral, the Duke sitting in the Dean's seat, " with a voluntary upon the organ, and before sermon a part of the first psalme was ordered to be sung these words: 'He shal be like the tree that growes fast by the river,'" &c. The Duke also went to Midhurst, where the Bishop reports that one of his (Monmouth's) partisans said with a loud voice, so "that the three gentlemen in the other room heard the words distinctly," which were these: "Well, for all that, the sword shall be drawn before May-Day, and I care not if the King stood by and heard me."

The sword *was* drawn, though not "before May-Day," and a sorry ending had these semi-Royal Progresses of poor Monmouth. They led him to the scaffold. His visit to Sussex and that of his father were of an utterly opposite character: Charles put on the garb of a groom, to rise a king; Monmouth assumed the Royal robes, to hide his head in a ditch and lay it at last upon the block.

James II., so far as we know, was a stranger to Sussex; it was on the Kentish coast that he met with that rough reception from the natives, when they recognised the fugitive King by his "lanthorn jaws," that he never forgave, even excepting the offenders from the later amnesties he put forth at St. Germains. His heroic nephew, William III., is only connected with Sussex by one recorded visit to it, to witness a fox-hunt at Charlton. Most of his visits of pleasure were to Hoo, in his own beloved Holland. His Royal partner, Mary, kept him close company; but her sister Anne, before she ascended the Throne, paid a visit to Petworth, and there is a tradition that the roads were so bad that cart-horses had to be fetched to drag her carriage through the Sussex mud.

The next Royal visit to the county was that paid by George, Prince of Wales (afterwards George II.), to Chichester during the absence of his father in Hanover and after the Jacobite rising in 1716. He passed through the city on his way to Stanstead, then the seat of the Earl of Scarborough, and great preparations were made by the Mayor and Corporation to receive him—a banquet being laid out in the Council House—"a fitting dessert of sweetmeats with a bottle of sack, and two dozen bottles of the best red and white wine:" an "oration," or, as it is termed in the city records, an "elegant speech," being also got ready by the Recorder. But the citizens were disappointed :—"Some hours passed in suspense. At length the Prince appeared; but neither listened to the speech nor tasted the viands." For the latter the Corporation compensated itself by devouring them after the Royal departure; but for the neglected speech, what could repair that *laches*?

It seems strange that George III. should not have visited the southernmost county of his dominions during his long reign. His Queen did, we know. She was the guest of her son, the Prince of Wales, at his Brighton Pavilion, and the Duke of Cumberland had a house in Brighton, and it was on a visit to the Duke, in 1783, that the Prince of Wales made his first acquaintance with the town. Of his after-visits and sojourns, and Royal doings, are they not chronicled in the History of the *Brighton Pavilion and its Royal Associations?* William IV. so far followed the example of his Royal brother as to make Brighton his marine residence, and he and his Queen visited Lewes and other towns of Sussex. So, for a time, did Queen Victoria, both as Queen and as Princess; indeed, in her youthful days, she and her mother, the Duchess of Kent, made Sussex their place of abode, occupying a house at

Bognor, where the Princess Charlotte had also previously sojourned for a time.   But it is now forty years (1843) since the Queen of England did more than pass through Sussex on a rapid railway journey, with the exception of the Queen's visit to the Duke of Norfolk at Arundel Castle; and the county has ceased to be a place of Royal residence, the Brighton Pavilion passing into the hands of the people themselves.   It has, however, been frequently visited by the younger members of the Royal Family, and by Continental Sovereigns, regnant and non-regnant—the latter list including Louis Philippe and Louis Napoleon, both instances of the mutability of human affairs.   Since a Norman Duke landed at Pevensey to snatch by force of arms the Crown of England, and the day when a King and Queen of France were brought over by an English steamer to a little Inn at Newhaven as Mr. and Mrs. Smith, in order to seek safety and hospitality in England, what a gap of time is there, and what a change of thought and feeling has been wrought as to things and persons Royal!   But we will forbear moralising.   Those who love to indulge in it may find some suitable material in this brief outline of Royal Visits to Sussex.

The Great Nobleman and the English Yeoman in Sussex.

ENGLAND no longer counts amongst its sons two classes of men who were once the pride and the back-bone of it; who fought together at Crecy, and Poictiers, and Agincourt; who met each other face to face in many a bloody encounter during the long contest of the Rival Roses — when English fought with English in the " tug of war," as " Greek joined Greek "— and who met for the last time in their old relationship of fighting lord and fighting retainer in the national array which gathered round Elizabeth at Tilbury. There, for the last time, the yeomen of England came forth as a national force to do " yeomen's service " under their Lords, the great nobles of the land, in defence of the Realm. It was the last great feudal gathering in England, and at the very moment of its proudest exultation its doom was pronounced. For amongst those who looked at it in its bravery was Aubrey De Vere, who had learnt to know what modern warfare and modern soldiers were in the wars of the Netherlands, between the Dutch and the Spanish; and he looked doubtingly on the scene. "What do you think of my army?" Elizabeth asked of him, as he rode through the ranks with her. " It is a *brave* army," replied the cautious old soldier. The Queen saw that there was a deeper meaning in the words than lay on their surface. She bid him speak out. He did so: "I have the reputation, your Majesty," he said, " of not being a coward, and yet I am the greatest coward here; for all those fine

K

fellows are praying that the enemy may land and that there may be a battle, and I, who know that enemy well, cannot think of such a battle without dismay."

To De Vere, doubtless, such a battle, between the undisciplined English train-bands, under their brave but inexperienced leaders, and the veteran troops of Spain, under Alexander Farnese, the first General of the age, could have had no other result than that between the brave but half-armed and undisciplined host of Harold and the well-armed and comparatively well-trained army of William of Normandy.   The English baron and the English yeoman had, in fact, played out their parts as warriors, and had to give way to the regularly trained soldier, to whom war was to be a trade or profession.   The classes themselves, as sections of society, were also doomed.   They did not, indeed, perish here, as the nobles did in France, by the violence of a Revolution.   They died out by the gradual operation of time —by the effect of changes which acted gradually on the frame-work of society, leaving the men themselves untouched, and even in possession of the same territory, but with relations to each other, and with individual habits and duties, of a totally different character.

The English aristocracy still remains as a great Order in the State, political and social.   But in the social life and political influence of the English nobleman of the present day there is nothing to remind one of the life and power of his predecessor.   We need not go for proof of this farther back than the age of Elizabeth.   The English nobleman of that day had ceased to be the rude and turbulent Baron, living in his own fortified Castle in a state of semi-independence, and ready at any moment to wage war against his King or on his neighbour.   His feudal Castle, perched like an eagle's eyrie on some high point, had been brought down from its " pride of place " to the level of the river bank or the plain which it had before dominated, and was now built for show, and comfort, and hospitality, not for offence and defence. His retainers were no longer knights and squires and men-at-arms, but peaceful attendants on the person or in the household of the great noble, who was careful to avoid, both in his residence and in his attendance, that appearance of independence of the Crown which was so dear to the old Baron. For the pride and power of the Barons of England had been brought down by many a heavy blow, received, first, in their own conflicts during the civil wars of York and Lancaster, and afterwards from the Tudor Kings whom they had helped to place on the Throne, and who had had too striking an example of the evil effects of aristocratic power to wish to uphold it, but rather favoured the newly-rising wealth and strength of the middle classes. Then, too, the invention of fire-arms had revolutionised the character of warfare—had done away with the heavy defensive armour which could only be worn by mounted men, and had transferred the real strength of armies to the infantry—to the men who fought on foot—in fact, to the plebeians, and who, being poor, necessarily received pay—were, in fact, mercenaries, or, in the language of our neighbours, *soldés.*

All these and other things combined to change the social and political position of the " Old English Baron," to strip him of his warlike power, and make him rather an appendage than a rival of the Crown. But still, in the time of Elizabeth, he retained, like Lucifer in his fallen state, some of his "original brightness;" he still kept up a personal state and show of magnificence in his household with which there is nothing to match in the present day. There was a pomp and a formality in his life, and that of his wife and family, that is now utterly unknown even in the highest nobility and dignitaries of the State, and is only reserved for the Sovereign. The households of the great Nobles still in the Tudor days resembled little Courts, and if the heads of them were no longer, like the Neviles and Percies, the Stanleys and De Veres and De Burghs of old, the chiefs of armies that acknowledged no other leader, they had little armies of retainers, who crowded their halls, waited on their persons, held offices in their households, and depended on their favour and bounty.   Whatever they did, at home or abroad, was done with a state and formality which, cumbrous and costly and troublesome as it must have been, upheld their dignity and importance in the eyes of the world and made them, after the Crown, the first Order in the State.

A lively picture of the pomp and state with which the great English nobles surrounded themselves in the days of Elizabeth is given in the "Booke of Orders and Rules" of Anthony Browne, Viscount Montague, a nobleman whose chief place of residence was in Sussex—at Cowdray House, Midhurst—now one of the most picturesque ruins of our county.   The noble author of this "Booke of Orders and Rules," "established by me, Anthony Viscount Montague, for the better direction and governmente of my household and family," evidently sat down to the composition of it in as grave a spirit as in later days a Locke or an Abbé Sieyes sat down to compose Constitutions for the government of nations. "For as moche"—so he begins the preface to this "Booke of Orders and Rules "—" as neither publique weale nor private family can continue or long endure without laws, ordinances, and statutes to guyde and direct them, nor without prudent and experienced ministers to execute the same, I, therefore, being desirous to live orderly and quietly within my lymytte, and to mayntayne the estate of myne honor and callinge, accordinge to my degree, have esteemed ytt meete for the accomplishmente thereof to sett downe and declare in this booke of orders ensewinge myne owne opinion, judgement, and resolution touchinge the manner and order of the government of my private house and family," &c., &c. This preface alone is a lengthy document, and the "Booke" which it preludes occupies twenty-seven pages of closely printed type in a volume of the Sussex Archæological Collection.   It is marshalled, with the "Conclusion," under *thirty-nine heads*, and each one of these heads is devoted to a minute description of the duties of an officer of the

Viscount's household.   Here is the list of them, in the noble writer's own order :—

THE TABLE.

1. My Stewarde of Householde.
2. My Comptroller.
3. My highe Stewarde of Courtes.
4. My Auditor.
5. My Generall Receaver.
6. My Solliciter.
7. My other Principal Officers.
8. My Secretarye.
9. My Gentlemen Ushers.
10. My Carver.
11. My Sewer.
12. The Gentlemen of my Chamber.
13. The Gentlemen of my Horse.
14. The Gentlemen Wayters.
15. The Marshall of my Hall.
16. The Clarke of my Kitchen.
17. The Yeomen of my greate Chamber.
18. The Usher of my Hall.
19. The Chief Cooke.
20. The Yeomen of my Chamber.
21. The Clarke of myne Officers Chamber.
22. The Yeoman of my Horse.
23. The Yeoman of my Seller.
24. The Yeoman of myne Ewrye.
25. The Yeoman of my Pantrye.
26. The Yeoman of my Butterye.
27. The Yeomen of my Wardroppe.
28. The Yeomen Wayters.
29. The second Cooke and the Rest.
30. The Porter.
31. The Granator.
32. The Bayliffe.
33. The Baker.
34. The Brewer.
35. The Groomes of the Great Chamber.
36. The Almoner.
37. The Scullery Man.
38. An order of Service att my Table.
39. My determination for Officers Fees.

The foregoing list will serve to convey an idea of the "Orders and Rules," which are too long for quotation in their entirety, though the vivid idea they convey of the strict order and pomp and ceremony in which the domestic life of great nobles in Elizabeth's day was conducted would almost justify their insertion.   But our readers must be content with a few passages as specimens.

And, in the first place, as respects "my Stewarde of Householde "—this was evidently an office of no little importance, either in the eyes of the Viscount, or of inferior functionaries, or, doubtless, of the Steward himself!   He is called to take upon him "the carriage and porte of my chiefe officer, and assiste me with sounde advice in matters of most ymportance and greatest deliberacon, and therein faythfully keepe all my secrettes."   By subordinate officers he is to be "obeyed in all things (excepte ytt be dishonest in ytt selfe or undutifull to the Prince or State, or directly to the manifest hurte of me, my wiffe, &c.)—Yea, and albeit he exceede the boundes of office. For, if he soe doe, yte shall lie in noe servantts or childes power to controule him. But I, who am his master, will have my eares open to heare any pregnant matter that shalbe brought against him, and by my masterly authoritye will correcte such matter as shalbe misdon to myself or any other by abuse of my authoritye." "But," he adds, "my forsight and care in my choyce of an officer in soe high authoritye, shall be such," &c., &c.

If a King had been inducting a Prime Minister, or a Caliph had been installing a Vizier, he could not have employed more solemn and high-sounding phrases than does Viscount Montague for "My Stewarde of Householde." And really, when we come to see what he had to order, and over whom he had to rule, we are not surprised. He was not only at the head of an army of officers and domestics in-doors— the Earl of Derby of that day had 240 servants—but over an army of bailiffs and keepers and purveyors outside. He had to provide provisions and fuel, "utensills or furniture," "when I lye att Cowdrye, att Chichester, Southampton, or other portes upon the sea costes"—was, in fact, Generalissimo over an army of retainers, some, like "my Comptroller," "my highe Stewarde of Courtes," "my Auditor," "my Generall Receaver," and "my Solliciter," with duties almost as responsible as his own.

Coming down from these higher dignitaries to humbler and more domestic ones, it is both edifying and amusing to observe how minutely the noble author of the "Booke" goes into lesser matters of dress and deportment, not thinking it beneath him to instruct his Sewer, "after he hath washed together with my Carver att the ewrye boorde, be there armed (videlt.) with an armynge towell layd uppon his righte shoulder and tyed lowe under his lefte arme, whence beinge by my Gentleman Usher comaunded to the dresser, he shall departe towardes the hall, attended there through with half a dosen Gentlemen and yeomen att the leaste and soe on to the dresser, where he shall deliver the meate to everye one according to their places, and then returninge with my service all coveredde to my table, shall there receave everye dishe and deliver them severally to my Carver;" and to direct the said Carver "that he doe stande seemely and decently with due reverence and sylence, untill my dyett and fare be brought uppe, and then doe his office." Also to instruct his Gentlemen of my Chamber, "Att night if I be out of my lodgeinges (ytt beinge dark) some one of them shall wayte for my comeinge in, with a candle to light me to my chamber; where, after I am, and woulde goe to bedde, they shall helpe me into ytt, and beinge layed to reste they shall either by themselves or some of the yeomen take care that the dores be all faste lockte."

So, if the great man wishes to ride out, he wills that his "Gentlemen of my Horse" "helpe me to my horse, appoynteinge the Yeoman of my Horse to holde my styrroppe, and my footeman to stande to his heade."

In fact, each of the 39 officers of the Viscount's Household is instructed by him in the minutest points as to what he should or should not do or allow to be done; and some of the things *not* to be allowed strike one as rather comical. For instance, "the Clarke of my Kytchin" is to "suffer none to stande unseemly with his backe towards my meate whilst itt is att the range"—a degree of respect towards the meat that is now scarcely required to be paid to the eater of it! The Viscount had also a quick eye as to those who might have too much liking for his meat as well as to such as might treat it with disrespect, for, under the head "Yeomen Officers," he says, "I will that he have a vigilant eye to the meate, to the entente that ytt be nott ymbezeled or conveighed * to corners without the appoyntemente of myself or Gentleman Usher." There were no carpets in those days, even for the floors of the greatest nobles; but cleanliness and sweetness were duly studied.

---

* "Convey, the wise it call," says Pistol, when anxious to qualify thieving by a more respectable title.

Thus, after dinner, which takes place before noon (!) or supper (which is at 5 !), the place is to be "sweptc, and kept cleane and sweete with perfumes, flowers, herbes, and bowes (boughs), in their season." A very necessary precaution when the number and character of the guests are considered; for the whole Household—some hundreds of persons—assembled in the Hall at these two meals; and the only distinction was, as to which of the four tables they should sit at.

The form in which these meals were discussed is well pictured by Sir Sibbald David Scott in the introductory matter to this "Booke of Rules," for which we are indebted to him :—

Ten o'clock has just struck, and the household is mustering in the magnificent Buck Hall, it being "covering time," or the hour for preparing the tables for dinner. The Steward in his gown is standing at the uppermost part of the Hall—over against his appointed table—surrounded by most of his chief officers and some visitors—occasionally also travellers who had availed themselves of the hospitality of those days. The tables are neatly covered with white cloths, saltcellars, and trenchers, under the supervision of the Usher of the Hall. The Yeoman of the Ewry and Pantry, conducted by the Yeoman Usher, pass through to the great Dining Chamber. When they arrive at the middle of that room, they bow reverently (although no one else be present), and they do the same upon approaching the table. The Usher, kissing his hand, places it on the centre of the dining-table, to indicate to his subordinate of the Ewry (who kisses the table), where the cloth is to be laid.

The Yeoman of the Pantry then steps forth, and places the salt, trenchers of my Lord and Lady, rolls, knives, "hefted with silver," and spoons, making a little obeisance or inclination of the head as each article is laid down, and a low bow when he has finished. The trio then severally make solemn reverences, and retire in the same order as they arrived. Next in succession comes the Yeoman of the Cellar, who dresses the sideboard or buffet ("cupborde") with wines, flaggons, drinking cups, and such vessels as are consigned to his charge. The Yeoman of the Buttery follows him, and brings up beer and ale, and arranges the pewter pots, jugs, and so forth, on the side-board or buffet.

It being "dynner-tyme," the Gentleman Usher ascertains that all is in readiness, and proceeds to take his Lord's commands. He does so, respectfully of course, being instructed, if his master should be in his private apartments, always to knock, although the doors may be open. Having received his orders, he sees that the carver and sewer perform the required ablutions, and that they are provided with clean cloths proper for their vocation.

The Usher of the Hall, standing at the screen, with loud voice exclaims, "Gentlemen and Yeomen, wait upon the Sewer for my Lord!" Half-a-dozen Gentlemen and Yeomen at the least are to accompany that officer to the dresser. When these return, the Usher of the Hall calls out, "By your leave my masters," and all who are present in the Hall stand up reverently, while the procession of the great Lord's dinner passes through, preceded by the Usher of the Hall as far as the Dining Chamber, where it is met by the Gentleman Usher, who sees the dishes placed upon the table. While the meats were being roasted, it has been the duty of the Clerk of the Kitchen to take care that no one should turn his back upon them.

Doubtless, the Viscount, having been apprised by the Gentleman Usher, next comes forth with stately tread, in doublet and hose, leading the Viscountess by the hand, followed by her gentlewomen. The same ceremonial accompanies the passage of each course from the kitchen to the dining-room.

Dinner over, and the cloth removed, the Gentleman Usher having kept a sharp look-out all the while that nothing be purloined, now comes forth with a towel, and basins and ewers are produced, for the lord's and ladies' ablutions, which the want of forks rendered the more necessary. The attendants are then dismissed, and depart with the accustomed reverences, to take their dinners with all those who have hitherto been occupied, and this is denominated "the second sitting" in the Hall. Whilst they are so pleasantly engaged, the Steward, and the individuals who sat at his table, repair to the Lord's dining-chamber, and remain in attendance until the Gentlemen-Waiters return, and all await there the rising of the Viscount from table.

The assemblage is now dispersed; those who have leisure, and desire it, are at liberty to call for cards in the Hall, which the Yeomen officers provide, each player bestowing a gratuity in the "play box" for this service, the contents of which are proportionately divided.

That great judgment and discretion was shown by Viscount Montague in the drawing-up of his "Book of Orders and Rules for the better direction and governmente of my house-holde and family," and that he was a wise and discreet nobleman, there can be no doubt. But the result of all his care shows that the stately and costly fashion of living thus described was beginning to be unfitted to the times and could not be safely kept up even by the greatest nobles; for it appears, by the fragment of a document found by Sir Sibbald Scott "among other papers and rubbish in one of the ruined towers of Cowdray House" *(sic transit gloria mundi!)* that this very nobleman, great, and wealthy, and wise as he was, fell into such straitened circumstances that he had to petition the Crown to assist him in the payment of his debts and the portioning of his daughters. Such cumbrous state and ceremony had become as unsuited to the times, and as burthensome to the estate, as the old feudal array at Tilbury, to which old Viscount Montague marched at the head of his retainers, with his grandson (the very Anthony Browne who drew up this "Booke of Rules," then a child, by his side) had become as a mode of warfare. Both were doomed, even in Elizabeth's days, and scarcely a shred of either now remains. What, we may ask, would be the effect upon the household of a modern Duke of Norfolk or Duke of Richmond (the Viscounts Montague have been extinct since the last Viscount, a young man, madly ventured to shoot the Falls of Laufenburg, on the Rhine, in 1793, and was, with his companion, Mr. Burdett, lost in the torrent) if this "Booke of Rules" were "publicley redde in the presence of all my servants, once in the yeare," as its noble author directed it to be ? Would they "stand" so much as the reading of it, much less heed it, or believe that England had ever owned masters who could give such orders or servants who could have obeyed them ? The simplicity of life which is the characteristic of modern society reaches up to the highest ranks, and there is little in the domestic arrangements of the greatest noble which now differs from that of the wealthy merchant or tradesman. Some of them may have more servants and carriages and houses than their fellow-subjects : but they exact very little, if any, more state or respect from their servants, and sometimes, indeed, get none at all !—perhaps don't wish for it. We may travel with a Duke or an Earl, and not know he is of higher rank than his banker, or lawyer, or even his cook ! We may pass him in the streets, and see nothing in his dress or deportment to induce us to turn and look at him. We may even encounter him, or his wife or daughters, in his own house, as we gaze at their pictures or furniture, and never be expected to bow reverently before them, or show any mark of special awe or respect for their persons or dignity. They do not expect it, and, if they did, would not get it even from their own servants. One instance, that we can vouch for, will suffice in illustration of this change : A noble Duke (the first on the roll after Royalty), who lives in Sussex, had occasion lately to go to London and ordered a carriage to take him to the rail. But at the time appointed no carriage was forthcoming, and, as the rail would not certainly wait for him, off the noble Duke, with "all the blood of all the Howards" in his veins, set as hard as his Ducal legs could carry him, to "catch the train." Fancy the noble owner of that stately household at Cowdray running through Midhurst on such an errand!

But it is not only the great and noble who have been affected by the revolutions of Time. Humbler classes, but still very important ones in the days of Elizabeth, exist now no longer. The "good yeomen, whose limbs were made in England," so gallantly led by the Fifth Harry to the breach of Honfleur—these have long ceased to be a class. Like the Nobles who led them their decay was gradual, and we can follow them, as we follow the Noble, in their transition state. The picture we have given of the Elizabethan Noble, as the connecting link between the Baron and the modern Peer, may find its parallel for the yeoman class in a diary left by Thomas Marchant, who lived at Little Park, Hurst, now the property of the widow of Colonel Smith Hannington, in the 17th and 18th centuries. In his introductory remarks to this "Marchant Diary," the Rev. E. Turner says, "The account which he (the said Thomas Marchant) gives of his daily proceedings may be taken as a faithful representation of the every-day mode of life of a substantial Sussex yeoman of the period in which he lived; *i.e.*, of a man farming his own land, and living an active and useful, and, at the same time, an independent life. He was also the possessor of other property in the county besides what he himself occupied in Hurst."

Of these daily proceedings we will give our readers a sample or two. But we warn them to expect nothing of a very elevating or exciting character. They are as commonplace—as hum-drum, to use an old Sussex expression—as the "daily proceedings" of an English tradesman or farmer would be in the present day, if not more so; for the world in which the "substantial Sussex yeoman" of the 17th and 18th centuries lived was a much narrower and more uneventful one than that of the English tradesman or farmer of the present day. There is an utter absence from it of all exciting or elevating topics: there is not a single allusion to war or to politics or to any of those higher themes which, if they do raise the passions of men, also lift them out of that lower self which is apt, in peaceful, uneventful days, to absorb and debase them. The English yeoman, in fact, if he can be called such, in the days of Thomas Marchant, had ceased to be a warrior; he no longer answered to the call of his feudal lord to take up his bow or pike and follow him to "the wars." His landlord or feudal chief himself was no longer the warlike Baron with a following of scores of knights, each bound to do him knightly service in war, as the Yeoman was bound to do "Yeoman's service" to the Knight or Baron. Both classes, without ceasing to exist as social grades, had slid into new places—rapidly during the latter years of Elizabeth, and during the long and inglorious reign of James I.; and when, after our civil dissensions—in which the Yeoman class vindicated against their old leaders their claims to be of the same mettle and pasture as their ancestors who had fought in France— we look at the picture drawn by Thomas Marchant of the "substantial Yeoman" of his day, we see in it as great a revolution in his "daily proceedings," when contrasted with the old fighting Yeoman, as distinguishes the great but peaceful and orderly nobleman of later days from the turbulent old Baron.

As Anthony Browne gave evidence in the one case, so shall Thomas Marchant be called into Court to testify to the truth of our statement in the other.

We may premise that "Little Park," Hurst, formerly part and parcel of the Manor of Hurstpierpoint with the "Great Park," from which, by some means or another not now known, it got separated, was bought, about 1680, by the father of our Thomas Marchant, of Albourne, yeoman, and was inherited by his eldest son. Both Little and Great Parks were originally the property of the Pierpoints—great lords in Sussex in their day: but their day was past, and their name is unknown in Sussex, except in territorial nomenclature. Thomas Marchant, Mr. Turner tells us, was largely connected by birth, as well as by marriage (he married a Stone, of "The Nunnery," Rusper), with many of the gentry of the neighbourhood; he lived in a good house, and held land in other places besides Hurst. Yet his "daily proceedings" and occupations are not of that character which we associate in this day with the gentry of a county, or even with the farming class, except of the smallest kind. They indicate a kind of material prosperity—abundance of food and drink, and other good things of this life; but there is nothing to relieve or vary this animal kind of life. The growing and selling of corn, the fattening and selling of pigs and oxen, the dining out at neighbours' or at public-houses and imbibing a little too much liquor, the *non*-attendance at church, the giving in marriage, the births, christenings, and deaths, the fishing of ponds, or a day's shooting and hunting: these are the "daily proceedings" which fill up the diary of Thomas Marchant. A slight reference to a contested election is the only glimpse we get from Thomas Marchant of the public life of the day, and this not a very edifying one. A record of the Coronation day of George I., and a false report of the landing of the Duke of Ormond (one of the Pretender's partisans) in Lancashire, and another of his presence on the Sussex coast, are the nearest approach to politics. Of things literary or artistic there is not a *soupçon* in the whole diary. As to science, we should not expect anything; but the wondering references to "unusual lights in the air" illustrate the Diarist's inability to describe, with any clearness, such common phenomena as the aurora borealis, or falling ærolites; for we cannot tell which he refers to in his entry; and his patronage of the travelling mountebank is another gauge of his depth in this direction.

Yet it is evident that Thomas Marchant was a man of some ability—superior in many points to his neighbours, or he would not have been called on as he was to fill various parochial offices, to act as executor to his neighbours' wills, or, still more, have been selected by his great neighbour, the proud Duke of Somerset—then the owner and occupant of Petworth House and its wide domains—to be his steward. Thomas Marchant was obviously a man of some parts and educated up to the standard of his day. But the educational standard of that day for "the substantial yeoman" was a low one. The spheres of war and of politics—one might almost say of religion on its controversial side, in which his predecessors had moved so freely—were closed to him, or only presented themselves to him in their lowest phases: such as the enlistment of a good-for-nothing young fellow or the eating of a tithe dinner or preaching of a Visitation Sermon. His life was passed in buying and selling, sowing and reaping, eating and drinking, marrying and burying—and little more. It was a time of great material prosperity—this commencement of the Georgian era—and of much social deterioration; for the vivid light which war used to let in on the most remote places and the most sordid lives had gone out, and the new light which literature, art, science—above all, politics—throw on all life in England in modern times had not yet struggled into existence. At least, it had not penetrated to Hurst in the year 1714, at which period Thomas Marchant commences his diary.

Apologising to our readers for occupying them so long with our own remarks, we will now proceed to borrow a few of the entries of Thomas Marchant, of "Little Park," Hurst.

The first—dated September 29th, 1714—records that four pigs were "set to fatting;" that four oxen were lent to James Reed; that five runts were bought of Thomas Jones (for £16); and that the diarist "drank with Thomas Vinal, of Cowfold, at J. Beard's."

Not very interesting items of information these! But we warned our readers in due time, and if they expect anything much better than this, they had better stop at once!

On October 1st "dined at Danny"—then, as now, owned by a Campion—"with Mr. John Cheal, Mr. Phill. Shore, John

Hill, of Nuthurst, and *a Frenchman*." This Frenchman is referred to several times, but never otherwise than as "*the Frenchman*." His name, whatever it might be, was too hard a nut for Mr. Thomas Marchant to crack!

On the 3rd October "Mr. Dodson preached." The rev. gentleman was the Rector of Hurst, and the ancestor of the Right Hon. J. G. Dodson, late Member for East Sussex, and now a Cabinet Minister (President of the Local Government Board). On the 4th an attendance at the Sessions at Lewes, in a case of disputed settlement, is only worthy of note by the purchase of a *quarter* of a pound of tea for *four shillings*.

The 10th October was a Sunday, and the manners of the day are illustrated by the entry that "after Evening Prayer Mr. Campion, Mr. Hay, Mr. Bateman, the Frenchman, Mr. Hart, and I, went to Mr. Whitpaine's, at West-towne, where we drank three bottles of beer and a small bowl of punch."

On the 14th Thomas Marchant went to Brighthelmstone, borrowing "old Thos. Farncombe's coat at Patcham." Brighton, indeed, under its old title, frequently figures in the diary as a place between which and Hurst there was frequent intercourse.

Fish-ponds and their fry occupied a good deal of Thomas Marchant's time and attention. He bought and sold largely in carp, tench, eels, &c., and it is evident that fresh-water fish entered, 150 years ago, much more than it now does into the food of the English people; doubtless, owing to the difficulty at that period of communication with the sea-coast. The buying of ponds of fishes, both by Thomas Marchant and others, is frequently noted, and "stews" were "watched" then as game preserves are now. Fresh-water fish fetched, too, a good price; *ex. gr.:* "We took 242 fish out of the stew for Mr. Edmead. Received £10 of Richard Baldchild for them. They were, one with another, about 13 inches long." No fresh-water fish would fetch this price at the present day.

Thomas Marchant was, evidently, a clever, active, thrifty, money-making man; he often had more money than he knew what to do with, and then he sometimes (doubtless from prudence and in the total absence of country banks) deposited it with neighbours. Thus, Nov. 17, 1714, "I delivered a bag of money to Stephen Bine. Its contents were £40. The bag was sealed with two seals, thus: 'T.' 'M.' I desired him to keep it until I called for it." And, again, "Lodged 100 guineas with Mrs. Beard."

Temperance was not among Thomas Marchant's virtues; but, like Thomas Turner, of Easthothly, he does not hesitate to record his failings. Thus, having dined at Danny —"the Frenchman" being of the party—"we staid late and drank too much. Mr. Beaumont came in the afternoon, but went away before supper. He wore my hat home instead of his own, and I sent for it the next morning."

Drinking was one of the accomplishments of that day, and the higher and middle classes set an example of intemperance then which the lower ones of the present day follow but too closely.

In another point Mr. Thomas Marchant was equally faulty, as he is equally frank; he seldom went to Church, and his invariable reason (when he assigns one) is, that "his head ached very much." This head-ache falls so pertinaciously on the Sunday that it is, to say the least, suspicious.

In keeping with these Sunday head-ache entries is the following: "Mr. Dodson preached. He read a Brief for the repair of a Church, *to which I gave nothing.*" And the Rev. Mr. Turner slily adds, between brackets, "Seemingly his wont." For which, as Editor of the Diary, he had, no doubt, good authority; but we do not meet with a non-giving entry again. It is clear, however, that in the beginning of the last century the affection of the landed gentry and farmers of Sussex for the Church did not extend to their breeches' pockets.

There is a touch of humour in some of the entries, but "few and far between," and of a matter-of-fact kind. Here is one : "Paid my brother Ede 27s. for a calf, which I verily thought I had paid for before ; *and so I think still.*"

Was there ever a better exemplification of the Hudibrastic adage :—

"A man convinced against his will,
Is of the same opinion still."

Another entry of this kind, with its comment, occurs at a later date :—"My father and mother, my wife and I were at Danny in the afternoon, and met Mr. Piggot and Mr. Osbourne there. Paid Mrs. S. Courthope £6. 5s. 5d., of which I received 10s. 4d. of my father. J. Parsons shaved my head and face. Pd. Mrs. Courthope 14s. for my whip. How soon, alas ! are a fool and his money parted."

Thomas Marchant was evidently so much of a philosopher as to obey the Socratic behest : "Know thyself."

On the 17th of this January, 1715, there is a county election, and Thomas Marchant sets out for Chichester, where, and where only, the poll was taken, "with about 110 voters." "The candidates," he tells us, "were Mr. Bertram Ashburnham, Mr. Eversfield, the Tory, and Mr. Butler and Mr. Spencer Compton, the Whig candidates. The two latter gained the day by a vast majority." And thereby Mr. Thomas Marchant lost his bet with the Rector of Hurst, for he had previously recorded : "I gave Mr. Dodson 1s., for which he is to give me 10s. if both the Tory candidates are chosen at the ensuing election." As the Whigs were chosen, Mr. Dodson kept his 10s. as well as Mr. Thomas Marchant's 1s.

Mr. Turner tells us, later on, that Mr. Marchant "was not a Whig." It is clear he was not. Let us hope that he was not a Jacobite ! But he records, on May 10th, the fact of "The Pretender's birth-day," and on the 1st of August he enters, "King George's Accession to the Crown. *My servants and workmen were all at Church. I was not.*" With a man so reserved as to his political opinions, this counts for some-

L

thing. On lesser matters he is more out-spoken. Thus, the above entry is followed by another: "*Received a very mean pig from Wanbarrow.*" A very mean pig! Poor Mr. Marchant! And poor little pig!

We have noticed, in commenting on a previous diary of the 18th century (vol. 1 of "Glimpses of our Ancestors in Sussex"), how great was the mortality among children, and here we have another case in point: "Paid William Nicholas 1s. 6d. for raising the graves of my four deceased children." Whose ages and dates of death Mr. Turner gives as follows:—

Ann, b. 1706, d. 1706.	Thomas, b. 1703, d. 1707.
Mary, b. 1707, d. 1707.	James, b. 1710, d. 1711.

The practice of calling in mid-wives, which prevailed at this time, may have had something to do with these frequent deaths of infants. The small-pox, too, as frequent entries testify, was very fatal, and was assisted, doubtless, by the practice, also noted, of moving the patients, as soon as the disease declared itself, to some other locality! Thus: "October 20th. May carry'd the Widow Gun to Charles Smith's in the chaise, the small-pox being come out on her." A ride in the open air must have been a good ally to the disease!

In the course of this year we encounter an old friend— "Mr. Osborne, of Poynings, buried to-day. I was at Mrs. Beard's in the evening. *Mr. Leonard Gale was there.*" Mr. Gale was one of the Sussex ironmasters, from whose diary we have already borrowed a few "Glimpses." Many other Sussex names—not a few of families still flourishing—occur in the course of the Marchant diary: as Burrell (the "Counsellor" who lived at Ockenden House, Cuckfield, and to whom Thomas Marchant paid many a fee, and records his death with regret), Scutt, Gratwick, Turner, Beard, Campion, Courthope, Tredcroft, Hart, Marten, Ellis, Willard, Lindfield, &c., &c.

As fresh-water fish were much eaten, so was cyder drank at this time in Sussex as a common beverage. Living must have been cheap, and teaching not dear, for (says Mr. Marchant), "I agreed with Mrs. Atkinson to board and teach Bett (his daughter) at the rate of £13 per ann." What are the "terms" for a year's schooling of a young lady at the present time? Ladies also in those days were content to ride behind their husbands: "They carried the pillion to Atkinson's to be mended."

Have any of our fair readers ever seen a pillion, much more sat on one? Who, too, among them can give us any information as to the article of female attire referred to in this entry—"Doomsday, of Horsham (what a name! is it still extant, to pair with Death, of Petworth?) brought my wife a pair of jumps instead of stays. She paid him 36s. 6d. for them." What are "jumps?"

Cricket was "coming in" at this time. It made up in some degree as a manly, healthy exercise for the loss of other national sports—"April 30, 1717. Willy (his son) went to see a cricket match." Again, June 12, 1717, "I was at the cricket match at Dungton (Duncton) gate towards night."

Duncton, near Petworth, has since been famous in the annals of cricket. The Broadbridges, Dean, Millyard, and James Taylor came from it, and Duncton was more than a match for Brighton forty years ago, when they met each other in Ireland's Grounds (now Park Crescent), and Dean bowled for the first time in Brighton.

As cricket came in, the ironworks were going out; but they still lingered in Marchant's time: "John Clerk told me that his iron cost him £19 a ton at a forge near Maresfield."

The Sussex roads were still at their worst, which was very bad indeed: *ex. gr.*:—

At Shoreham, to meet my team, which did not come. They were *mired* down at the foot of Mr. Osbourne's, Holt Hill; and, like blockheads as they were (!), they left the load there, and went home again.

All home-produce was plentiful and cheap—Mr. Marchant bought Cheshire cheese at 3d. per lb.—but foreign was dear: Bohea tea, 16s. and even 18s. 6d. per lb.

An obsolete and not very edifying practice is set down under the date January 31st, 1720 : "Mrs. Beard had two stray ewes *cried at Church*, which turned out to be mine."

In connection with this lady we have a reference to that smuggling on the Sussex coast which, under the stimulus of Protectionist legislation, flourished for the next 150 years, to the ruin of rustic morals :—

"Sept. 30th, 1719. Talked to Mrs. Beard for Allan Savage, about her horse that was seized by the officers at Brighton, running brandy." It is well known that the farmers often " winked " at their horses being taken for this purpose, and were paid in " kind."

Some obsolete words are, as might be expected, to be found in this old diary. " Bargained with Edward Morley at 35s. until Michaelmas, and if his *vailes* (gifts to servants) be not 5s., I have promised to make them so." The custom of making presents to servants on festive occasions was carried to a high point at this time. In London, indeed, they were ruinous to diners-out, and Pope refused the invitation of his patron, the Duke of Montague, unless the noble host paid his (Pope's) vailes to his own servants ($£10$ a dinner), which he did ! It is well that "vailes" are obsolete!

Here is another old word : " George and May *thwarted (i.e.,* cross-ploughed)." Is this still used in Sussex ? Then " Friar's Oak," near Hurst, is called " Freize Oak." But what does " Freize " Oak mean ?

Amongst other matters past and gone, there was "a publick fast on account of the plague," and "a smock race in our field," and "went to Ditchling Fair. Carried Nanny behind me."

But we must come to an end with this curious, and, in some respects, instructive old diary of a Sussex yeoman, in the 17th and 18th centuries. In the latter part of it the yeoman and the great nobleman, whose parts and relations in life had been so completely revolutionised that they could scarcely know themselves, much less recognise each other, as they existed 100 years before, were brought face to face; for, as we have said, the Duke of Somerset, known as "the proud Duke," wanted Mr. Marchant to be his Steward at Petworth, and at last he consented, and went to Petworth. He saw the house allotted to him as Steward, and liked it. But his wife also saw it, and liked it not. Perhaps this had something to do with the short duration and apparently unsatisfactory character of the relations of the Duke and Mr. Marchant. Here is a record of one of his interviews with the great man : "I talked with his Grace, and he found much fault about the grates he ordered me to have made. But he was in a cursed bad humour about the dung carts, &c., having cut up the land ; and he sent the teams for hay to William Keen's at 7 o'clock at night."

"In a cursed bad humour!" Now, let the reader only turn back to the "Book of Rules" of Viscount Montague, where that nobleman defines the office and duties and dignity of Steward in his day, and the relations of lord and servant. What a revolution must have taken place in these relations before the Duke of Somerset's steward could have made such an entry as that!

Mr. Marchant "kept on" his stewardship ; but it was not for long. In the course of the next month we have these entries :—

February 25th (Sunday). A very wet day. Jack went to Hurst. I was at the House, and answered my Lord Duke's letter, received this day.

March 13th. Mr. Elder returned from London. Recd. of my Lord Duke, £15. 12s. 4d., in full of my salary to next Wednesday. Dined with Mr. Elder.

March 14th. Took my horse out of my Lord Duke's stables.

March 19th. Went to the Duke's to take leave of the family.

March 21st. Returned to Hurst.

And with a few more memorandums (one of them, curiously enough, to this effect, "Copley, the painter, here," —the only reference to Art or artists in the whole diary), the diary comes to a close, on the 20th June, 1728 ; the death of the diarist taking place in the September of the same year.

Unconsciously, Thomas Marchant, Yeoman of Sussex, has recorded, in his matter-of-fact diary, a great social change. The English Yeoman had not only ceased to be a fighting man—a feudal retainer; he was also beginning, in Marchant's time, to pass from a holder of land into a cultivator of the soil: a farmer. A division of labour was going on, on all sides. Fighting, once a duty which every man owed to the State or his Lord, became a profession, as distinct from the social life of a Noble or a Yeoman as any other calling; and the gentry, once only Yeomen of a higher grade, became a class by themselves, holding land and not cultivating it; whilst the farmer cultivated it and ceased to own it. Society is, doubtless, the richer for these divisions; they were the necessary result of the development of modern Society, so rich in its multifarious phases. But, for all that, we feel that we have lost as well as gained by these changes, and, in retracing our footsteps in the company of Anthony Browne, great Nobleman, and Thomas Marchant, substantial Yeoman, of Sussex, we may be pardoned for regretting some things that have passed away never to return, and for admitting that, if we have gone a-head very fast indeed of late days, yet in some respects they had the advantage of us, and that we are not altogether " wisest, virtuousest, discreetest, best," as we are accustomed to think ourselves!

Christmas in Sussex in the Olden Time.

 NATIONAL Festival reflects the character of a people. If an accurate picture of the way in which Christmas has been observed in England for the last thousand years could be drawn, it would, without doubt, convey a pretty good notion, not only of the religious institutions of the times, but of the social and moral condition of the people. In the early and purely Saxon days we should, in all probability, find a good deal of Paganism and the grossness of heathen idolatry in the festivities of the season. There had been a feast of Yule long before the festival of Christmas, and an element of the old heathen holiday long mingled with the rejoicings of the new festival, and, perhaps, still does so. Yule cakes or dough are still to be met with in the North of England; the Yule plough is not quite obsolete; and the Yule log still burns on our hearths. It was, and still is, the wont of the Roman Priesthood to smooth the conversion of a heathen people by grafting the rites of the new religion on those of the old. In Italy it was the worship of the gods of "high Olympus" that was thus tenderly dealt with. In the countries which, like England, had been wrested from Rome by the Northern barbarians, it was the gods of Walhalla—Odin and Friga, Woden and Thor—that had to be superseded by a higher faith, and the same policy was pursued: the people's habits and customs were disturbed as little as possible, and if a festival of the new religion happened to concur in season with or to resemble in character a feast of the old religion, the transition from one to the other was made as easy as it could be by the preservation of the olden forms. Conversions

in those early days were made wholesale—an entire people
following the example or obeying the command of their King;
and in such cases national customs, even if they partook of a
heathenish nature, had to be respected. Their rooting-out
was left to a more enlightened day.

A good deal of trouble was, without doubt, given to later
ages of the Roman Church by this lingering element of
Paganism. It worked up in the new and purer faith in the
same manner that the idolatries of Egypt and of Canaan—
also respected for the same politic reasons by the earlier
rulers of Israel—worked up in the chosen people, leading
them back to "the flesh-pots of Egypt" and to the worship
of Baal and of Ashtaroth—the serpent and the golden calf.
It was at Christmas in particular—that recognised season of
feasting and rejoicing, in the new faith as in the old—that
the heathenish instincts and traditions of the people cropped
up, breaking out into very strange excesses. As if to mark
the religious origin of these, the churches themselves were
made the theatre of them, and the clergy were obliged to
suspend their functions and to permit an impious mockery of
them to be carried on in the very centres of religious worship,
and with an imitation of all its forms. Mock Popes, mock
Bishops, and mock Priests were set up, with the tacit sanction
of the Church itself, and often with the participation of the
ecclesiastics. Chosen from and followed by the lowest
classes, they invaded the churches, and turned its most
sacred rites and ceremonies into ridicule. "The mock
Pontiffs," says Strutt, in his description of these "Festivals of
Fools," which, he adds, were always exhibited at Christmas-
time, or near to it, "the mock Pontiffs had usually a proper
suite of ecclesiastics who attended upon them, and assisted
at the divine service, most of them attired in ridiculous
dresses resembling pantomimical players and buffoons; they
were accompanied by large crowds of the laity, some being
disguised with masks of a monstrous fashion, and others
having their faces smutted; in one instance to frighten the
beholders, and in the other to excite their laughter: and

some, again, assuming the habits of females, practised all the wanton airs of the loosest and most abandoned of the sex. During the divine service this motley crowd were not contented with singing of indecent songs in the choir, but some of them ate, and drank, and played at dice upon the altar, by the side of the priest who celebrated the mass. After the service they put filth into the censers, and ran about the church, leaping, dancing, laughing, singing, breaking obscene jests, and exposing themselves in the most unseemly attitudes with shameless impudence. Another part of these ridiculous ceremonies was, to shave the precentor of fools upon a stage erected before the church, in the presence of the populace; and during the operation, he amused them with lewd and vulgar discourses, accompanied by actions equally reprehensible. The bishop, or the pope of fools, performed the divine service habited in the pontifical garments, and gave his benediction to the people before they quitted the church. He was afterwards seated in an open carriage, and drawn about to the different parts of the town, attended by a large train of ecclesiastics and laymen promiscuously mingled together; and many of the most profligate of the latter assumed clerical habits in order to give their impious fooleries the greater effect; they had also with them carts filled with ordure, which they threw occasionally upon the populace assembled to see the procession." *

It will be recollected that Sir Walter Scott introduces one of these "pious orgies" into his novel of "The Abbot," where it was made use of by the Scotch people, then about to fling off the yoke of the Roman Church, to insult the heads of the old faith.

"A Boy-Bishop" was another form taken by the spirit of defiance of religion, or of ecclesiastical discipline, after the "Festival of Fools" had been put down.

---

* This description is given by Strutt from a circular addressed to the Clergy of France; but he says that similar grotesque ceremonies certainly took place in England, though not carried to such an extent of impiety or so grossly offensive to decency.

In all the Collegiate Churches of England it was customary for one of the children of the choir, completely apparelled in Episcopal vestments, with a mitre and crozier, to bear the title and state of a Bishop. He exacted a ceremonial obedience from his fellows, who, being dressed like priests, took possession of the church and performed all the ceremonies and offices which might have been celebrated by a Bishop and his prebendaries. In the statutes of Dean Colet for his school at St. Paul's it is expressly ordered that the scholars " shall, every Childermas, come to Paul's Churche, and hear the Childe-Bishop's sermon." This was, with other ceremonies and processions, abrogated by a proclamation issued in the thirty-third year of the reign of Henry VIII.

If such scenes as these, in very mockery of religion, were carried on in churches, it is easy to conceive that the people were not slow to imitate them in their own houses. And such was the case. " Cards, dice, tables, and most other games prohibited at other seasons of the year, were (says Strutt) tolerated during the Christmas holidays, as well as disguisements and mummeries," and he distinctly traces one of these mummeries, the " Fool's Plough "—which, in the North, was, and, perhaps, still is, dragged about by sword-dancers attired in antic dress, and with which the soil is ploughed up before those houses where no reward is given—to the "Yule-plough" of Pagan days.

Royalty itself, in the time of the Plantagenets, set the example of Christmas revelries; and as the Church had its mock-Popes and mock-Bishops, so the Court had its " Lord of Misrule." " At the feast of Christmas," says Stow, " in the king's court, wherever he chanced to reside, there was appointed a lord of misrule, or master of merry disports; the same merry fellow made his appearance at the house of every nobleman and person of distinction, and among the rest the Lord Mayor of London and the Sheriffs had severally of them their lords of misrule, ever contending, without quarrel or offence, who should make the rarest pastimes to delight the beholders."

The most graphic description of the reign of a people's "Lord of Misrule" is given by Philip Stubbs, who wrote at the close of the 16th century. As a picture of Christmas doings before the Puritan Revolution it is very suggestive :—

First of all, the wilde heades of the parish flocking togither, chuse them a graund captaine of mischiefe, whom they innoble with the title of Lord of Misrule; and him they crowne with great solemnity, and adopt for their king. This king annoynted chooseth forth twentie, fourty, three-score, or an hundred lustie guttes, like to himself, to waite upon his lordly majesty, and to guarde his noble person. Then every one of these men he investeth with his liveries of greene, yellow, or some other light wanton colour, and as though they were not gawdy ynough, they bedecke them-selves with scarffes, ribbons, and laces, hanged all over with gold ringes, pretious stones, and other jewels. This done, they tie aboute either legge twentie or fortie belles, with rich handkerchiefs in their handes, and some-times laide acrosse over their shoulders and neckes, borrowed, for the most part, of their pretie mopsies and loving Bessies. Thus all thinges set in order, then have they their hobby horses, their dragons, and other antiques, together with their baudie pipers, and thundring drummers, to strike up the devil's daunce with all. Then march this heathen company towards the church, their pypers pyping, their drummers thundring, their stumpes dauncing, their belles jyngliny, their handkerchiefes fluttering aboute their heades like madde men, their hobbie horses and other monsters skirmishing amongst the throng; and in this sorte they go to the church, though the minister be at prayer or preaching, dauncing and singing like devils incarnate, with such a confused noise that no man can heare his owne voyce. Then the foolish people they looke, they stare, they laugh, they fleere, and mount upon the formes and pewes to see these goodly pageants solemnized. Then after this, aboute the church they go againe and againe, and so fourthe into the churche yard, where they have commonly their sommer-halls, their bowers, arbours, and banquetting-houses set up, wherein they feast, banquet, and daunce all that day, and paradventure all that night too; and thus these terrestrial furies spend the Sabbath day. Then, for the further innobling of this honourable lardane, lord I should say, they have certaine papers wherein is painted babelerie or other imagerie worke, and these they call my Lord of Misrule's badges, or cognizances. These they give to evey-one who will give them money to maintain them in this their heathenish devilrie; and who will not show himself buxome to them and give them money, they shall be mocked and flouted shamefully; yea, and many times carried upon a cowlstaffe, and dived over heade and eares in water, or otherwise most horribly abused. And so besotted are some, that they not only give them money, but weare their badges or cognizances in their hates or cappes openly.

Of course, Philip Stubbs was one of those new sectaries to whom the Reformation gave rise, who, by the severe way in which they looked at religion and life in general, were dubbed Puritans, and who were destined to give quite a new character to Christmas in England, and powerfully to influence its celebration down to our own days. The Reformation, in fact, though it had put an end to the most flagrant abuses of Christmas revelling in the churches themselves, had left the people to follow pretty much the old paths, as we see by Philip Stubbs's description, and as we know also by the goings-on at the Courts of Edward, Elizabeth, and James I. But the higher minds of the English people were rapidly waking up to a sense of the inconsistency of this spirit of license with the objects and aims of the religion they professed, and which they were now able to realise for themselves. A sober and severe spirit grew upon the people more and more, operating equally upon manners, morals, political opinions, and faith, until it attained its full development, first, in the ascendancy of the Presbyterians in Scotland and in England, and then in the rule of the Independents under Cromwell. Of the two, probably, the Presbyterians were the most hostile to that religious laxness which had tolerated, if not encouraged, the license and abuse of Christmas and other festive seasons. They were very severe disciplinarians and made short work of the games and sports, religious and secular, which had given to this country the title of " merrie England." The Cavaliers endeavoured to keep up this vein, in their dress, poetry, and mode of living; but they were beaten out of the field by the fanatics, as their enemies called them—by the elect of God, as they called themselves; and England became, for a time, a very sober, and, on the surface, at least, a very moral and religious country. To reverse the lines that Shakspeare puts into the mouth of Glo'ster, " its merry-meetings were turned into stern alarums;" its bear-baitings and cock-shyings into prayer-meetings and psalm-singings; its Festivals into Fasts. Christmas Day itself was made a strict fast-day, and if English-men eat roast-beef on that day, during the reign of the saints, they had to do it " on the sly." That many did so, we do not doubt; for the work sought to be done by the exalted spirits of these Puritan days was too much in advance of the times to carry the great body of the people with it. A vast number sighed for the flesh-pots of Egypt, and with the Restoration there was a strong re-action to olden ways. But the Puritans of the 17th century left their mark on the nation and on its chief festival of Christmas. Their purgation of the old heathen license was very effectual. They went too far, no doubt; most Reformers do so; but they succeeded in giving a new and a higher character to the English people in their religious life, and a new aspect to the Church in its religious festivals. It is only since the Commonwealth that England has presented that strong contrast to the Continent in its Sunday aspect which strikes all foreigners—even when those foreigners are Protestants—with astonishment and not a little dismay.

Christmas Day shared at first with the Sunday in the almost ascetic character given to it by the Puritans. But there has been a tendency of late days to emancipate it from this strict discipline and to restore to it a part, at least, of its original, and, as some may think, its appropriate character of a festival. After going, first, too far in one direction—that of license and profanity—and then too far in another—that of asceticism— the national pendulum seems to have swung into a medium movement, in which the spirit of religion and the spirit of enjoyment mingle with and temper one another. In fact, the great festival is becoming, as festivals are wont to become, a reflection of the character of the people themselves. As they become more refined—more intellectual—more spiritual—so are their national demonstrations, religious or secular, apt to present these aspects and be purged of that grossness which marked them in early ages—ages fresh from the contact of barbarism and idolatry.

The advance has been gradual. There was, doubtless, a re-action in the days of the Second Charles from the extreme rigidity of the Commonwealth. From a severe fast-day, Christmas again became a joyous festival. We find the evidence of it in the journal of the Rev. Giles Moore, Rector of Horsted Keynes, who, though a Royalist at heart, had been "admitted" to the Sussex living by the Commissioners appointed by Cromwell and his Council to "try" the efficiency of such as presented themselves. Not a word do we find in the journal about Christmas Day until Charles II. has been restored, and then, on December 25, 1662, the Rector tells us :—"I gave an entertainment to Mr. Hale and Mr. Citizen, at Bachelor's [the village public-house?] and I paid for 3 pecks of barley malt, 2s. 7d.; for 11lbs. of beef 2s. 2d. [2½d. a lb. for beef! think of that, ye modern consumers of beef!] Being Christ-masse daye, I received of John Burtenshaw, at the Parsonage, 8s., whereof I did give him back again 1s. *Christi gratiâ.*" For what the eight shillings were paid we are not told— perhaps for tithes or some other ecclesiastical dues. The gift of the shilling was clearly in the nature of a Christmas-box.

We have to pass over several years before we meet with another entry by the Rev. Giles Moore on a Christmas Day, and then it is a somewhat laconic one :—"25th Dec. I sent to Mr. Hely a ribspare and hoggs puddings, for which he returned me a box of pills and sermons." We wonder whether the Rector of Horsted Keynes considered himself the loser or the gainer by the transaction ?

The next reference of the Sussex Rector to Christmas is of a similar character—only with a change of persons. Perhaps Mr. Moore had had enough of "Pills and sermons!" "25th Dec., 1677. I sent Mr. Herryman a faire large ribspare and hoggs pudding worth 4s., for the which he returned mee 24 oranges and 6 lemons." This was a decided advance upon Mr. Hely's pills and sermons, but whether it was a fair piece of barter we can't determine, not knowing the value of oranges and lemons 200 years ago.

With the exception of a gift of 6d. to "the howling boys" on the 26th December [how many sixpences have we to give now-a-days both to howling boys and girls!], these are the only references to Christmas in the journal of a Sussex country clergyman in the time of the Commonwealth and the Second Charles ; and it shows that the great festival did not occupy much of his time, thoughts, or labours. It had not recovered the double blow given to it, first by the Reformation and then by the Puritans.

This view is borne out by other Sussex diaries. Their references to Christmas are very few and far between. In the minute and voluminous diary of Thomas Marchant, of Little Park, Hurstpierpoint, there are only three meagre entries on the 25th December:—In 1714, "Mr. Martin preached. Thos. Norton, of Edgerley, Nich. Stacey, and I spent 3d. a-piece at Smith's." This was certainly a very modest expenditure for Christmas rejoicings! In 1719, "Mr. Dodson preached. My father and mother, and *the workmen*, din'd here (at Little Park). Mr. Burry and my brother Peter stopped and spent the evening here." And again, in 1721, "Our workmen all dined here." These last entries mark an improvement. The workmen of the farm are invited into the house and partake of Christmas fare with their master. There is no record of any special festivities—of the old games and mummeries and carol singing which used to characterise the day. Eating and drinking were the solid shape which Christmas festivities assumed in Sussex farmhouses in the 18th century.

It was pretty much the same in the mansions of the gentry. The feasting and hospitality in these latter were of a higher kind; but Christmas rejoicings were confined to this solid shape of eating and drinking. In 1691, Mr. Councillor Timothy Burrell, of Ockenden, Cuckfield, "for the first time," we are told by the editor of his journal, "invited a number of his humbler neighbours to dine with him at Christmas," and he kept up the practice to the year of his death. He has left us not only the names of the guests on these occasions, but the bills of fare; and we subjoin two of the latter, to show to later—shall we say, more degenerate times?—the materials of a Christmas dinner nearly 200 years ago :—

1st January, 1706. Plumm pottage, calves' head and bacon, goose, pig, plumm pottage, roast beef, sirloin, veale, a loin, goose, plumm pottage, boiled beef, a clod, two baked puddings, three dishes of minced pies, two capons, two dishes of tarts, two pullets.—2nd January, 1706. Plumm pottage, boiled leg of mutton, goose, pig, plumm pottage, roast beef, veal, leg, roasted pig, plumm pottage, boiled beef, a rump, two baked puddings, three dishes of minced pies, two capons, two dishes of tarts, two pullets.

It will be remarked that plum-pudding, without which no Christmas Day festivities would be now complete, does not figure in Mr. Timothy Burrell's bill of fare. Its place is supplied by "plumm pottage" (sometimes called plumm broth), which occurs thrice in each bill, and which, no doubt, stood in the place of and was the embryo of its more famous successor. Minced pies had arrived at maturity; but plum puddings had yet to be invented!

Such entertainments as these of a gentleman to his poorer neighbours, and of farmers to their men, at which all met and feasted at the same board, have fallen into disuetude. The poor are feasted, doubtless, at Christmas; but they feast apart from the rich. Classes are more divided, and carry on their tasks and pleasures by themselves.

One illustration of the way in which Christmas was kept by the middle classes in Sussex in the age succeeding Timothy Burrell's is furnished by the diary of Thomas Turner, general dealer, of Easthoathly, who flourished in the middle of the 18th century :—

On Sunday, December 25, 1756 (writes Thomas Turner) myself, the two boys, and servant at Church : I and the maid staid the Communion. This being Christmas Day, the widow Marchant, Hannah, and James Marchant dined with us on a buttock of beef and a plumb suet pudding. Thos. Davey at our house in the even, to whom I read two nights of the *Complaint*, one of which was the "Christian's Triumph against the Fear of Death:" a noble subject, it being the redemption of mankind by Jesus Christ!

Here we have the elements of feasting and Puritan piety in pretty equal proportions. The struggle of these two "fell opposites" is illustrated by the following entry of Dec. 25th, 1758 :—

This being Christmas Day, myself and wife at Church in the morning. We stayed the Communion; my wife gave 6d.; *but they not asking me, I gave nothing. Oh, may we increase in faith and maintain and keep the good intentions that I hope we have this day taken up.*

What Thomas Turner's "good intentions" were, we can only guess; but his acts were very shortcoming! As years went on the feasting at Easthoathly obtained the ascendancy, until at length the Christmas doings of Thomas Turner and his neighbours, including the parson himself, ended in down-right debauchery. For weeks after Christmas Day they met at each other's houses to play " brag," eat and drink to excess, and then dance and shout and play pranks with each other—such as carrying home the ladies pick-a-back and dragging each other out of bed—which bordered closely on indecency.

This occurs for some years, on each successive Christmas, the clergyman, the medical man, and the chief people of the parish taking part in the orgies, and one of them (a Mr. French, who, his friend Turner estimates, drank for several years "not less than twenty gallons of spirituous liquors a year!") at last succumbed to it; Mr. Turner's wife also died; and he himself then "turned over a new leaf." But his very frank confessions expose to our view the gross and sensual way in which Christmas was kept in Sussex villages (and Sussex was a county of villages) in the middle and latter part of the 18th century. There was a modicum of church attendance infused into it; but the rule was "eat, drink, and be merry."

There is no reason to believe that the Christmas of Sussex, as here depicted, was different from the Christmas of other parts of England. It was a time of gross material prosperity, in which Court, nobles, clergy, and people gave themselves up to the enjoyment of the senses. The sports, both of high and low, partook of the same character. Bull-baiting, cock-fighting, and prize-fighting were the popular sports; the clergy hunted, shot, gambled, and went to the play like other people, and the Parson Trullibers were, we are afraid, much more numerous in the Church than the Parson Adamses. Thomas Turner, a man of education and with literary tastes, joined in the revelry whilst deploring it, and lets us see that the example was set at "the great House" of the parish, Halland House, where the great Duke of Newcastle, the head of the Pelhams and the first statesman of the day, lavished his vast wealth with an excess and profuseness that was imitated on a smaller scale by his humbler neighbours. There was a

M

spirit of hospitality and even of charity to the poor in this Christmas feasting of the 18th century; but it was overlaid by grossness and immorality, and in the midst of it the rich lost the power and respect and influence which they used to possess and the poor their virtue and independence. Again it was the Protestant or Puritan spirit that came to the rescue, and, in the Wesleyan and other religious movements, battled with the heathen coarseness of the times. With vast numbers of Churchmen as well as Dissenters the Christmas Day again became a Fast-day, or, at least, was shorn of its festive character—only differing from the Sunday in the intenser degree of gloom that overspread it. But against this there was also a re-action, and the spirit of asceticism has had to yield in later times to an infusion of a brighter and more festive, and what may be called a more æsthetic spirit. With the growing refinements of the age, its chief Festival has become more refined: the graces of Art and the beauties of Nature—flowers, music, painting, embroidery, &c.—are brought to the aid of religion, and temper that love of "the good things of this world" to which the nation is prone. All cruel sports and coarse amusements are banished, and if the bulk of the community still make the day a holiday, and, like Justice Greedy, "eat abundantly," it is in a less objectionable form than that of the 18th century.

Thus the great Festival of the year—it is considered so in England more than it is on the Continent, where the first day of the year vies with and, perhaps, surpasses it—has followed the various changes which the nation itself has undergone. It has been, at different eras, Pagan; half-Pagan; half-Christian; Presbyterian, Puritan, grossly material, rigidly ascetic; and now, if it can be classified at all when its phases are so various, it is Eclectic; for it borrows something from all of these interpretations of it. In the devotion of the misletoe, the yew, and the holly to its service, there is still a particle of Paganism; in the carol-singers, the "waits," and, in some parts, the "mummers," we have a remnant of the old Catholic plays and apologues and buffooneries; in the sober appearance of our streets, and the church-going habits of our middle classes, we have the Puritan element asserting itself; in the universal feasting going on we have a manifestation of our material nature and tendencies; in the floral and artistic decorations of our churches, and in the interchange of "Christmas cards," and the pouring forth of Christmas tales and Christmas lays, the æsthetic tastes of the age peep out; in the wide-spread charity and spirit of kindness and benevolence, and goodwill to men, which walks abroad at Christmas, we have the great substratum of Christian feeling, which supports all these varieties of national character, blending them into one whole and making up, with the central Divine idea, in which we all "live and move and have our being," the ideal Christmas Day.

The Knights Templars in Sussex.

S the great Earl of Chatham confessed that he drew a large portion of his historical knowledge from the Chronicle Plays of Shakspeare, so a good many modern readers might own that they derive no small amount of their notions of the Middle Ages from the romances and novels of Sir Walter Scott. The figure of Brian de Bois Gilbert, in particular, stands forth in Ivanhoe as the popular type of the Knight-Templar, when that military Order was at the apex of its strength and wealth and fame. How far the Templars were sinners or victims is still a problem of history. It may well be doubted, if they had not been very rich, whether they would have been attacked by the Popes and the Monarchs of that day. But then these very riches are a proof of the probability of guilt. It has been said that no man can grow rich of a sudden by fair and innocent means; and this holds true of bodies quite as much as of individuals. Judged by this rule, the Knights-Templars must be condemned, for in less than 200 years they had risen from affected poverty to a point of wealth that enabled their Grand Masters to vie with Princes and their chief officers to take rank with the Barons of England and France, whilst their forces were equal in number, and superior in discipline, to the armies of Princes, and their military stations, or Preceptories, as they were called, scattered as they were throughout Europe and Asia, drew to them the most active spirits of the day, and not a small portion of the wealth of the pious.

There were two of these Preceptories in Sussex, though all traces of them have long since disappeared. One was at

Shipley, near Horsham, in West Sussex; the other in East
Sussex, at Sedlescombe, four miles to the north-west of
Brighton, and lying within the parishes of Newtimber, Hurst,
Twineham, and Bolney. At the time of the dissolution of
the Order, at the close of the 13th and the commencement
of the 14th century, by Philippe IV. of France and Edward II.
of England, at the instigation of Pope Alexander, these two
Preceptories had extensive possessions in Sussex, with valuable
privileges granted by previous Sovereigns. In addition to
lands, houses, tithes and manors, including the churches of
Sompting, Southwick, and Woodmancote, they had a large
quantity of live and dead stock in the shape of corn, cattle,
sheep, horses, ducks, geese, fowls, &c. In fact, they seem to
have been very good farmers; but there is no evidence—at
least, in the inventory of the Sussex " plant "—of luxurious
living, consisting as it does chiefly of agricultural implements,
and the wardrobe and armoury being poorly furnished, and
the church furniture on a mean scale. Literature, too, was
not in high esteem amongst the Sussex Templars: the Shipley
library consisted of " two books—of Kings and of Beasts
(*liber Regum, liber bestiarum*) which are not valued, because the
jury do not know their price." A strange conjunction this
of Kings and beasts! and a very naive, and, doubtless, true
confession on the part of the jury. The only articles at all
betokening the gentle blood of the Knights were 20 silver
spoons, valued at 10d. each, three rings of gold at 1s. each,
and three silk purses at 1s. each.

Not much here to tempt the cupidity of Kings! But the
Sussex Preceptories were in remote and rural districts, to
which, perhaps, the pomp and luxury of which the Templars
were accused had not yet penetrated. At all events, nothing
of a very heinous nature was proved against the Knights and
their servants seized at Shipley and Sedlescombe. The
measures for the dissolution of the Order in England were
taken with great secrecy and promptitude, the Knights themselves being arrested and sent to prison on one day, the 8th
of January, 1308, and their goods confiscated; a summary

proceeding that has no parallel in English history, though not uncommon in that of France.   The orders for the arrest of the Knights and seizure of their goods were delivered to the Sheriff of Sussex and Surrey (and to all other Sheriffs) by priests, who exacted an oath of secrecy.   It was, in fact, a plan devised by the Pope himself; and when the King of England (Edward II.) hesitated to apply torture to these unfortunate men, to extort confession, it was the Pope (then Clement V.) who overcame his scruples.

Among the knights thus arrested and sent to the Tower of London were the Preceptor of Shipley (William de Egendon) and five others who had taken part in the solemn ceremonies of the Order in Sussex.   The Preceptor of Sedlescombe appears to have made his escape, for his name does not figure in the after-proceedings.   These were little to the credit of the authorities of the day.   There appears to have been little or nothing beyond vague and credulous reports adduced against the Order in England, and it was only by the confessions extorted by torture, or fear of it, that sufficient grounds were obtained for a condemnation. One charge against them was that of secret burials, which was generally denied; but " one knight, who had been thirty-eight years in the Order, gave the striking answer that he had never witnessed any burials except of those who had died in the Tower.   One of the accusers was a Templar, John de Gertia, and he bare witness that he had heard from a woman named Cacocaca that a servant, fourteen years ago, had secretly seen and watched the Templars while they placed an idol upon the crucifix, and that one brother who had refused to do so had been confined inside a well with the lid shut down *(clauso puteo cum cooperculo);* and he also deposed that one Walter Salvage, of the household of the Earl of Warenne's grandfather, had, two years after entering the Order, been so removed away that neither the Earl nor his other friends could ever learn what had become of him."

After three years' imprisonment it is not to be wondered at if the Templars were tired out and glad to regain their liberty on any terms. They made a general confession (in Latin, French, and English) "that though they were sincere Christians, they were in such evil repute, as to having denied the Saviour, and treated the Cross with contempt, and other heresies, that they were unable to prove themselves innocent: and therefore submitted themselves to the discipline of the Church and implored its pardon."

Upon this submission, the English Grand Master (William de la More) and many of his knightly companions, including the Preceptor of Shipley, who abjured in French, received absolution, which was given by the Bishops of London and of Chichester; "and this (we are told) they did with much pomp, seated at the west door of St. Paul's, surrounded by priests and people, while the Templars on their knees before them publicly abjured all heresies, some with cries and weeping."

Upon this they were released from their prisons, but not set at liberty, being sent, by direction of the Bishops, into divers monasteries to perform penance. But there was one exception. The Grand Master, William de la More, it is added, though included among those who confessed, alone refused to admit himself guilty of what he had not done, and was doomed to be shut up in the vilest prison, confined with double irons, and from time to time to be visited and importuned to confess. He did not long survive this treatment. In France, the Templars escaped far less easily. They were subjected to the greatest cruelties, and large numbers expired under horrible tortures: inflicted upon the plea of heresy or impiety. The Order was finally dissolved by the Pope; the Bull of Clement V. being published in England by the Archbishop of Canterbury on August 15, 1312.

Of all "the gold, silver, and riches" popularly attributed to the Sussex Templars, the only relic now remaining is a beautiful reliquary, still the property of the parish of Shipley. "It is" (says Mr. W. H. Blaauw, to whose paper in the Sussex Archæological Collections we are chiefly indebted for these facts of the Knights-Templars in Sussex) "seven inches long by six inches high, and its wooden frame still preserves some of its coverings of gilt plates, ornamented with enamel, which appear to be of the thirteenth century. They represent the Crucifixion, with the Greek letters X P E over the cross, the Virgin Mary and St. John standing near, and other saints under semicircular arches on each side and at the ends."

The landed property of the Templars was transferred to the Hospitallers, who undertook to perform their duties, whatever these were. The Knights Hospitallers, too, have long disappeared, with all the other ponderous machinery, religious and military, by which the Roman Church supported itself in the Middle Ages, doing in a rough way a necessary work. As civilization advanced, these bulwarks of Faith, as they were deemed, became mere encumbrances and clogs to religion, too often full of gross abuses, and they have been swept away as so much rubbish—never to be called back again.

When the lands and goods of the Knights Templars in Sussex were confiscated by the King, a valuation of the property was ordered to be made, and several juries were sworn in by the Sheriff of the County for the purpose. The names of these jurymen still appear on the record in the State Paper Office, and they are interesting as supplying a clue to many names still familiar among us. Thus there were on these old juries John de Dene, John le Post, Andrew de Sonde, Adam le Fraunk, Robert de Hales, Robert Santys, Paulin de Nitimber, Walter le Shepherd, John Sieth, John Scrace, William de Risbrigge, Walter Tenereday, John Ottehale, Philip de Heyworth, John atte Helegrove, Ralph de Saggeworth, Walter de Brenteregge, Osbert Giffard, Simon de Warbilton, Richard de Seles, Thomas de Sheryngton, Robert le Husiére, Henry Gilebert, Walter Colekyn, Robert de Birche, Nicholas Garlaunde, Thomas le Heye, John de Gissyngham, Hamo le Neem, Simon de Seldemerse, Richard atte Delve, and Reginald de Compton. Some of these names, as the last on the list, are, of course, taken from the places at

which the jurymen lived, and Walter le Shepherd was, probably,
or some of his ancestors had been, a tender of sheep. The
number of these juries was irregular: one—held at Horsham
—was unusually large—twenty-one. Their duty was to take
an inventory of the goods and assess the value of the lands
of the unfortunate Knights.

The names of the Sussex benefactors of the Order have
also been preserved, with the witnesses to the deeds; and
they also throw a light on the County Patronymica. In this
category we have Sir Luke de Poynings, Sir Robert de
Cokesfelde, Henry de Wayvell, John de Pierpounde, William
de Perchinge, Hugh Waldefare, Philip de Holeburn, William
Bisshop, of Stanninges (Steyning ?), Finian de Schorham
(Shoreham ?), William le Mercer, John de Swele, Peter of the
Wood, Walter le Fre, Walter le Wrenge (afterwards changed
to Walter de Farncombe, because, doubtless, he held land in
" Farncombe, near Sadeliscombe "), Thomas Belhomme, &c.

One very curious fact is brought out by these old deeds.
It is, that the Sussex Templars admitted a married lady into
their Order: a fact which, if it had been introduced into a
modern romance, would have been ridiculed as a solecism in
history. However, here it is upon record in black and white,
and we may as well say at once, that it involves no scandal to
the Templars. The order for the reception of the lady came,
it would seem, from a foreign Archbishop, and the bearer of
it was the lady's own husband! It ran thus :—

Reception of Johanna Chaldese as a sister of the Templars. To the
very dear to him in Christ, S. Master of the Brothers of the Temple of
Jerusalem in England, Azo Archbishop greeting in the Lord. Know that
Johanna the wife of the bearer of this present letter, Richard de Chaldese,
knight, who by the grace of God has proposed to submit herself to the
yoke of the rule of the Temple, although worn out by age (*se jugo regule
Templi subdere proposuit licet confecta senio*) insomuch that no sinister
suspicion can henceforth arise concerning her, has promised in the presence
of my officers to preserve her chastity, and has promised finally that she
shall submit to the rule of the Temple ; wherefore we, desirous of bearing
our testimony to the truth, have throught it right to certify this to you
with my letters hanging outside (*cum literis meis extra pendentibus*).

This is all that is known of this remarkable circumstance,
the reception of an elderly married lady into a military order

of bachelors !   It is a proof of advanced ideas in the 13th
century, which may cause the strongest-minded woman of the
present day to open her eyes with astonishment.   Who the
lady was—what her motives were for selecting a Sussex
Preceptory of this military Order as her place of refuge, and
how she behaved and what became of her, we do not know.
But we do not doubt for a moment that Johanna Chaldese,
wife of Richard de Chaldese, knight, religiously kept her
vow of chastity "as a sister of the Templars."

Liberty of Speech in Sussex in Times Past and Present.

WE are in the habit, in the present day, of congratulating ourselves on the privileges we possess above our ancestors in what we call "the liberty of the Press," to the overlooking of the still greater privilege which we claim and exercise, in "liberty of Speech." Where one person sets up the one, how many thousand use, or abuse, the other! It is the prerogative, so to say, of every man, woman, and child—of every soul that can speak the English tongue, and it is a prerogative that is not allowed to lie idle. It is, indeed, a "chartered libertine"—it bloweth like the wind whither it listeth—now in accents so soft that the ear can scarcely catch the passing sound, but not the less deadly for that; at other times in all the blusterous fury of the hurricane—sweeping every thing before it. Now it is a bastard report — a scandal — that no man will own for his child, and now it is public opinion, which has its parentage in a nation and acknowledges no superior—no tribunal which can call it to account.

It is curious to think how mighty this power of free speech—this license of the tongue—is, and yet how little account we take of it. We English accept it now as the ancients did the right of air and water, as an indefeasible attribute of our birth, without which we could scarcely be what we are. And yet this great right, prerogative, privilege—call it what we will—did not always exist in the unshackled form in which we now enjoy it, and abuse it. In the days when men did not write and print so much as they do now, they had to be much more careful about what they *spoke*. Written matter was, doubtless, always more grave than spoken. But not one man in a thousand, if so many, could write 300 years ago,

whilst every man had a tongue to be wagged more or less idly;
and so the tongue was looked after more sharply in those days,
and men had to be careful what they said, as well as what they
wrote and printed.

In our Sussex annals, so carefully collected by the members
of the Archæological Society, we find some striking instances
of the state of things to which we are adverting, and of the
danger which our ancestors ran in allowing their tongues to
run too idly.   Both the Crown and the aristocracy—nay, the
class below the nobility—had the power to call such offenders
to a strict account.   There was a special Court to take account
of any words in derogation of the honor, or rank, or character
of the upper classes uttered by the coarse-speaking rural or
mechanic class; and a man might find himself "clapt up by
the heels" in a very summary fashion for criticising the
appearance, or expressing his opinion of the character or
conduct, of his grander neighbour in a style that would now
excite no notice, or only call forth a laugh.

But to our Sussex instances.   The first has reference to
"good Queen Bess," and if our readers exclaim, with Puff, in
the *Critic,* "No scandal, I hope, of Queen Elizabeth," we
must leave them to form their own opinion on the point.
She herself did think there was scandal in it, and that her
liege subjects had no business to indulge in idle gossip at her
expense.   Only think if Queen Victoria had such a notion as
this and could bring to account all the idle tongues who have
indulged in idle tales—we will not say at her expense, for they
took nothing from a character so pure and unimpeachable;
but still, if a Queen Elizabeth had had to deal with a John
Brown gossip, Heavens! what an issuing forth of warrants,
what a sallying forth of Marshals, and what an opening and
shutting of prison-gates, perhaps a shortening of ears and noses
—to say nothing of heavy fines and long imprisonments—
there would have been!

If the reader doubts, let him note the fate which befel
Arthur Gunter, an ancestor of that famous Colonel Gunter,
of Racton, in West Sussex, who gave shelter, in his house, to

the fugitive, Charles Stuart, after Worcester, and accompanied him to Brighthelmstone, and found out the means of his escape to the opposite coast of France—all which shows him to have been a true-hearted and loyal Englishman. And so, doubtless, was his ancestor, Arthur Gunter, or Gounter, as the name was spelt in Elizabeth's day. But this Arthur seems to have been over-fond of gossip, and one day, when he " chaunced to be a huntynge with divers gentlemen " (we quote his own words), " I fell in Taulcke with a Jentleman named Mr. George Cottone, who towlde me that hyt chaunced the Quene's Hynes to be at supper on a tyme at my Lorde Robert's Howse, wheare hyt chaunced Hyr Hyghness to be nyghted homeward, and as hyr Grace whas goynge homeward by Torchelyght, hyr Hyghness fell in Taulcke with them that carryed the Torches, and seyde that hyr Grace wolde make ther Lorde the best that ever whas of hys name. Whereuppon I seyde that hyr Grasee must macke him then a Dewke, and he said that the Reporte was that Hyr Hyghness sholde marry hym ; and I answered—I praye God all men may tacke hyt well that there might rysse no troble thereof, and so I have seyde to dyvers others synce that Tyme."

Whereby Arthur Gounter did manifest that he was a very indiscreet individual, and that it would have been better for him if he had held his tongue ; for if trees have tongues, so have they ears, and this " taulcke " in the Sussex hunting field came in time to the knowledge of the Royal lady whom it concerned, and not a little wroth, doubtless, was she that " base churls " should make free with her maiden fame, and her intentions towards matrimony or otherwise. So, indeed, Master Gounter found out, for he was speedily " clapt up by the heels," in other words, incarcerated, and made to speak out more plainly as to what he meant by the above " taulcke," and hereupon he made the following

Confessions of A. Gunter, concerning Lord Robert Dudley (Earl of Leicester).

Pleseth your Honor, further to understande, that the sayde Mr. George Cotton seyde, that hyt was rumored heretofore ; that my Lorde my Master shoolde have maryed the Quene's Hyghnes ; and I seyde, that, yf hyt pleased hyr Hynes, I thought him as mette a Man as any in Inglande; and further he asked me, yf I herde of any Parlement towarde; and I seyde, No;—but, yf ther wer eny, I thynke every Nobleman wyll geve his opinion, and then they that be my Lord Robert's friends wyll seye that he is a mette man; and so hyt maye fortune there wyll rysse troble amonge the Noblemen; which God forbede. And then he asked me, who was my Lorde's Frends? and I seyde, my Lorde Markes of Northampton; my Lorde of Pembroke; Mr. Treasurer; Mr. Laefelde, with many others. Further I seyd, I trust the *Whyght Horsse** will be in quiet; and so shall we be out of troble; hyt is well knowen hys Blode as yette whas never attaynte, nor he was ever a man of Warr, wherefor ys hyt lycke, that we shall syt still; but yf he shoole stomache hyt, he were able to make a great Powre. All these things befoore rehearseed I have spoken unto dyvers other, as unto Mr. Robt. Palmer, Mr. Stowton, Mr. Benyon, and others. Further as towchynge my Lord Robert, I have seyde to Mr. Cottone that I thought hym to be causse that my Lord my Master (the Earl of Arundel) might not marry the Quene's Hyghnes, wherefor I wolde that he had bene put to dethe with his father, or that some roffen wolde have dyspatched hym by the way as he hath gone, with some dagge or Gonne. Farther I seyde that yf hyt chaunced my Lord Robert to marry the Quene's Hyghnes, then I dowted whether he woolde remember my owlde matter passed heartofore, and so be turned unto my Lord my master's displeasure and hindrance.

By me ARTHUR GOUNTER.

A good deal of these "Confessions" is not very intelligible to us at the present day. But it is obvious that it had reference to the Queen's marriage either with the Earl of Arundel ("the White Horse") or Robert Dudley, afterwards Earl of Leicester, and that the sudden and mysterious death of the wife of the latter, the ill-fated Amy Robsart, happened about this time, and had its bearing on the reports afloat, for, in one of the Hatfield MSS., under the date 1560, occurs this entry:—"The saying of Arthur Gunter to George Cotton," that "ere this my Lord Robert's wife is dead, and she broke her neck. It is in a number of heads that the Queen will marry him. If she do, you will see a grand stir, for my Lord Arundel is sure of the Earl of Pembroke, and the Lord Rich, with divers others; to be ready with the putting up of his finger; and then shall you see the White Horse bestir him; for my Lord is of great power."

Gunter, it is evident, was a follower of "the White Horse," the Norfolk or Catholic interest, whilst Leicester was the head

---

* The well-known badge of the Earls of Arundel.

of the Protestant party, with a tendency to Puritanism. So that, in this "taulcke" between two gentlemen "huntynge" in Sussex, the deadly rivalry of two great religious parties was, doubtless, shadowed forth. So, indeed, might it be in the present day, without that danger to body and estate which Arthur Gunter ran, and from the consequences of which he narrowly escaped. For, as our chronicler tells us, after being incarcerated and questioned, he was only pardoned on making a written "Confession," in which he declared that for the "unfytting wordes" uttered by him, he had been "most worthely punished;" and was "very hartely sorry," that the like should never again enter into his heart, and much less pass his mouth; and that he would study by all means "to reduble and recompence" his former offence.

Now, let us turn from this somewhat exalted instance of the danger of "taulcke" about Queens and Earls and Lords, and let us take a humbler case and one nearer to our own times. It occurred in the reign of the First Charles, and the principal actors in it were Master John Wilson, *Esq.*—"as," says Mr. Blencowe, "it was the custom to call an esquire in those days"—of Searles, in the parish of Fletching—the proprietor of several iron furnaces in Sussex and Kent—and a certain fellow, named John Tye." For some reason or other—perhaps because he was unusually prosperous in his undertakings—Master John Wilson, Esq., drew upon himself the ill-will of some of his humbler neighbours, and this was shown in several "causeless aspersions" and "scandalous reflections"—so we are assured—upon his worth. But of the exact nature of these aspersions and reflections we are not informed, except in the case of John Tye, "the most notorious of his slanderers," and who, as such, was selected for punishment.

And what was the heinous offence of this "base fellow, John Tye?" Well, the "head and front of his offending" consisted in his having uttered the following words:—"As for this Wilson, I am as good as he, nobody knows where he came from;" "accompanied," we are told,"by some certainly very coarse and offensive terms of contempt."

Very annoying, doubtless, for a gentleman thus to be spoken of by a "common fellow." But only imagine such words as these in our days being made the subject of indictment at the County Sessions! Such was the course adopted by Master John Wilson, Esquire, and, failing to obtain redress here of his fellow-justices—not, it seems, because the Court was unequal to the task or unwilling, but because Sussex was not Mr. Wilson's county—he had recourse to "the Court of Honour"—a Court of which the very name and memory have now died out, but which, in the 17th century, was in great vigour—"much," we are told, and, no doubt, correctly, "to the satisfaction of the nobility and gentry in such cases as were not to be redressed by the strict rules of common law." No doubt of it! "But," proceeds our authority, "I must take notice that this Court did not exert itself in favour of persons who were not truly gentlemen. I mean by birth—or an office legally entitling them to that title." In fact, common fellows like John Tye might abuse each other as much as they liked; but if they came between the wind and the nobility of their superiors, let them look to themselves! John Tye soon found out that he had to do so. A "Court of Honour" was constituted to take cognizance of the case. "Mr. Serjeant Amherst, Mr. Thomas Challoner (a member of the family which was shortly to see its head, Colonel Challoner, sit on that High Court which doomed to death Charles I), and Mr. Anthony Fowle were appointed by the Earl Marshal to inquire into the case." Such was the composition of the Court of Honour. In that day men were not always tried by a jury of their peers. John Tye, "base fellow" as he was, had to answer for his offence to these three gentlemen, all of the same rank as his accuser, Master John Wilson, Esq. Who can doubt what the verdict of such a jury was? "As might be easily supposed," says Mr. Blencowe, "John Tye was soon convicted. He begged for mercy, and was forgiven, upon condition that he made his humble submission and a public recantation of the calumny before the inhabitants of the parish, in the porch of the church at Fletching."

To make assurance doubly sure, we learn that one of the Court of Honour, Mr. Serjeant Amherst, wrote as follows to " his loveing cosen and friend," Robert Foster, Esq. :—"Mr. Wilson always lived and carryed himself as a gentleman (as he is), of a good and ancient descent; I pray you let him not be abused in so base and false a manner, and Tye be suffered to escape without punishment; *you know hou irksome it is for a gentleman to be abused by a clowne.*"

Poor John Tye ! He was born an age too soon ! Had he belonged to our times, he might have boasted his equality with any Esquire in the county, or Duke or Earl for the matter of that, as much as he liked. But "the Age of Chivalry is gone," and "Courts of Honour" are sunk into the dust! "Common fellows" have come to the surface, and whoever chooses to call himself a gentleman or esquire may do so to his heart's content, and take no harm. Not so in "the brave days of old."

In the time of the Stuarts, however, if gentlemen had their own Courts of Honour and peculiar privileges, it was not so easy a thing to set up a title to gentility, and the man who set about proving it had to undertake a work of some trouble, and, unless his claim was well founded, some risk. This was the process :—

A commission was granted by His Majesty to the Provincial King at Armes to visit the county, which was performed in a very solemn manner. Sir Richard St. George, Knight, was then Clarencieux; and pursuant thereto, in the year 1634, in person he visited the county. The end of these visitations was to take an account of all the familys of the nobility and gentry of the county lawfully bearing armes; and also to take notice of all such persons who bore armes that had no right, and of others, who assumed and usurped the title of gentlemen or esquire, having no right to be so called according to the laws of the land. A jury was usually summoned *ad inquirendum* . . . . . . Those who assumed armes were obliged to prove their right before the Lord Marshal; and those who suffered themselves to be styled gentlemen or esquires, not having lawful right thereto, were (according to the words in the commission, in the last visit to this county in 1668), to be made infamous : their names were usually posted up in the market-place of the chief towns there, with a signification that they were not what they were called; or otherwise stigmatised according to the laws of honour and the Earl Marshal's authority.

N

So that there was a *pro* and *con.* to the case, and the man too anxious to become famous might find himself proclaimed infamous. Gentlemen of the present day run no such danger!

It is not without its advantage that we can thus contrast the past with the present. We are inclined sometimes to envy our forefathers some of the advantages which, doubtless, they enjoyed, and which we have lost. But there were other things in which the balance inclines to our side. Most certainly that is the case in regard, not merely to the freedom of the Press (as is sometimes thought), but to the much larger domain included in the liberty of speech. As Tennyson so eloquently says of England in the present day,

> " It is the land that freemen till,
>   That sober-suited Freedom chose,
>   The land where, girt with friends or foes,
> *A man may speak the thing he will.*"

And, having this great liberty, who will gainsay that, for the most part, it is wisely and nobly used by the English people, and that, with little check on their tongues except that which their own sense of propriety imposes, there is, perhaps, as little—nay, perhaps, less abuse in the way of " taulcke " in the days of Victoria than in those of Elizabeth or of the Charles's ?

A Sussex Sedition: An Episode of Brambletye.

WHEN Brambletye House is named, the thoughts of the speaker or hearer naturally revert to the romantic incidents that the genius of Horace Smith has associated with all that now remains of that old residence of the Lewknors and the Comptons—incidents, we need hardly say, almost totally due to the novelist's invention. But there are curious events connected with Brambletye long anterior to the days of the Cavaliers and Roundheads, whom Horace Smith deals with in his story, and one of the most curious is that which brought it under the notice of Elizabeth's Council of State as the scene of a sedition.

How quick of growth seditions were in those days—how easy it was to swell words into matter of dangerous import to those who uttered them, and to give to the most innocent acts a treasonable aspect, we have already given a notion of in the proceedings which were taken in the same reign against Arthur Gunter, of Racton (an ancestor of the Colonel Racton who escorted Charles II. in his flight through Sussex), for certain words spoken by him during a hunting-party in West Sussex, with respect to the probable marriage of Queen Elizabeth with the Earl of Leicester. To that illustration of the suspicious nature of the times may be well appended the "Proceedings against John Turner for seditious words spoken on livery and seizin of Brambletye Chapel to Lord Buckhurst's use in May, 1579."

The chief mover in these proceedings was a lady, and a lady, it is pretty clear, well able to take her own part—by name Katherin Pickas. Her antagonist, and the party charged with sedition, was John Turner, by profession an attorney, and in the service, it would appear, of Lord Buckhurst. And it was whilst in the performance of one of his professional duties, namely, taking livery and seizin of Brambletye Chapel (that is, the lands belonging to the charity which had been founded there in Catholic times by the owners of Brambletye, but which chapel, at the Reformation, had been dissolved and the lands taken by the Crown) that John Turner came into contact with Katherin Pickas, or rather, we should say, that Katherin Pickas came into contact with John Turner, for the lady was the more active party.

But we will quote, from the Paper in the State Paper Office, a description of the scene and act of sedition as it is reported to " the Right Honable and our verie good Lordes the Lordes of her Majestie's most honourable Privee Counselle " by six Magistrates of the Lewes Sessions, including a Buckhurste, a Pelham, a Gorringe, a Covert, a Colepepper, and Sackevylle, all good Sussex names, and some still current amongst us :—

" There came before us," report their Worships, " at the late sessions, holden at Lewes now after Ester, on Katherin Pickas, who among other matters then and there declared by her unto us, did affirme that on John Turner in seking to make liverie and sesin of a dede made from John Farnam of a chapel and certein landes to the Lord Buckhurst, in which the said John Turner was atturnie for that purpose, did speke certein evell and unsemely wordes toching the Quenes majestie such as she thought fit to impart unto us. The effect whereof was thus : whan the said Katherin Pickas and vj others with her had found the said John Turner and v others with him, at a place being nere to the hous of on Steven Frenche within Grnsted parishe in Sussex, she asked of the said John Turner what he and the rest did there. The said John Turner answered " to take possession for my Lorde of Buckhurste for the chapel of Brambletie, and land which (as he said) pertanied thereunto ; " the saide Katherin answered " by what authoritie ? " and the said Turner answered " by authority from John Farnam." " What hath he to do here ? (said the said Katherin). This matter is ended by the Quene, God save her highness." " Yt makes no matter for the Quene " (said the said Turner). "No (said the said Katherin). Is my lord of Buckhurst above the Quene ? " " Yea (said Turner), in this respecte." Upon the informacon of which saide wordes unto us some of us were of opinion that we shold consider of the matter among ourselves, and accordinglie to procede as to the same caus upon the statute made against suche as shalle use any fals seditious or slaunderous wordes against the Quenes highness ; others were of mind that in a matter thus concerning

her majesty, we ought rather to remit the judgement thereof to the order
and wisdomes of your honorable lordships: unto which presentlie we all
assented. And therupon we toke the examinacons by othe of all such as
were said to be present at the said place and time, whan the said wordes
were supposed to be spoken, save of the said John Turner, and of on
Alexander Middleton, being but a boy of xiiij yeres of age: unto bothe
which we forbare to offer any othe, becaus the on was the partie acused,
the other of so yonge yeres: but how far furthe the same wordes are
proved or disproved by the deposicons of thos that were present, or how
they are to be understode or expounded, we do most humbly referre to the
judgement of your Lordships, to whom we send herewithall the examinacons
of the said parties at large, and so doe most humblie take our leave. ffrom
Lewis in Sussex this second day of May, 1579.

And to this general description of the seditious act (a kind
of Counsel's opening speech!) are appended the depositions
of the several witnesses on each side. These depositions, as
being " more exquisite " than the other, we also give:—

Katherin Pycas, wife of James Pycas, about forty-four years of age,
deposed that she being at Stephen Frenches door in Grinsted, there being
then also present John Turner, Gilbert Sackvylle, Gent., Robert Fryer,
Edmund Tomson, Robert Payne, Evans Flud, Henry Cropper, John Cotty,
Edward Matthew, Richard Knight, Alexander Mydelton, and John Grame,
the conversation passed as set out in the letter: adding that Turner spoke
the words very vehemently: she added "I hope my Lord of Buckhurst
will take nothing away from us wrongfully." "No, I warrant you," said
Mr. Sackevyll, "there is never a right further from you;" and then she
related a further talk with Mr. Sackevyll, who did not deny that the words
were used. (Signed by the aboue six justices, and also by Richard Shelley,
Laurens Levat and Henry Bartlet.)

Henry Cropper, of Bramblety, servant to Mr. Pycas, confirmed his
mistress; as did also other servants, viz., John Cotty, Edward Marten,
Richard Knight, Alexander Mydelton, and Jone Greme.

John Turner, gentleman, aged thirty-eight years (unsworn), stated that
by virtue of a letter of attorney by John Farnham, Esq., to Gilbert
Sackvyll and himself, jointly and severally, to make livery and seizin of the
chantry and chapel of Bramblety to Lord Buckhurst, they came to a green
between Stephen Frenche's house and the chapel, intending to make the
delivery to Robert Fryer to his lordship's use, in the presence of Evans
Flud, Edmund Tomson, and Robert Payn, but were set upon by Cotty,
Matthew, Cropper, and others; and after some blows Turner, seeing
Katherin Pycas coming towards them in great haste, and others following
her with staves and other weapons, Turner and his party departed from
the green to a lane a little beneath Frenche's house, and then Katherin
Pycas asked Turner "what have you to do here? and will you shew
your authority?" Whereupon he referred to the deed and grant to Lord
Buckhurst, and the letter of attorney to deliver seizin. They then asked
how Mr. Farnam came by it? and he said by the Queen's Majesty's letters
patent. Then she said that her title was good, and that she had proved it
before the Queen's Majesty's commissioners. Whereupon Turner answered
that if her title were good, that which he did could do her no hurt, and
wished her, if her title were good, to shew it to Lord Buckhurst by her

counsel; and he thought if her title fell out better than his lordships, she would find that favor that he would not shew her. She said that she would shew it to my lord and my lord's betters, and to them that would not be afraid to shew it him, and that it was but a private thing, and that my lord would stop a poor man's living. Turner then said "there is a better way," and then went into a field, and she remained in the lane, and then went again after Turner and his friends with her company with staves. Turner asked her what she made in that ground, and she said it was her land, and Turner said it was Henry Payne's during his lease, and she answered, he should not enjoy it, and bid her men drive them out, and follow them, "you Berkshire gentlemen, you think to make me stoop to you, but I will never do it;" whereunto he answered, "no, good gossip, I mean it not," and so departed homeward and returned not.

Gilbert Sackfyle, aged sixty-eight years of age, said he was not present near Frenche's door where the words were supposed to be spoken, but he did hear the portion about it not being further from her, if her title were good. And afterwards meeting with her again, she said "we may thank you for all this," and further, "will not you say as yonder Jack hath saith?" "What is that?" "Marry," said she, "he said my Lord of Buckhurst is above the Queen," whereupon Sackville answered "he has too much wit to say so." "And will not you say so?" quoth she twice together. "No, marry, will I not," said he; but whether she said that the words were concerning the Queen, that the Lord Buckhurst was above the Queen in this respect, he knew not.

John Fryer confirmed the memorandum of the conversation as set down by Turner a few days after the discourse.

Edmund Tompson denied that those words, nor were the like spoken in his presence, and he was near enough to hear; and Payne and Flud confirmed him.

As no measures were taken by the Privy Council against John Turner, either for sedition or anything else, we may conclude that Mistress Katherin Pycas failed in her little plot. What her interest, or that of her husband—who never appears in the affair at all, but leaves all to the management of his wife—was in the land in dispute, we are not told. In all probability the land of the dissolved Brambletye Chauntry, or its usufruct, had fallen in some way to her; she told Turner that "it was *her* land," and "that her title was good and that she had proved it before the Queen's Majesty's Commissioners," adding "that it was but a private thing, and that my Lord (Buckhurst) would stop a poor man's living." To maintain her hold upon the land, and keep out the attorney of the opposite party, it was not a bad device of Mrs. Katherin Pycas to set up a charge of sedition. A very little foundation was sufficient in those days, when the air of

England was full of sedition, or the suspicion of it, for such a charge, and half the time of Elizabeth's Council was occupied in detecting or enquiring into conspiracies against her person or Government. In this case, however, the motive was too obvious and the grounds of the charge were too trivial; and the "Sussex Sedition" never went beyond the above stage. The Chantry lands of which John Turner "made liverie and seizin" for my Lord Buckhurst by virtue of a deed from John Farnham, to whom they had been granted by the Crown on the dissolution of the Chantry, passed doubtless into the hands of that powerful nobleman, and Katherin Pickas, after fighting a stout battle for her rights, or those of her husband, whatever they were, had to smother her griefs and put up with her loss.

Witchcraft in Sussex.

E need hardly remind our readers that, in the 17th century, the most enlightened men believed in witchcraft, and that Judges like Sir Matthew Hale sent poor old women accused of dealing with his Satanic Majesty to the stake. It is not, therefore, to be wondered at that country Justices fell into the same delusion; it was a part of the religion of the day. Sussex was never the scene of such wholesale witch-drownings and burnings as disgraced Lancashire and some other counties; the infamous witch-finder, Hopkins, did not travel so far south. But that, if he had done so, he would have found the soil ready for him may be judged by the curious narrative contained in the MS. collections relating to Sussex, left by the Rev. W. Hayley, rector of Brightling, to the British Museum. The date of the incidents referred to is supposed to be about 1662. We give it *verbatim et literatim :—*

AT BRIGHTLING, IN SUSSEX.

As touching ye Relation of ye Brightling Story, which is in substance undoubtedly true, however some circumstances of it may vary, be pleased to take ye following account.

On Monday was three weeks at or near ye house of Joseph Cruttenden, of Brightling, an old woman about noon came to a servant girl of the said Cruttenden's and tells her sad Calamities were coming upon her Master and Dame, their house should be fired, and many other troubles befall them, but tells this Girl withal, That if she spake of what she had told her, ye Devil would tear her to pieces, otherwise she need not fear, for no hurt should come to her.

The same night, as the man and woman lay in bed, Dirt and Dust was thrown at them, but they could not tell whence it came; They rise and pray, during which the disturbances cease. Some say they went to bed again, but finding ye same trouble they are forced to rise. Tuesday, about noon, Dust and Dirt, and several things are thrown at them again; before night, a part of one end of their house fired; they rake it down, it flashes somewhat like gunpowder; as they stopped it there, it began in another place, and then in another, till the whole house was burnt down. Some say something like a Black Bull was seen tumbling about; ye certainty of which I aver not. The house, though it burned down to the ground, it flamed not. The night was spent in carrying away goods, or one thing or another, to one place or another, they I think remaining most without doors. Thursday Colonel Busbridge (whose house the former was, being acquainted with ye man's sad accident, bid them go into another of his Houses in ye Parish, whither, when ye Goods were brought, such like Disturbances were there also; ye house fireth, endeavours are made by many to quench it, but in vain, till ye Goods are thrown out, when it ceased with little or no help.

In this condition none durst let them into their doors; they'abide unde-a Hut; ye Goods are thrown upside down; Pewter Dishes, knives, Brickr bats strike them, but hurt ym not. Mr. Bennett and Mr. Bradshaw, Ministers, came to pray with ym, when a knife glanced by ye Breast of Mr. Bennett, a Bowl or Dish thrown at his Back, but while at Prayers quiet; they were without doors, there being very many present, a wooden *Tut** came flying out of ye air, by many, and came and struck the man; as likewise a horse-shoe; which was by some laid away, and it was observed of its own accord to rise again and fly to the man, and struck him in ye midst of a hundred people.

Upon strict examination ye man confesseth that he had been a thief, and did it [the theft?] under ye Colour of Religion, Sabbath day. Ye girl told her Dame ye former story of ye woman's discourse; she is sent for and examined before Capt. Collins and Mr. Busbridge, and she is watched and searched twenty-four hours; the girl saith she is like ye woman, but I think will not swear it is the same. This woman was formerly suspected to be a Witch, had to Maidstone about it, but got away, and hath lived about Burwash some time since; her name I know not. Tuesday Four Ministers kept a Fast, Mr. Bennett, Weller, Bradshaw, and Golden. Since I hear not of any trouble. 'Tis said that they are in a Barn or Alehouse. While they lay without doors, ye woman sending some meal to a Neighbour's to make some bread, they could not make it up into Loaves, but it was like Butter, and so they put it into ye Oven, but it would not bake, but came out as it went in.

This relation came from Mr. Collins, who was an Eye-Witness to much of it.

The late Mr. Lower, in sending this curious narrative to the Sussex Archæological Society, adds that the Captain Collins and Colonel Busbridge referred to in it were "both men of good family and county magistrates." They, as well as the four Ministers, Messrs. Bennett, Weller, Golden, and Bradshaw, were evidently firm believers in the existence of witchcraft, and any unfortunate old lady who had been accused before them of that crime would have stood a very poor chance of escape. In this instance, as in so many others, it seems most likely that the inventor and actor in the above incidents was a girl. It was to the servant-girl of Joseph Cruttenden, the supposed victim of witchcraft, that

* *Tut*, I suppose to be a word used in Sussex for scoop to lade water.—[M. A. Lower.]

"an old woman" comes and discloses the "sad calamities" that were coming upon her "Master and Dame," and, of course, in due time, they *do* come, and the house is burnt down, and all kinds of pranks are played at the expense of her master and mistress.   They remove to another house, and the same "disturbances" take place. Of course the servant-girl was present on these occasions, and she was the only person interested in making her story of the old woman's prophecy come true. " Ye girl told her Dame ye former story of ye woman's discourse," she (the woman) is sent for and examined before Captain Collins and Mr. Busbridge, and she is "watched and searched twenty-four hours ; the girl saith she is like ye woman, but, I think, will not swear it is the same." This passage, by the unknown narrator, refers to some old woman, who, on the girl's testimony, was taken up on suspicion, "watched and searched twenty-four hours," and had, it is evident, a very narrow escape from conviction as a witch, having been "formerly suspected to be a witch, had to Maidstone about it, but got away, and hath lived about Burwash some time since."

Poor old lady ! She was nearly falling a victim to a cunning girl's tricks and love of mischief. Not only in the witchcraft of olden days, but in the spirit-rapping and other delusions of modern times, it is remarkable how readily children and young people have lent themselves to the imposition and taken a delight in making fools of their elders.   If the great majority of so-called supernatural visitations, from those which troubled the household of John Wesley's father down to our own times, could be traced to their real source, they would, we believe, be found to lie, as they did in this case at Brightling, in the morbid craving for excitement and love of deception so often found in children and servant-girls.

The Antiquity of Brighton as a Health-Resort.

BRIGHTON, as a place of resort for health or pleasure, is older than most of our "Guides" and "Handbooks" give it credit for. Dr. Russell, of Lewes, has long enjoyed the fame of "discovering it," because he wrote a book on the salubrious effects of sea-bathing, as though *that* were new to the world! But the fact is, Brighton is referred to as a place of resort—for health or pleasure, or both—long before Dr. Russell's time.

One of the earliest references to it as a place of resort is contained in a letter written from Brighton in July, 1736, by the Rev. William Clark, rector of Buxted, to a friend of his (Mr. Bowyer) in London :—

We are now, he says, sunning ourselves upon the beach at Brighthelmstone, and observing what a tempting figure this island must have made in the eyes of those gentlemen who were pleased to take the trouble of civilising and subduing us. The place is really pleasant; I have seen nothing in its way that really out-does it; such a tract of sea, such regions of corn, and such an extent of fine carpet, that gives your eye the command of it all. But then the mischief is, that we have little to do; we have little conversation beside the *clamor maritimus,* which here is a sort of treble to the plashing of the waves against the cliffs. My morning's business is bathing in the sea, and then buying fish; and my evening occupation is riding out for air, viewing the old Saxon camps, and counting the ships in the road and the boats that are trawling. Sometimes we give the imagination leave to expatiate a little; and to fancy that you are coming down; and that we intend next week to dine one day at Dieppe in Normandy. The price is already fixed, and the wine and lodging there tolerably good. But though we build castles in the air, I assure you we live here underground almost. I fancy the architects actually take the altitude of the inhabitants, and having done so, they lose not an inch between the head and the ceiling; and then, dropping a step or two below the surface, the second story is finished, something under 12 feet. I suppose this was a necessary precaution against storms— that a man should not be blown out of his bed into New England, Barbary, or God knows where. But as the lodgings are low they are cheap. We have two parlours, two bed-chambers, pantry, &c., for 5s. per week; and if you really will come down you need not fear having a bed of proper dimensions, and the coast is safe, and the cannons all covered with rust and grass, the ships moored, no enemy apprehended, &c.

And in a letter written from Brighton to another friend in London, a few years previous to this, he says :—

Do come and join us here, if you can bear the dullness of this place. We shall be right glad to see you. Here we do just what we like ; we are bound by no conventionalities. We dine at one o'clock, and take our tea at five ; and when we have nothing better to do, we roll about on the beach, interrupted by no one, &c.

This anticipates Dr. Russell, who came to reside in Brighton (from Lewes) in 1750, by 14 years or more.

Another early reference to it we find in a letter written by Sir Edward Wilson, F.S.A., dated the 18th of December, 1759. The writer resided at that time at Bourn Place, Eastbourne. It was in reply to some genealogical question addressed to him by another member of the Wilson family, living in York-shire. Speaking of Bourn Place, which he calls a very fine house, and "the principal seat" of the Earl of Wilmington, he proceeds as follows:—"After his (the Earl's) death it came to his nephew, Lord Northampton, who made it his residence in this country (*sic*), and he dieing, his brother, the late Consul Compton, had it, whose son, now Earl of Northampton, possesses it, who lately married the Duke of Beaufort's sister, with whom he got acquainted, whilst at Bourn (Eastbourne), at Brighthelmstone, in this county, *of late so much resorted to in this county for the sea-water*, as Scarborough is in your's."

This passage, in a letter written in 1759, and referring to a period anterior to that as one in which Brighthelmstone was much resorted to for its sea-water, cuts away some of the feathers usually placed in Dr. Russell's cap.

A still earlier reference to Brighton, but not of so flattering a character—indeed, the reverse of flattering, and with no mention of sea-bathing—is that of Dr. John Burton, a very learned man—a scholar of Corpus Christi College, Cambridge, and tutor and Greek lecturer there for 15 years. He paid a

visit to Sussex in 1751, to visit his mother, who had married
the Rector of Shermanbury, and he kept a journal (of 52
pages) in Greek! with a Latin addendum of 14 pages! There
is something very comical in this "most learned Theban"
coming into a county which, for its backwardness in learning,
had been dubbed the Bœotia of England, and setting down
his experiences of it in Greek and Latin! Was it as a precaution against the prying eyes of the natives, who, if they
could have suspected the Doctor of being "a chiel among
them taking notes," and such notes as the one we are about
to quote, might have had thoughts of tarring and feathering.
Here it is :—

> Proceeding (from Lewes) by the valleys and rideable country [there
> seems to have been no road] towards the west, about 70 furlongs, we arrived,
> just as the day was fading, at Brighthelmstone, a village on the sea-coast,
> lying in a valley gradually sloping and yet not deep. It is not, indeed,
> contemptible as to size, for it is thronged with people [was it the season?],
> though the inhabitants are mostly very needy and wretched in their mode
> of living, occupied in the employment of fishing, robust in their bodies,
> laborious, skilful in all nautical crafts, *and, as it is said, terrible cheats of
> the Custom House Officers.* [An allusion, doubtless, to the smuggling
> proclivities of our predecessors!] The village near the shore seemed to
> me very miserable—many houses here and there deserted, and traces of
> overthrown walls. For that most turbulent of all winds with us, the
> south-west,—
>
>> " The stormy blast across the boundless sea
>> Lifts high the waves, while trembles all the earth
>> Beneath hoarse Neptune's heavy-footed tread;"
>
> Or, to speak in plain prose, the waves at times dashing violently upon the
> shore, had shakened and loosened some of the rotten foundations; the
> ground above had given away; and all the dwellings on it had been at
> once dragged down and thrown forward into the sea.

This is, we think, by far the most minute and graphic
description left to us of the condition of Brighton in 1750, a
century and a quarter ago, after the destructive storms with
which it was visited in the early part of the 18th century.
But even at that early period the most effective mode of
battling with the sea, namely, by groynes, had been discovered
and put in practice; for Mr. W. H. Blaauw, the translator of
the learned Doctor's journals, tells us that "the wooden groins,
built to retain the drift of the sea (the shingle?) as a protection
against such inroads, are then described with much praise, and
Dr. Burton enjoys a delightful walk on the sands, in the purple

glow of a calm sunset, until he is warned by a messenger from the inn that supper is ready."

Only think of the Old or New Ship (perhaps both in existence at that time), or the Bedford or the Albion or the Grand sending to tell *their* visitors that supper is ready!

But we have not done yet with our learned journalist, or, rather, he has not yet done with our forefathers, nor they with him! For, he proceeds, "Departing therefore to the inn, like the heroes of Homer after a battle (!), so did we perform our part most manfully and then turned to bed, intending to sleep; but this sweet lulling of the senses was begrudged us by some sailors arriving all night long, and in the middle of their drink singing out with their barbarous voices, clapping and making all manner of noises. The women also disturbed us, quarrelling and fighting about their fish."

> "Nor lacked there in the house
> Mad-footed Thetis with her briny friends."

Now we see the wisdom of Dr. Burton in jotting down his opinions of Brighton and the Brightonians in Greek!

An Institution of the Past.

THERE are numerous institutions of the Past the memory of which is fast fading from us, and in some cases the very name is almost lost. The cock-pit, the bull-ring, the whipping-post, the stocks—where are they? As to the last-named, however, Echo is not without an answer. The stocks still linger amongst us. We believe they are to be seen in some Sussex parishes; we *know* that a year or two ago they still graced the entrance to the Parish Church at Shalford, two or three miles from Guildford, for we saw them there in a sound state of preservation. The whipping-post, as an out-of-doors institution, is, we believe, quite extinct, and so is the cucking-stool, the seat of penitence for scolds and slanderers. Who, too, of living men, has ever seen a human being "in irons?" The gallows itself is, happily, now hidden from our sight, with all its horrors; human suffering, in any shape, is no longer held to be a means of softening the human heart, or even of deterring it from the evil of its ways. "The stake," to which men and women true to their faith, and poor old ladies accused of witchcraft, were bound and burnt to death, has long been put away from us as accursed of men, though it is not so long since it went out of use. But, of all the devilish devices used by men to torture one another in countries calling themselves civilised, surely that was the worst which lingered amongst us until nearly the middle of the last century, and the last-recorded infliction of which was in our own county of Sussex.

We refer to the punishment—torture, rather—of "pressing to death." It was resorted to when a man would not plead to a charge, in which case the old judicial system held that the trial could not be proceeded with! It was one of those imaginary difficulties which learned men, like poor idiots, raise up in order, it would seem, to show the littleness of human wisdom. In the present day we jump over the straw, and, if a prisoner will not plead, proceed all the same to try him. A little more than one hundred years ago the law subjected him to *peine forte et dure*, that is, they placed him, naked, on his back, on the bare floor of a low, dark chamber, and there it was ordered that as great a weight of iron should be placed upon his body as he could bear—*and more.* And this process of torture was a long one. At different periods of it he was questioned, and, if he refused to plead, the weight was increased. It might be prolonged for days, and so it was charitably directed that on the first day he was to have three morsels of the worst bread given to him, and on the second day three draughts of standing water; this alternation of diet so to go on, from day to day, till he answered, or, as the judgment ran in later times, "till he died."

It will scarcely be credited that this horrible punishment was inflicted on a man in this county in the year of our Lord 1736. But such was the fact. It is quoted in a pamphlet by Basil Montague upon the debate in the House of Commons (April 5, 1813) upon Sir Samuel Romilly's Bill on the punishment of treason; and the victim of it was a man indicted at Lewes for a murder and robbery, and who pretended to be dumb. When brought to the bar, it is said, he would not speak or plead, though often urged to it, and though the sentence inflicted on those "who stand mute" was explained to him. Four or five persons in Court swore that they had heard him speak; and a boy, who was his accomplice, and had been apprehended, was there to be a witness against him; yet he continued mute. On which he was carried back to Horsham Gaol, to be pressed to death if he would not plead. And this piece of barbarity was thus carried out :—

They laid on him first 100 weight; then added 100 more, and then made it 350 lbs.; yet he would not speak. Then, adding 50 lbs. more, he was just about dead, having all the agonies of death about him, when the executioner, who weighs about sixteen or seventeen stone, laid himself upon the board which was over him, and, adding to the weight, killed him.

This is believed to have been the last instance of "pressing to death" in England. It was time enough! As a consequence of the man's refusal or inability to answer, his name remains unknown. The charge against him (and of this there is little doubt he was guilty), was for murdering and robbing one Elizabeth Symonds, at Bognor.

The torture was inflicted at Horsham, where the County Gaol then was; and there is a tradition of the place which indicates the horror with which the deed was regarded. The body of the man he had killed was placed by the executioner in a wheelbarrow for interment in the churchyard. But, in passing the spot where now stands the King's Head Hotel, he threw it out of the barrow, and then, taking it up again, proceeded to the churchyard, where it was buried. The story now runs that, some time afterwards, that very executioner, passing the spot where he had thrown the body out, dropped down dead.

This was the peculiar way, in times gone by, of showing the popular sense of diabolical acts. They could not prevent them, but they called down God's vengeance upon them.

o

GLEANINGS in EAST and WEST SUSSEX.

Lindfield: Its Colony, Schools, Church, &c.

S Midhurst may be taken as a typical country-town of West Sussex, so Lindfield may stand for a typical country-town of East Sussex. Both have many things in common: rivers, commons, and woods. But the woods, common, and river of Lindfield are widely different from those of Midhurst. Both, too, have the Downs in their close vicinity; but the Downs of West Sussex and the Downs of East Sussex have each a beauty of their own. The Downs of West Sussex are dotted with parks and enriched by the foliage of the beech, the elm, the plane, the chestnut, and the tulip tree. The Downs of East Sussex (Brighton being the point of division between the two) are virtually treeless; and as much of the beauty of the Western Downs undoubtedly lies in their woods, so the peculiar charm of the Eastern Downs lies in the absence of trees—in the unbroken lines in which they sweep along, rising and sinking in every variety of rounded and undulating form, and answering in their play of light and shadow to every change of the atmosphere, almost as much as the sea itself does—now illumined by floods of light, or frowning beneath ominous thunder clouds, or wrapped in a vapoury mist; more frequently, perhaps, presenting a combination of these effects of light and shadow—the former on the high crests of the hills, the latter in the deep hollows—contending with each other for supremacy. Happy the eye and the mind which can appreciate the charms of both these aspects of

A COTTAGE OF "THE COLONY."

THE MANOR HOUSE OF THE CHALLONERS.

Nature—those which the wooded Downs of West Sussex present and those which characterise the unwooded Downs of East Sussex.

Lindfield is bounded on nearly all sides by the unwooded Downs, which form a feature in the *points de vue* from its more elevated sites, and it has woods on every side; but not the stately woods of West Sussex. At Lindfield we are in the heart of the old Sussex Weald, or Wild, the Sylva Anderida of the Romans, and we touch, to the north, on the relics of that great primeval wood which still exists in the Forests of Tilgate, St. Leonards, and Ashdown, finding their point of junction at Balcombe. The very name of Lindfield* indicates that it was originally a clearing made in this great wood, before it was thinned by the axe to smelt the ore of the iron-masters whose mills and forges came close up to Lindfield. One, at least, of the families that drew their riches from this source (the Burrells) still have a residence (Ockenden) in the neighbouring parish of Cuckfield. By this cause the original woods round Lindfield were swept away, and those that have partly replaced them are on a smaller scale and consist of firs and larches, with a scattering of oaks and beeches. The hedge-row timber is chiefly oak, of a small kind, but famed for its hardness, and the enclosures being small, it makes a feature in the view; but there are few, or none, of those giants of the forest which meet the eye at Cowdray and Easebourne,† or those imposing masses of foliage which darken the hill-sides or fill up the glades and valleys round Midhurst, Goodwood, and Arundel. These latter, and, indeed, West Sussex generally, are aristocratic in their character. Lindfield, and, as a rule, East Sussex, are democratic. There has not been for some centuries past a " great family " in or near Lindfield to impress a character of exclusiveness on it, to hedge it round and impress on its visitor a sense (often an oppressive one) of

---

* It is, says Mr. Lower, pure Anglo-Saxon, and a simple combination of *lind*, the lime tree, and *feld*, a field—" the field where lime trees grow."

† The principal exception, the well-known " High Beech " on the Ardingly Road, was blown down in the great gale of 1882.

greatness, such as Midhurst and Petworth, Goodwood and Arundel rejoice in or suffer from! Lindfield has not grown up "under the cold shade of aristocracy," but with a kind of natural freedom, which shows itself in the long and mixed line of houses and cottages, of all sizes and characters, and every style of building, which form its High Street, and most of which are faced by a garden. Midhurst, as we point out in the paper on that place, is without this feature, and, as at Arundel, the close-pressing park swallows up one side, at least, of its main street. But Lindfield is free, open, and unconfined on all sides, and it has grouped itself in a natural manner on the little hill that, winding downwards from the church for some quarter of a mile, ends southward in the village pond and the beautiful Common.

The absence, for a long period, from the neighbourhood of Lindfield of any great family—the decay and disappearance of the original owners of Pax Hill, Board House, and Wakehurst Place, the De la Bordes and the Culpeppers; the dismantlement and virtual destruction of Kenward's, the chief residence of the Challoners; and the desertion of East Mascalls, formerly the family-house of the Newtons and the Noyes — these facts have doubtless had their effect on the present state, and even appearance, of Lindfield; leaving the land round it more free and open, and affording room for those smaller landed proprietors whose houses, such as Sunt, Buckshalls, and Bedales,* are scattered around, to which have been added of late years more modern erections on the many beautiful sites in or round the village.†

But the decay of the old families left the lower classes without that protection which they found in earlier days under the great nobles, such as West Sussex possessed in the Howards,

---

* The respective residences of Mrs. George Catt; Lieut.-Col. Dudley Sampson; and the Rev Frederick Willett.

† Of these numerous modern mansions that stand in or about Lindfield we may name "Finches," the residence of James Procter, Esq.; "Summer Hill," of Chas. Catt, Esq.; "Beckworth," of Wm. Blaber, Esq.; "Great Walstead," of S. C. Gibbons, Esq.; "Milton House," of Robert Caudle, Esq.; "The Welkin," owned by C. B. Warre, Esq.; "Gravelye House," by Mrs. A Lawrie; "Walstead House," by Mrs. A. H. Davis, and "Norrington," by Chas. Fleet, Esq.

the Percies, the Brownes, and the Lennoxes. The Pelhams, who succeeded the Challoners as Lords of the Manor of Lindfield, lived at a distance, and their landed interest in the place was not great. The result was, that when "bad days" came for the farm labourer, as they did after the great struggle with France, he fell into a state of pauperism and ignorance which threatened to demoralise the class. Education at Lindfield for the people there was none. The living (a "Peculiar," under the Archbishops of Canterbury) was a very poor one, the great tithes being owned by a lay impropriator; the Church was dilapidated; there were no schools; and the labourers' thatched cottages were becoming more and more squalid, and were over-run by dirty, neglected children, who were chiefly valued by their parents because they gave them an increased claim on the poor-rates. The parish, to use an expression of the day, was "eaten up with pauperism"—the truer version of the case being that pauperism was eating it up—when a new aspect was given to this deplorable state of things by the fact of Lindfield being selected as a field of experiment in Sussex for what was called the Allotment System: a benevolent attempt to rescue the working-classes from pauperism by giving them a share in that land which had passed so completely out of their possession.

Three gentlemen joined in this patriotic and philanthropic enterprise: the then Earl of Chichester; Mr. John Smith, Member for Bucks; and William Allen, a Quaker of London. The latter was the active spirit of it. He had been associated with Clarkson and Wilberforce in the movement for the abolition of slavery; with Humphrey Davey and Babington in the diffusion of science; with Brougham in the extension of popular literature; with Elizabeth Fry in the improvement of our prison system, and with Mackintosh and Romilly in the reform of our criminal code; and he now, in the period of agricultural depression between 1820 and 1830, diverted his labours to the difficult task of improving the condition of the agricultural labourer.

It was thought that if the labourer were provided with a

tidy, well-arranged house. and if to this house were attached an acre or two of ground, he might, by his own efforts, keep himself from going to the parish, and also be enabled to pay such a rent for the tenement and the land as would return a fair interest upon the outlay.   To test this, a couple of farms—Gravelye farm and Scamp's (afterwards called Penn's) farm—were bought at Lindfield; the greater part of it poor land, lying between woods upon the slope above the Common south-eastward.   Here three sets of cottages— six to a set—were built: the first of a superior character, and let at 3s. a week; the second middling, and let at 2s. 6d.; the third inferior, and let at 2s.; but all much better in every respect than the ordinary labourer's cottage; and to each cottage was attached a bit of land ranging from an acre to two acres or more, according to the character of the cottage.   On their completion, Mr. Allen went to a parish meeting and told the parish officers that he had built some cottages and wanted tenants for them, and that the tenants he wanted were industrious men with large families, and he didn't care how large the family was, provided the man was industrious.   This, it need hardly be observed, was the very class who were the recipients of parish relief.   One man and his family had had above £80 in three years; he became a tenant of the "Colony," and from that day forward he ceased to be a pauper.   Others followed; for there was a comfortable home and land to be had for a mere trifle, and the strongest love of an Englishman is, for a home and land.   And so, in a short time, all the tenements of what was by some called "The Colony," and by others "America," were occupied, and a social revolution commenced in Lindfield.

We visited these cottages in 1852, and described them at the time in a series of papers in the *Brighton Herald* from which we will take a few passages, which are still a correct description of "The Colony:"—

I visited one of each class, beginning with the lowest—the 2s. a-week tenements.   They are long, low, thatched cottages, with a good-sized kitchen, and three bedrooms connected by a long passage—all on the ground-floor. These cottages are only one room deep, and no staircase. The inconvenience is, the length of the house—50 or 60 feet, and the distance between the extreme rooms. This is remedied in the second or 2s. 6d. a-week cottages, the rooms of which are two-deep, and so lie more compactly together. The out-houses to both consist of bakehouse (with good oven and copper), woodhouse, piggery, well, wash-house, &c., with plenty of spare room at the back; whilst in front run the long slips of ground, averaging an acre to each, cultivated either as garden or arable ground—with fruit trees, or wheat, beans, vegetables, &c.

In one of the 2s. tenements I spoke to a woman—healthy and strong—who said she had been a widow five years, and had brought up nine children—two were with her now. She had grown wheat upon part of her ground, and there was the produce in a neat little stack; and there were beans, &c., for the two fat pigs in the sty. She said she could manage to keep herself pretty well with her pigs, her fruit, her bees, &c., though this year the help she needed cost her more than usual. She seemed cheerful and contented. Her next-door neighbour—an intelligent-looking, tidily-clad man, of about 40—was standing at his door. He and his father had been tenants ever since the cottages had been erected. He got, he said, 12s. a-week as a labourer, and did not see why a man should have less than 2s. a-day. From enquiries I had made in other quarters, I found that 10s. was the average wages in the neighbourhood, and in winter 9s. or 1s. 6d. a-day. But the men who got these wages were not in a situation, like our friend of the Colony, to demand higher; they had not, like him, an acre of good land to fall back upon; they must either take the 9s. or 10s., go to "the house," or starve.

The next set of cottages, at 2s. 6d. a-week, are much superior to the 2s. tenements. They are slate-roofed, with stuccoed fronts, instead of mere mud and beach; and their rooms, though all on the ground-floor, are, as I have said, two-deep. These tenements, like the other sets, stand by themselves, and are built two and two—each couple in the form of a ⊤—the down-stroke representing the out-houses—woodhouse, bakehouse, piggery, wash-house, &c.—facing each way, so that one building provides out-houses for two tenements. These are strongly built and well arranged. So are the cottages themselves. I went into one at random. The mistress of the house—a good-looking woman—was busily engaged in drying her clothes (the day having been wet), and being surrounded by half-a-dozen little children, who had just come from school, she was, as might be supposed, in a little bit of a pother—yet all was clean and neat; the woman was cheerful; the children happy; and there was that unmistakeable air of comfort which bespeaks abundance. The wife opened the doors of the sleeping-rooms—three in number—and the bed-hanging and bed-clothes were as white as snow. The husband showed me his woodhouse and piggery and garden—the latter full of fine fruit trees, planted chiefly by himself. Half his garden was so occupied; the produce of the other half stood in the shape of a plump little stack of wheat. He had grown, he said, two quarters on half-an-acre. He intended to thrash it himself, and smiled when I asked if he sent any to market. He had, he said, seven children, and they did not let any crumbs fall under the table. He, too, had held his tenement from the time of William Allen, and spoke of him as one the like of whom he did not expect to meet in this world.

Passing on to the third set of cottages, 3s. a week, which stand on a higher elevation, on a line with Gravelye House (the former residence of

William Allen, but at this time, 1852, the residence of the Rev. Mr. Johnson, the Incumbent of Lindfield), a still higher degree of comfort met the eye. These cottages are such as any member of the middle ranks might be happy to occupy—indeed, two of them were now tenanted by respectable tradesmen; but the others were still occupied by the original occupants, and one of these, Edward Cook, was a labourer on Gravelye Farm when William Allen bought it, and went from the farm to his present home, in which he has brought up seven or eight children, now all out and settled but one, who lives with his parents. Edward Cook is still a healthy, stalwart man, with handsome features, and of frank, open address. When asked by my companion (a patriarch of the village) what he thought of William Allen?—"What do I think of William Allen?" he replied, "Why, William Allen was the best man that ever I knew. He was the poor man's friend. Many a time has William Allen come to me and said, ' Well, Edward, dost thee want a little money?' Mayhap I did, but I couldn't tell when I could pay it back again. 'Never mind that, Edward; there is £10, and after harvest I dare say thee will be able to pay it.' And he would never ask me for it again, though I always found a way to pay the money, in bits." So spoke Edward Cook. I should observe that this tenant rented seven acres of land in addition to the acre attached to his house. It was a rule with William Allen that a man should have as much land as he could cultivate properly, but then, to ensure proper cultivation, these extra acres were let at the usual rent, 30s. an acre; and of these Cook had, and still has, seven—consisting of a meadow and some corn-fields, to raise oats for his horses—he being a carter.

I was anxious to know what kind of land the "Colony" was when it was first planted; and my companion told me an anecdote illustrative of the point. After Farmer Simmonds—who must have been a shrewd old customer—had sold the land to William Allen (or to John Smith, Member for Bucks, and father of John Abel Smith, M.P. for Chichester—for not even the tenants of the land or the builder of the cottages ever exactly knew which was the owner—William Allen or John Smith—such bosom-friends were they)—but when Farmer Simmonds had sold Gravelye Farm, he said to William Allen, pointing to the land between Bent's Wood and Sergison's Wood, down which run the plots of the Colony, "The best thing you can do with that, Sir, be to turn out colts on it. 'Tis a hungry soil, and eats up everything you put into it, and makes no return. It owes me £200, does that piece of land." The object, however, of the purchaser was to turn out men—independent men—working for themselves, upon it, and not colts. Perhaps he recollected the saying of Arthur Young—"That a sure holding will turn a rock into a garden; an insecure, a garden into a desert;" for though the land was not given in fee to the occupants of it, nor is it even held on lease, yet the rent was never raised, nor was the tenant ever disturbed during good conduct. The estate passed away, at the death of William Allen, into the hands of the Rev. Mr. Scutt, and is now held by his son-in-law, the Rev. Mr. Johnson, Incumbent of Lindfield; but, to the honour of that gentleman be it said, the colonists remain undisturbed—many, indeed, work for him—and the rent of their cottages and ground is the same as that paid to the founder. However, whether William Allen thought of Arthur Young or not, he turned out his men, and the place only fit for colts was soon converted into a garden. Not that he left all to the tenants' unaided efforts. Allen was a practical chemist; he preceded Liebeg in the application of science to the cultivation of the land. He had a pit in which he tested various substances as manure, as whale's blubber, &c., and the land of the Colony had, doubtless, the benefit of his experiments, as the tenants had of his counsels and encouragement. Was there an empty pig-sty? "What! no pig?" said the kind-hearted old man, "thee must have a pig." And lo! there was a grunting in the stye. After another visit, the village shoemaker (I have his word for it) would suddenly make his appearance in the Colony, and begin measuring the ill-shod feet of half-a-dozen children. He had his orders, and no bill was ever sent in to the parents—no name breathed.

From his house at Gravelye, William Allen looked down on his Colony, and it flourished beneath his eye; for he appealed to the best feelings of Englishmen—the love of home and independence; and I believe it is a fact that no member of the Colony ever went to the parish for relief.

One condition the tenants of the "Colony" amply fulfilled: they all had tremendous families—six, seven, eight, nine, and even ten and twelve children. It is so still: children swarm in the "Colony" to such an extent that it has been nicknamed "the Warren." But the founder of the "Colony" was not the man to encourage the growth of population and let it run to seed. Jointly with the homes for the parents he raised schools for the children—a plain, humble-looking building, facing the Common, and in this the benevolent effort of the philanthropic triumvirate to reclaim the farm labourers of Lindfield was carried out with complete success for above 50 years—up, indeed, to the year 1882, when the School was closed as a voluntary institution, owing to the election of a School Board and the erection of Board Schools in the parish.

A description of these schools (which were opened in 1825 by the then Earl of Chichester), as we saw them in 1852, will, we think, still be read with interest :—

These Schools are in as full and efficient operation now (1852) as when they were first founded. In 1851 they were attended by 175 children, who came from all parts of the neighbourhood—from Hayward's Heath, Wivelsfield, Worth, Ardingly, and even as far as Ditchling—distances of three, four, five, and even six and seven miles. On a fine morning—aye, and even when the sky looks black and threatening—you may meet the little travellers trudging along the country lanes and roads, with their dinners in their little baskets slung before them, with clean and cheerful faces, tidy clothes, and those rosy cheeks and blue eyes which attest their Saxon origin. Question them and you will receive a ready answer, and a bow or a curtsey, by the fashion of which you may soon know a scholar of the Lindfield Schools. As nine o'clock approaches they gather together in front of the Schools—on the Common and on the wide roadsides, and at nine they enter the spacious school-rooms, from the walls of which are suspended well-selected lessons in which the great truths of Christianity are taught in the simplest and yet most sublime of language.

The Schools are divided into three compartments—the first and largest for the boys; the second, for the girls; the third, for infants of both sexes. The system of instruction is adapted from that of Joseph Lancaster, and the copy-books of the lads, their slates, and their ready answers to questions in arithmetic, geography, &c., speak for the progress they make. The boys generally have an intelligent look. Some of the elder ones have their little classes around them, and boys in round frocks, and with ruddy, rustic faces, such as one generally sees at the plough's tail, act the part of school-master to a little circle with a gravity and a readiness which prove them to be masters of their part. I asked the names of one or two of the boys, and soon found that it is not only the labouring classes who avail themselves of these schools. The sons of respectable tradesmen and of substantial farmers were seated at the same desk with the children of labourers. A day or two afterwards, falling into discourse with a farmer who has the reputation of being the "heaviest" tenant-farmer in the parish, I found that he had a son at the Lindfield Schools, and he said the boy got on very well—better, he thought, than he had done at the Hurst College, from which he had taken him. I do not know what they teach at the Hurst College, or what the scholars pay; but at these Lindfield Schools, the boys are taught to write and read and cypher well—in the latter department they go as far as algebra, mensuration, &c., and they understand what they are taught; and for this education the boys pay 3d. per week; the girls, 2d.; and the infants, 1d. This rate, however, is reduced if there are more than one child in a family. Thus, if two attend from the same family, they pay only 2d. each; if three, only 1d. each; and if there are four, they pay nothing. So, too, as a premium for regular attendance, if a scholar attend every day in the week, he may claim his money back again. The above scale is so low that there are few labourers who cannot now-a-days send their children to receive a good English education.

Passing through the girls' room, where all is order and industry, we come to the Infant School—perhaps the most interesting of the whole. Here there were some 40 or 50 little things ranged in rows upon seats rising one above another at one end of the room: from the mere baby of eighteen months up to four or five years old. When one reflects upon the task of managing one child of such tender age—to say nothing of two or three—by what species of discipline can 40 or 50 be brought into anything like order? If, one would think, a "reign of terror" were justifiable any where, it would be here. Yet, so far from this, there is an utter absence of all severity—all rigid discipline, all restraint or monotonous order—and yet there is no noise or disorder. The little things, boys and girls, little and big, sit together on tiers of seats, and are free to shift themselves about and indulge in that restlessness which is the characteristic of childhood, and to curb which is to torture them. They may vary their position—turn and twist about as much as they please. But the mode of instruction adopted is such as to satisfy this very restlessness, and to gratify that desire of motion and change which is peculiar to childhood. Either the little hands or the little feet are constantly in motion, or there is something for the eye to rest upon or the ear to listen to. Imitative action (acting, in a humble sense), rhymes, pictures, music—these are the agencies by which the mistress of the Infant School instructs and occupies her little pupils. As you enter, at a word they are all on their feet to welcome the lady or gentleman who is come to visit them. Then, the mistress, placing herself in front, repeats some rhyme, with suitable action, descriptive of the many familiar objects, or figures, or occupations about us, and a forest of little hands and arms are engaged—perhaps in describing circles, semi-circles, parallel lines, &c., &c., which one wonders at seeing thus made a source of amusement, as they evidently were, to children scarcely able to hold up their little arms. Some little things, unable to keep up with their elder and more advanced school-fellows, showed their sense of the fun by clapping their little hands together; and one, more ambitious than the rest, in a desperate attempt to illustrate

"This is what I do when I tie my shoe,"

turned a summersault right over, displaying as sturdy a pair of legs as ever carried so little a body. How strongly these games interested the children was shown by a little incident which fell under my notice, and which I cannot help telling, though I fear it is a terrible breach of confidence. When the game commenced, the mistress observed that one of the youngest infants—"baby Saxby" she called her—was amusing herself by sucking a piece of pipe which she had brought in with her from the play-ground. "Put that down, baby Saxby," said the mistress, and baby Saxby's hand instantly disappeared behind her, and her large blue eyes were fixed hard upon the mistress, who very quietly took the pipe away from baby Saxby and went on with the game. But I had noticed what the mistress had not —that baby Saxby had a piece of pipe in each hand, and no sooner was the mistress's eye off than up went the pipe again to the little mouth, and baby Saxby looked as if she had half-a-mind to be a naughty baby. But as the game went on, and as the children proceeded to describe "This is the way the miller goes," &c., baby Saxby got so thoroughly interested in the part she was playing, and into such good humour with herself and all her baby-world, that, by-and-by, she stepped out of her place, and, going up to the mistress with the other piece of pipe in her little hand, laid it on the table. The good genius of the game had triumphed over the evil genius of the tobacco-pipe! Then there was a march round the room, after the mistress, still repeating instructive rhymes; and then, the infants resuming their seats, one bright-looking little fellow, some three years of age, was called down from the ranks and placed in front of his fellows, who were invited to test his powers of spelling, which they did by putting words to him which would have staggered many an elder scholar, and I could scarcely believe my ears as I heard one little urchin of four or five require another still younger to spell elephant, rhinoceros, and even hippopotamus, each of which was rattled off, with a vast number of other words of smaller calibre, as quickly as they were put. Then a slate was produced, on which the visitors were invited to write what figures they pleased, in tens or hundreds, and no sooner were the figures chalked up than a dozen little figures were signalling their eagerness to answer. Questions in addition and division were equally well resolved, by boys and girls—and all with the most evident delight and without the slightest appearance of envy. The girls were less forward than the boys in offering to answer questions, but when called on by the mistress they were equally quick in replying. Some of the children were perfect specimens of Saxon beauty—large blue eyes, flaxen hair, and cheeks as red and white as the softest peach. One or two, however, were little dark gipsy beauties, with sloe-black eyes and raven hair. All the time these exercises were going on, one little thing was snuggled up in one corner of the room on a bed which is always kept for children too young to keep awake during the hours of school.

If William Allen (who died in 1843) could have witnessed this scene—and it was continued until our own days under the admirable mastership of Mr. J. Wells—and could have marked the change for the better which was wrought by his "Colony" and schools in the moral and physical condition of the labouring classes of Lindfield and the adjacent parishes, he would have held himself well repaid for all his labours and outlay. Seldom has a scheme of philanthropy been better and more successfully carried out than that of the Earl of Chichester, John Smith, and William Allen, at Lindfield. If Lindfield is now one of the neatest, cleanest, and most prosperous, as well as prettiest villages or towns (it now boasts itself a town by virtue of the powers under the Local Government Board by which it is paved, lighted, drained, and "governed") in England, it owes it in no small degree to the work of William Allen and his coadjutors. Of course, since the Elementary Education Act, and even earlier than that, by the waking-up of the Church and nation to their duties of instructing the people, other rural parishes vie with Lindfield in the excellence of their elementary schools. But, in a day of darkness, indifference, and general depression, Lindfield and William Allen led the way in the work of raising the status of the labourer and educating his children; and it still "marches on" in it.

The "Colony" and the schools have taken us somewhat away from Lindfield itself, to which we will now return. Approaching it from the Hayward's Heath Station, from which it is distant about a mile, Lindfield street can scarcely be said to commence until we reach the village pond—a large sheet of water, round which the road makes a bend, and then the street runs up in a somewhat winding fashion to the Church, with that intermixture of houses, high and lowly, old and modern, square and pointed, wood and brick and stone, gables and non-gables, shops and private dwellings, which marks a true English village. And we doubt if a more perfect or favourable specimen of an English village can be found in all England than Lindfield. Where there are gardens in front of the houses, they are neatly kept and full of flowers and shrubs. But on the western side of the street a grassy slope runs from the footpath down to the road, with here and there rows of limes and poplars in front of the houses; and down this grassy slope you may see children rolling and tumbling with that delightful sense of security which can never be enjoyed by a juvenile population within a dozen miles of those mystic letters "H. C. S." The road is a good road, as it ought to be, if only for its past fame—for did not the far-famed " Times," and "Age," and " Comet," roll along this road on their way to London ?— and did they not pull up amidst admiring groups of villagers and ostlers at the " Red Lion " (Callow, who kept it at one time and still lives at Lindfield, was one of Crossweller's best whips), the " Bent Arms," and the " Tiger " Inn ?—inns that still show their signs to passers-by, but the glories of which passed away with the days of coaching and posting. One other remnant there is of the days of turnpike-road greatness, and that is, a turnpike gate, nearly in the middle of the village, which takes a toll of 3d. or 6d. from every hapless traveller that drives up Lindfield street.

On arriving at the top of the street, the Church meets the eye, with its spire of oak shingles, which, whitened by the sun, forms a conspicuous object for many a mile. The high-road passes by it on to London ; but in a diversion which it makes round the Church is to be found the most interesting feature of Lindfield in an archæological point of view. This is the ancient Manor or Dower House of the Challoners—built in the reign of Elizabeth and occupied by that family until their growing fortunes led them to build a more stately and solid house on the opposite side of the road. This, called " Kenward's," no longer exists, whilst the more lowly Manor House, after many ups and downs, still stands in almost its original freshness. It is, in its external aspect, almost a *fac simile* of Shakspeare's house at Stratford-upon-Avon, and in its interior it has one relic of its palmy days in a room completely panelled with oak. The exterior has been well restored within the last twenty years by the then owners, the Noyes, and it is admirably kept up by its present owner, Mr. Kempe. Previous to that it was in danger of utter ruin. For a time it was the workhouse of the parish; on its abandonment for that use, labourers occupied it until it became too dilapidated and dangerous for the poorest of these, and then it remained empty until, as we have said, the late Mr. Noyes, with a spirit that did him honour, restored it, as well as the adjoining cottage of the same date.

Being now close to the Church, we will enter it, though, in an archæological point of view, it will be only to be disappointed. The fabric itself is in good repair, and is very complete in its proportions, with its nave, aisles, and transepts. But, at a restoration which took place in 1848, it was swept clean of the tombs and memorials of the Challoners, the Newtons, and the Bordes, which then existed, in stone, metal, and in glass. An artistic curiosity which was discovered at the time, in the shape of some mural fresco paintings (one representing St. Michael weighing a sinner's soul, the dragon at his feet, and with St. Margaret standing by as a witness of his equity) was also effaced, but not before a drawing of it had been made by the late Mrs. Bigge and transferred to the pages of the Sussex Archæological Collections.

About half-a-mile to the west of the Church stood Kenward's, the great house of the Challoners; but the only portion of it that now remains is the stables, turned into a farm-house. The fall of the family, whose possessions are said to have extended in the 17th century from Lindfield nearly to the sea, was a sudden one. The last owner of Kenward's, Robert Challoner, was a Major in the Parliamentary Army and a warm supporter of the Protector. In the old Parish Register, which records the christenings, burials, and weddings of the good people of Lindfield from the year 1558 to 1690, there is one whole page and more, from 1655 to 1659, occupied by the record of the labours of Major Challoner in marrying and giving in marriage. The entries are brief enough,

as doubtless was the Major's Service. The first on the list is
" Edward Bannister, of Hartfield, to Margaret Ogborn, of the
same, married, at Kenward's, by Major Challoner, Oct. 1655,"
and then follows a long list of couples from Clayton, Ditcheling,
Lyndfield (so spelt), Chiltington, Bolney, East Grinstead,
Cuckfield, and even from Danefold, in Surrey, and Marden,
in Kent—showing how, far and wide, the people must have
come to Kenward's to be married "by ye Major," as the
registrar expresses it for brevity. These marriages all seem
to have been solemnised at Kenward's, the Major's house,
and not in the Parish Church of Lindfield, and of course
the Service was looked upon as a civil contract, and not a
religious rite. At the Restoration, Major Challoner had
to seek safety in flight, and he seems to have failed to
make his peace with the new powers. The Kenward's
estate and the Manor of Lindfield passed eventually to the
Pelhams, with whom the Challoners had intermarried, and
the Challoners themselves, once so numerous and flourishing
in Sussex, passed, like the Culpeppers, the Lewknors, the
Shirleys, the Coverts, the Bordes, &c., out of the roll of
Sussex gentry. The Bordes, however, lingered to a later
date, thanks to their loyal proclivities. The last male representative of the family, William Borde, or Board, as the name
came to be spelt, was still remembered by old residents of
Lindfield in 1850. He resided at Pax Hill, the most picturesque
building in Lindfield, with its seven gables; the two large
flanking ones covered (in 1856) with ivy, from which it was
difficult to distinguish the dark grey sandstone of which the
house is built. At this time, and for some years afterwards,
there was an air of decay and neglect about Pax Hill, as
though it were about to suffer the fate of East Mascalls. On
the death of William Borde the estate was divided between
his three daughters, one of whom brought Pax Hill to her
husband, Capt. Gibbs Crawfurd, as her dowry. The son of
this Capt. Crawfurd only left daughters, the eldest of whom
became the wife of Arthur Smith, Esq., the brother of the
well-known Albert Smith, by whom at this time the Swiss Châlet

adjacent to Pax Hill (now owned by the Hon. Mrs. Needham) was built and occupied; and here he was visited by Charles Dickens, and other literary celebrities. But Mr. Arthur Smith dying without issue, his widow parted with Pax Hill, which passed first into the hands of the Noyes, the owners of East Mascalls (deserted at this period); then into those of Mr. Northall Laurie, by whom it was restored and enlarged—its character, indeed, altogether changed; and eventually it was bought by William Sturdy, Esq., by whom it is still owned and kept up in a style worthy of its pristine glories.

So Pax Hill has been more fortunate than Kenward's, though the Bordes, like the Challoners, have disappeared from the roll of Sussex gentry.

Pax Hill was not the earliest dwelling-place of the Bordes in Lindfield. They had another and older house, which still exists, and which was called, after them, Borde or Board House. It was not till 1622 that Pax Hill House was built, and its name betrays its ecclesiastical origin, and only becomes intelligible when we learn that a religious house of some kind once stood on this spot—not, indeed, on the site of the present house, but, as tradition points out, beneath it, nearer to the banks of the river Ouse, in the meadows between the present house and the London road. But here, as at Kenward's, it is in vain that we look for any vestiges of the past. The chapelry has been swept away even more completely than the house. A tradition of a Priory or Nunnery having stood here still remains; but Mr. M. A. Lower rejects it as unfounded, though not without some grounds for belief.

Lindfield (he says) being an outlying and important Manor of the Canons of Malling, they would naturally establish here a manor house or grange, to which, in all probability, a chapel would be attached, where service would be performed for the benefit of tenants and dependants. Such a little household, presided over by a canon, and including a few serving brethren, would not unnaturally come to be regarded as a Priory. Indeed, in the statutes of the College of Malling, it is expressly stipulated that the Dean himself may reside at Lyndefelde, "for the collection of the autumnal fruits and for the better edification of the people," three months in every year, without infringing the oath of residence at the College which he took at his appointment. This shows the importance of the Manor at that period, as does also the fact that, in the Seventeenth year of Edward III., the Dean and Canons obtained for it a Charter for a market and two annual fairs.

Lindfield and its vicinity are rich in roads and woods. Go which way you will—north, east, west, south—you will find yourself going over a good sand-bottom road, bordered on each side by an over-hanging wood or else beautiful hedges, almost as high as those of Jersey. The soil doubtless is peculiarly favourable for roads. It is generally of sand, and the water drains off it so quickly that you may walk immediately after the heaviest rains. But if you happen to be caught in a shower, you can never be at a loss, in this well-wooded country, for shelter. Even the hedge-rows are full of fine timber, chiefly oak. It is, indeed, an oak country. To many people perhaps the English oak, as typical of the country in which it is supposed to grow so abundantly, is a myth. The elm, the beech, the chestnut, and other trees are much more common all round London and in most of our noblemen's parks. To see a thorough oak wood and oak country, we would advise a visit to Lindfield and the neighbourhood. There you may see the noble tree by itself, growing straight and sturdy out of a hedge-row, with its thick, short stem, its rough coat, and its wide-sweeping branches, or you may see it with hundreds of others, growing to a greater height, as oaks will when planted together, but yet of a bold, rugged freedom and wildness of culture as opposed as can possibly be to the straight, regular, stiff-looking pine or the aristocratic elm and chestnut. We know of no stronger contrast in the aspect of Nature than is presented by the two woods—Oate Hall or Bent's wood, and Petlands or pine wood—which lie between the " Colony " and the Common, and by which Lindfield may, in summer, be more pleasantly approached from the Railway Station and over the Heath than by the high road. Enter the oak wood, and there is an irregular mass of foliage before you, mixed up with the sky and distance in charming variety and confusion—the very artless beauty of Nature, careless how she stands, confident in her attractions.

P

It is a rustic beauty, with sturdy limbs, ruddy hue, scattered tresses—beautiful in the absence of art.   Pass on a few yards, and you come to the pine wood.   Enter that, and what a different scene strikes you !   Equally beautiful, perhaps, but a beauty made up of such different elements.   The tall shafts of the trees rise up to a height of a hundred feet or more, without leaf or limb, and stand in regular order, like rows of columns in a vast temple ; and turn which way you please, long vistas run before you, and the air is as still, and the ground as smooth, as though you were shut in by a roof ; only by looking up you perceive that overhead there is a covering of leaves, in which the birds chirrup, and on which the sun shines, but neither the birds nor the sun ever visit the still, quiet, lifeless atmosphere of this pine wood.

We have wandered from our way.   Had we gone on without pause, we should have reached ere this the Holy Well, which, though in Horsted Keynes parish, is not above a mile and a half from Pax Hill, and is well worth a walk, through high hedge-rows, with ever and anon a peep of the beautiful country that lies stretched before you, taking in the forests of Ashdown and St. Leonards, the villages of Horsted Keynes, Ardingly, and Easthoathly and their churches, and presenting a perfect specimen of that undulating country, well covered with wood, which characterises the Weald of Sussex.   The Holy Well—a place of no small reputation in the neighbourhood, and with its traditions of wonderful cures —is a mineral spring, that rises in an open basin some six or eight yards in diameter, in a field by the road side.   The line of the spring is marked by the bushes which grow on its banks, till it flows, about thirty yards on, into one of the tributaries of the Ouse.   The basin is circular, and not quite in the centre you perceive, at a depth of about four or five feet, an orifice about half-a-foot wide and perhaps a foot long, and from out of this fissure in the earth bubbles up the spring, at the rate, it is said, of two butts a minute, and certainly in such quantities that it supplies a stream of water nearly sufficient to turn a mill below.   The water is of beautiful clearness; but the mineral matter with which it is charged colours everything that it flows over, and the fallen leaves at its bottom are as yellow as gold, being encrusted with the mineral substance deposited by the stream. The well, properly so called, is reported to be unfathomable; but on thrusting in a pole lying near, as if intended for that purpose, at about seven or eight feet there was an obstruction—the pole would go no further; but whether because it had reached the bottom or stuck against the side of the well, we will not undertake to say. In all probability the spring has its fountain-head in the forest to the north, and takes up the oxide of iron which enters so largely into the soil in this part of the country.

There are few districts in which the eye can take in at one glance so many village spires. Looking from Skames Hill— the high point at the eastern extremity of the parish—16 churches can be counted in as many villages, and we do not know a more interesting tract of country than that overlooked from this point, taking in as it does the beautiful range of South Downs running from Lewes to Brighton, on a spur of which stands Lewes; and, turning to the north and the low wooded country which stretches as far as the eye can reach in that direction, we may easily trace the *route* by which the army of Simon de Montfort marched from London upon Lewes, encamping for the night upon Fletching Common, and attacking the town and Castle, defended by the army of Henry III., on the western side, now called the Wallands.

There is only one other point of view near Lindfield which exceeds that from Skames Hill in picturesque beauty, and that is from the highest point of Hayward's Heath. Here, standing in the centre of a beautiful country, the view is on every side —from the South Downs on the south, with a peep of the sea at Newhaven and a glimpse of Chanctonbury to the west, to the forest of Ashdown on the north. The Heath itself a few years ago was a wild and most picturesque spot, covered with beautiful gorse and ferns, and dotted with clumps of Scotch firs, which still stand and give a character to the spot. But, since the erection of the Sussex Lunatic Asylum and the easy

access given to the Heath by the London and Brighton
Railway, nearly all the traits by which Hayward's Heath used
to be distinguished have disappeared. Instead of the gipsies,
poachers, and other not very reputable classes by whom the
Heath was once frequented, a town with church (St. Wilfred's)
and schools has sprung up on the spot, and roads have
been laid out by Enclosure Commissioners, not in the best
taste, and villas of all sizes and styles of architecture have
been built, until the Heath presents few or none of its primitive
features. Twenty years ago the only way across it from Lindfield to the Railway Station was by an ill-defined foot-path,
through ferns and gorse and over beds of sweet-smelling
camomile. Now there is a road (Sydney road) with rows of
cottages and villas on each side, and in a short time nothing
of Hayward's Heath but its name will remain. This name,
by the way, has been a frequent subject of discussion among
etymologists. Some ascribed it to the Saxon Chief, Hereward,
who kept up a partisan war against the Normans after all
organised resistance to them had ceased. Others associated
it with a highwayman named Hayward, said to have been
hung in chains here; whilst some only saw in it a corruption
of High Wood. But there is no doubt that the real etymon
of the name comes from a remoter and humbler source than
any of these. In an old charter and in manorial records the
spot is designated as "Hogwarden's Hawth," and this points
to it as a spot in which the herds of hogs which used to be
kept by our Saxon ancestors were turned out to feed on the
mast of the beech-trees and the acorns of the oak. It was at
this time the centre of a vast forest and the point where several
manors and tithings joined. Several parishes still touch each
other here, and the divided jurisdiction doubtless contributed
to preserve for the Heath that bad character which it long kept
from the practices of those who frequented it. The hogs,
however, and their wardens or keepers had long disappeared,
with the forest and the fruits on which they fed, and in course
of time the name was abbreviated to " Hogward's Hawth,"
and thence, by an easy process, corrupted to " Howard's

Hawth,"* then to " Yeward's Hawth," and ultimately to its
present form of " Hayward's Heath."

The population of Lindfield is now 2,000, and it is a
growing one, though not to the same extent as that at
Hayward's Heath. Even in 1558, to which year the parish
register of "christenyinges, weddinges, and burryinges" takes
us back, there were 23 christenings, and in 1850 there were
but 50, whilst in 1559 the burials (38) exceeded by six in
number those registered in 1851 (32). Most of the names in
the register are still common ones in the village or its neighbourhood, such as Huggett, Chatfield, Comber, Martyn, Pellatt,
Carter, Wood, Boxall, Bannister, Verrall, &c. The Challoners
occur early on the register. They were during the 16th and
for a considerable portion of the 17th centuries the largest
landholders in the parish, and they also flourished in other
parts of Sussex. Their decline was a rapid one, and as complete as rapid. " I believe," wrote the late Mr. M. A. Lower,
" that the name of Challoner is now wholly extinct in Sussex.
The younger or Chiltington branch dwindled from gentry
to yeomanhood, and from yeomanhood to absolute poverty.
The last members of the family were two brothers, Christopher
and Nicholas, but more commonly known as Kit and Nick.
Kit kept a miserable little school at Ripe, some seventy years
ago, and died in Hailsham workhouse; and Nick sustained a
wretched existence by attending fairs and other public gather-
ings as a fiddler!" The Challoners of Lindfield, says the
same authority, " became extinct in the male line in 1689 or
1690, and a co-heiress carried the manor to John Studley, Esq.,
who died in 1703, and whose representatives conveyed it
to the family of Pelham. It now belongs to the Earl of
Chichester." † We have not to go far, however, to find a

* It has been surmised that the name of the famous Howard family is only a corruption of Hog-warden !

† And all well-wishers to Lindfield may exclaim, "and long may it belong;" for in
all matters relating to the well-being of Lindfield the Earls of Chichester have always
been forward and active. The last act of munificence on the part of the present Earl
has been to give a piece of land (adjoining his former site for the Church Schools) on
which to build the necessary addition to the Lindfield Board School. Except for such
public purposes as this the Common is never encroached upon.

parallel for the fortunes of the Challoners. The Culpeppers, the former owners of Wakehurst Place, in the adjoining parish of Ardingly, could boast of an earlier origin, as far back as King John; their fortunes rose higher; and their name was even more widely spread and their family more numerous than the Challoners. One of them (Sir William Culpepper, whose widow died in 1647) had eighteen children—ten sons and eight daughters; and the effigies of the whole family, in full apparel, from 1633 to 1678, still exist in brasses, let into their tombs of Sussex marble in Ardingly Church. But the Culpeppers are as extinct in Sussex as the Challoners, and if their Sussex residence, Wakehurst Place, which they obtained by marriage with the Wakehurst family, still stands (though not in its integrity), it has long passed into other hands.

Having named Ardingly and its great house and church, it would be a strange *laches* on our part not to take notice of one of the "lions" of this part of Sussex: viz., "the Rocks," as they are called, which rise in a valley running parallel with the high-road to London. They now belong to a gentleman named Hill, who has built a house at the northern head of the valley and who allows the public to visit "the Rocks" on entering their names in a visitors' book. It is as curious a spot as Nature, in one of her wildest freaks, ever wrought out. Although, at a distance, the rocks seem to run in a straight line, this order is lost as you get among them, and you see on every side rocks of from 30 to 40 feet in height, and 400 or 500 tons in weight, and of every shape, overgrown with beautiful heath and mixed up with varied foliage. In a country of rocks, this might excite no wonder; but the Weald is an open, gently undulating country, with nothing rocky or ragged about it; and these huge sandstones, thus starting up amidst fern and foliage of every kind, strike you as a phenomenon. It is one, however, not difficult to explain. They are not like the stones of Stonehenge, which stand unconnected with the soil beneath and about them. They are part and parcel of the original soil. They are clearly the result of the action of water upon the soft sandstone which forms the substratum of so much of the Weald. At some period or another in the world's history a mighty stream poured over and past these rocks, sweeping round the base of some, boiling and eddying and making passages for itself between the huge but not very solid masses; in some instances producing very fantastic shapes, as in the case of the stones called "Big-upon-Little," where a huge rock is so nicely poised upon a smaller one that it seems as if the smallest exertion of power would overset it. Yet there it has stood for centuries and there it is likely to stand if man do not disturb it. These rocks have doubtless a common origin with those of Uckfield and Tunbridge Wells, and add another proof to the theory of geologists that the Weald of Sussex was at one time the bed, first, perhaps, of a vast estuary, which then sank into a river before the waters were finally drained off and left the limits of land and water as we now find them.

East Mascalls and Its Owners.

IT is difficult to say which is the sadder spectacle of the two: the decay of an old house or of an old family. The former strikes the senses more forcibly; there it yet stands with all the signs of past strength and prosperity about it: solid walls that almost defy time—deep embrasured windows, in which one can fancy many a love-tale to have been told—large chimney places, within and around which generations of youth and age were wont to assemble, with all the means of mirth and merriment which we associate with these large low-roofed dining halls. The silence, and cold, and gloom that now prevail in these once noisy and well-warmed rooms, the signs of neglect and decay that meet the eye on every side depress the mind of the visitor, and lead him to sympathise with the fabric that has seen such a change in its fortunes, without any reference to the fate of its owners. These may, perhaps, for aught we know, have abandoned the old house for a newer and a better one ; they may have thrown it aside, as rising men do the ladders on which they mount to fortune—

"Scorning the base degrees by which they did ascend."

They may be joyous and flourishing, whilst the "old house" is slowly sinking into ruins. This may be so; and yet the old house itself appeals to our sympathies almost like a living thing, and almost utters a cry against the neglect or forgetfulness of those who have left it to so melancholy a fate.

The chances, however, are that if the visitor of the old house enquire into the history of its former occupants he will find that its crumbling walls and sinking floors do but reflect the fallen fortunes of the family which raised them; that we

East Mascalls: The Road Front.

East Mascalls: The River Front.

may look at the old house as a visible representative of the old family, and include both in that feeling of compassion which naturally arises at the sight of an object, which was once strong and beautiful, falling into decay and ruin.

Such we believe to be the case with respect to East Mascalls, near Lindfield, one of the oldest and most picturesque "Houses" that are to be found in Sussex, which was occupied within the memory of man by the descendants of those who built it nearly 300 years ago, but which is now a mere wreck and is rapidly sinking into that squalid state arising from non-occupation which, in the course of a few years, will often degrade the gentleman's mansion into the abode of the pauper or the vagrant.

The house called East Mascalls is believed to have been built about 1560 or 1570 by a member of the Newton family, the same family from which the great Sir Isaac traced his descent. But the estate itself had been, for many years previous, in the possession of the Mascall family, and hence the name of the place. Even this name of Mascall is, however, held to be only a corruption of Michelborne, the two earliest-named members of the Mascall family being styled (in the entry of a Visitation) as Michelborne *alias* Mascall.

It is not, however, with the fortunes of these original possessors of East Mascalls that the present house is associated. They, after a legal contest with the Newtons for the possession of the estate (which the Newtons themselves had bought of Thomas Middleton, to whom it had been sold by a Mascall)— a contest in which they got worsted—pass away altogether out of sight, leaving nothing but a name attached to a spot on which they had lived for centuries. A new house was, in all probability, built by the Newtons out of the remains of the old one; evidence of this being furnished by the quantity of cut stone used for the foundations of the walls and farm-buildings about the premises.

The style of the new house was not the characteristic one of Sussex; its architecture rather resembles that of Cheshire, in which county a branch of the Newtons were early settled; the projecting eaves, the curious wood-work that decorates the face of the house, the wooden gables, and the low, rambling cottage-like form of the structure all calling to mind the quaint architecture of Chester, rather than the solid and castellated style of building that prevailed in Sussex 300 years ago, of which Amberley Castle, or, at a more recent date (1606), Pax Hill, may be cited as specimens. And nothing more opposite in architecture can be imagined than Pax Hill and East Mascalls, though standing within half-a-mile of each other, and built within the same half-century. Of the two, East Mascalls approaches more nearly to the shape of the Swiss *chalet*, built a few years ago on the Pax Hill property by Albert Smith, than it does to the ancient residence of the Borde family: the reason, doubtless, being that Pax Hill represents the true Sussex mansion of the period, whilst East Mascalls was an importation from a distant county, like the Newton family itself.

The Newtons, however, soon naturalised themselves in Sussex. They intermarried with the Challoners, of Kenward's, and the Bordes, of Pax Hill, the two principal families in the neighbourhood, and both now extinct—at least in the direct line. The Newtons also intermarried with the Erley or Earnley family, of Brighton, and so became possessed of the Manor of Erlyes, in the parishes of Brighton, Lewes, and Edburton, and of the Manor House of Ernley, at Brighton— a fabric of which we now know nothing.* The Newtons, in fact, became a Sussex family, one branch of it living at East

---

* With reference to this Ernley family the following note is appended to a genealogical notice of the family of Newton, by T. Herbert Noyes, jun., Esq , in vol. ix. of the Sussex Archæological Collections:—"The family of Ernley is said to have been originally Erley, and to have derived its name from the village of Ernley or *Erley*, so called from Erlege—the eagle's nest. The origin of this Manor of Erleyes at Brighton appears from a fine, passed in 1197 for Sussex and Berks, between Matilda, daughter of Robert de Erlege, deforciant (petitioner), and John de Erlege, plaintiff (tenant), of two hides of land in Herlege, Reading, and Sunning, for which the said John has granted to the said Matilda a capital messuage in Brietelmeston, and 7 virges of land in the said vill, of which one verge is now in the occupation of William, 1 virge of Seredus, 1 of John Ruffus, 1 of Ketere, 1 of Alfstan and Wulwin, and the 2 virges which the said John holds in his demesne, et 3 "coterias," with all liberties and free customs appertaining to the half of his whole fief, *i.e., manor,* in the said vill, in the land, in the sea, and in all places, to be held of him and his heirs by the service of 24s. yearly, to revert to the heirs of the said John, failing heirs of the body of the said Matilda."

Mascalls, Lindfield, and the other at Southover Priory, Lewes, another house, not unlike East Mascalls, erected by the founder of the family in Sussex, William Newton.

We cannot follow the Sussex Newtons for the 200 years during which they flourished in Sussex. They ran their course. As a modern poets sings—

"They drank the same stream—they felt the same sun,
They ran the same course their fathers had run."

They had their ups and downs, until at last, as is the case with so many great families, the Newtons of East Mascalls merged into a female representative, who married, in 1695, William Noyes, of Reading, the representative of another ancient family. This lady had to establish her claim to the estate by an action against the Southover Newtons, who had taken possession of it. She succeeded in doing so at the East Grinstead Assizes, July 24, 1741, and the estate descended in 1800 to her grandson, Thomas Herbert Noyes, by whose eldest son, Thomas Herbert Noyes, the house of East Mascalls was occupied about 30 years ago, and the old people of Lindfield still remember and speak of the merry goings-on there. The old house must have been well filled then, for Mr. Noyes had a family of twelve children—seven sons and five daughters, and if these could not enliven a house what could ? But other "means and appliances to boot" were not wanting. Openhanded hospitality was exercised at East Mascalls; the large dining-hall was often filled with guests. "There was a band at Lindfield in those days," said our informant, "and we used to go to East Mascalls when the Squire had visitors, and they used to draw a large screen across the hall, and we used to play and sing behind it. Those were merry days at East Mascalls. The old house looked very different from what it does now."

Looked very different! Yes, it must have done so. Now the chimney places are empty; the walls have been stripped not only of their paint or paper, but of their wainscot and battens; in some places the ivy from the outside has grown through them; the oaken floors have sunk; the ceilings have fallen; the windows are broken. There is not a piece of furniture in one of the numerous rooms which were inhabited by that numerous family. Yes, we mistake. In two of the ground-floor rooms, when we visited the house a few years ago, there was a wretched bed, a table, and a chair or two— the goods and chattels of two poor women whom the bailiff or agent had kindly allowed to house themselves for a few nights in the family mansion of the Newtons until they could find better lodgings elsewhere. Instead of the twelve little Noyes's, there were three half-starved and almost clothes-less children, whose pinched features and attenuated limbs matched well with the squalid aspect of the old house. The women seemed half scared, half delighted to see visitors less wretched than themselves at the place. But in a short time even this wretched shelter ceased to be afforded by East Mascalls, and it was not, and is not, safe to venture within its ruined walls or under its falling roof.

A glance from some of the higher windows discloses a beautiful view over the wooded country which surrounds East Mascalls; but the front view into the meadows, through which runs the river Ouse, is somewhat melancholy—the grounds being neglected, the grass rank, and the garden walls dreary. It wants life, and that neatness and cheerfulness which only life can impart.

The precise date at which Mr. Noyes left East Mascalls we do not know. It had other tenants after him, but not of a class to maintain its olden character. One, we were told, was an adventurer, who hunted, shot, drank, and ran away in debt. Another was a farmer, who was a careful man and did well; but his son, who succeeded, was not careful and did ill, and the farm-buildings, and the water-mill near them, went to decay. They are now mere ruins. The old house sank lower and lower, until it lost all its mansion-like aspect, and nobody, as they now pass its entrance from the road, would suppose it was anything better than a deserted cottage. All the ground about the entrance is broken up; the palings have long been carried off; even the huge yew, which must have been a veteran 300 years ago, when the house was built, is now a mere wreck. When we saw it one huge limb lay at the foot of the bare and splintered trunk; like the Newtons of East Mascalls themselves at the foot of Time!

A more recent visit (in 1878) disclosed to us a still lower degree of degradation than is described above. The house was now become too dangerous for occupation of any kind, even by tramps or vagrants. The rafters had fallen in; the flooring had given way. So far from shutting out cold or rain, there was a clear view right through it—not through the once solid window-frames, which were gone, but through great holes in the walls themselves. It was not a very safe or easy experiment to make our way over heaps of rubbish and under falling timbers from the entrance which fronts the road to the opposite or more private face of the house, looking to the wooded meadows that skirt the Ouse; but the feat was not without its reward, for on that side some idea is still to be gained of the original character of East Mascalls: the outline, indeed, of the house is perfect in its projecting central porch and its flanking sides which make up the Elizabethan initial; and a little glass still remained in the upper latticed windows. In this front are the curious oaken scroll ornaments, let in, as it were, into the outer panels of the house; and the Horsham tiles and the yet solid wooden eaves still give an air of solidity to what, in every other respect, is, without and within, a squalid ruin: the skeleton of a once happy and comfortable Sussex mansion.

Midhurst, Cowdray, Woolbeding, &c.

THE name of Midhurst* points to its chief characteristic. It is a town of woods. They surround
it as the waves do a boat. Look which way you
will, there are the majestic heads of mighty
trees peering above the roofs of the houses. Issue from
what street you will, in a moment you are in the shade
of oak, lime, chestnut, beech, or yew. But, as a good mariner,
much as he loves the water, carefully keeps it out of his boat,
so have the good people of Midhurst carefully guarded
against invasion by the leafy ocean which surrounds their
town. In the whole town there is scarcely a tree to be found
—and the houses are wholly without that characteristic
ornament of our villages and modern towns—a front garden.
The main street is broad and spacious; but it is all thrown
into road and pavement: the latter of unusual width,
composed of the sandstone which the district abounds in,
with white slabs of limestone for a central walk. This gives
to Midhurst more the aspect of a French than an English
town; but then its excessive cleanliness, and the want of
uniformity in the houses—some built of modern red brick,
some of the aforesaid sandstone, and the most ancient of
wood—some mere cottages, and some fit abodes for the
grandees of a country town, the lawyer and the surgeon—
redeem Midhurst from the charge of Gallicism, except, as we
said before, in the one point of the absence of the English
garden. Singular, thought we, as we sauntered down the
street, the sole promenader in it†—in our modern towns, such

* "Hurst" is Saxon for Wood; "Mid" is supposed by some to be derived from a
Roman station called Mida.

† The reader will be kind enough to bear in mind that this was written in 1860, since
which Midhurst has been taken into the systems both of the London, Brighton, and
South-Coast and the South-Western Railways, and rejoices in Stations of both!

as Cheltenham and Brighton, the trees, shrubs, and flowers are in the streets; get beyond the houses, and you are in a bare waste. But in such old towns as Arundel, Chichester, and more than all, here in Midhurst, the inhabitants keep all green things out of sight as much as possible: like children who have been surfeited with sweets, they turn their backs on trees and flowers.

But *we* wont do so, and we warn such of our readers as do not love trees not to go to Midhurst. No matter to what particular species his aversion inclines—whether to oak, lime, ash, beech, elm, chestnut, yew, cedar, or such exclusives of the forest as the tulip-tree and the plane—here he will find it in a luxuriance that will appal him as much as the sight of Birnam Wood did Macbeth. In magnificent avenues, a mile long—in towering clusters, visible for miles around—in still, secluded "closes," that for hundreds of years have kept out all but a few faint, struggling lines of light—in the hill-side copse, closing in the corn-field—in scattered groups, and in solitary majesty, in every form and shape does the foliage of trees present itself to the eye, puzzling the taste as to which form is the most beautiful.

Nature must always have been prodigal of its gifts in this district. The soil—a light red sandstone, so favourable for the growth of trees, watered as it is by a small winding river, the Rother, and by a hundred sparkling rills, that run singing along the road-side; the situation—the centre of a basin made by the curvature of the Southdowns, which here strike inland between Sussex and Hampshire, and almost join hands with the Surrey hills to the North; the temperature—so soft that, to one who comes from a more bracing air, it is like velvet to the cheek—soil, site, and temperature all combine to make this a famous country for trees.

So, doubtless, thought Sir William Fitzwilliam, K.G., and Earl of Southampton, when, in 1553, he obtained the Royal licence to impark 600 acres of land in Easebourne and Midhurst, and to call the same Cowdray Park. Not less

favourable, too, must have been the Earl's opinion of
Midhurst as a residence for man; for on the skirts of the
Park, with only the river between it and the town, he built a
stately edifice—there are the *ruins* now before us, scarcely
distinguishable from the ivy which has climbed up and now
waves victoriously over them : * the ruins, these, not of Time,
or of Man's hand, but of a casualty which befel the edifice
almost in our own days.

But we are anticipating events. From the Earl of
Southampton the estate of Cowdray passed into the hands of
Sir Anthony Browne, K.G., and Viscount Montague, and it is
with the fortunes of this family that Cowdray is most closely
connected, and from which it derives both an historic and
a romantic interest. Sir Anthony Browne, first Viscount
Montague, was one of those Roman Catholic noblemen who,
like the noble Howard of Effingham, were at the same time
bons Catholiques and faithful subjects to the Crown. His
religion did not impair his loyalty. He was "of the Council"
both to Mary and Elizabeth ; he went to Rome for the elder
and to Parma for the younger sister, as Ambassador of
England, and performed many other services both in the
field and in the Cabinet. In acknowledgment of these
Elizabeth paid him a visit in one of her Royal Progresses
(in 1591), and stopped five days at Cowdray. A spot—an
open circular space—is still pointed out (in the Close Walks)
where the Virgin Queen partook of refreshment in a summer-
house overshadowed by hundreds of yew trees, amidst
which the Queen doubtless strayed, listening now to her
sage statesmen—her Cecils, her Bacons, and her Brownes ;
and now to her sighing lovers—her Dudleys, her Raleighs,
and her Devereux. But all earthly glories must have a term.
Sir Anthony Browne died, and was laid in Midhurst church
by the side of his two noble wives, whose virtues and his own
services are still recorded upon the family mausoleum, which

* Recently, by direction of the present possessor, the Earl of Egmont, the ivy has
been removed from a portion of the ruins, showing more distinctly the stonework of
the windows, &c.

has been removed from Midhurst to a small chapel erected for its reception and that of later monuments of the family near the church of Easebourne.

The Lords Montague who succeeded Sir Anthony seem to have remained stedfast to the old religion until the seventh of the line, and he became a Protestant. He also enlarged the Park, and tradition still points to one magnificent clump of chestnuts, close to the town, as having been planted by him. He left two children—a daughter and a son—the last Lord Montague. The story of this young nobleman's death has often been told; but such incidents never lose their hold upon the mind. The last Lord Montague, then, whilst still in the prime of youth, left England (in 1793) on a Continental tour. His companions were a Mr. Burdett, and an old and faithful servant. On arriving at the falls of the Rhine at Lauffenberg, he and his friend formed the rash project of passing the rapids in a boat—a feat which had never been accomplished, or even attempted, by any visitant. The project, it seems, came to the knowledge of the authorities of the place, and they, knowing that inevitable destruction would overtake the rash adventurers, placed guards to prevent the attempt. Lord Montague, however, and his friend found means to elude these, and were entering the flat-bottomed boat they had provided, when the young nobleman's servant instinctively seized his master by the collar, declaring that he should forget the respect of the servant for the duty of a man. His efforts, however, were in vain; the young nobleman extricated himself from his retainer's grasp, with the loss of part of his collar and neckerchief, and the two young men pushed off. They got over the first fall in safety, and began to shout and to wave their handkerchiefs in token of success. They then pushed down the second fall—by far more dangerous than the first: after which they were no more seen or heard of. The supposition is that they were carried away by the violence of the rapid and their boat jammed between the two rocks. The servant of Lord Montague remained three weeks near the falls, bewailing the fate of his beloved master, who

Q

had thus, in the prime of life, fallen a victim to a spirit of rash adventure.

The intelligence of this melancholy accident, by which the direct line of the Viscounts Montague became extinct, had not yet reached England when the family mansion at Cowdray was destroyed by fire ; originating, it is supposed, in the carelessness of the servants engaged in cleaning it. When this paper was written there were yet old men living (the day of the calamity was September 24, 1793) who remembered seeing the reflection of the fire at many miles' distance. Little or nothing was saved of the magnificent pictures and valuables—the accumulation of ages—with which the house was filled. Many of these, impaired by the flames, are said to have been concealed by the country-people who flocked to the spot ; some few, of little value, are still preserved in the houses of the Steward and the Gardener. The frescoes with which the walls were covered, of course, perished with them ; and all that now remains of the magnificent edifice, erected by the Earl of Southampton and ornamented by the Browne family, are the ivy-covered fragments of the walls, by which the extent of the building may still be judged.

The letter bearing the intelligence of this calamity to Lord Montague crossed, on its way to Germany, another letter, bearing to England the news of the death of the Viscount at Lauffenberg.

The calamities of the race did not end here. We have said the seventh Viscount Montague left a daughter as well as a son. This young lady, on the death of her brother, inherited the vast property of the Brownes. She became the wife of W. S. Poyntz, Esq., and the mother of two sons and three daughters. Although no attempt was made to rebuild Cowdray House, Mr. Poyntz lived on the estate, in a lodge which he built on a higher point in the Park about half-a-mile from the old House, going at certain periods with his family down to the sea-coast, where he had a pretty place, called the Pavilion, at Aldwick, near Bognor. It was here that a catastrophe occurred which put the climax to the misfortunes of the Browne family. Mr. Poyntz and his two boys were fond of boating, and were in the habit of making excursions on the sea in the vessel of an experienced boatman, named Allen. So close was the house to the water, that from the drawing-room windows Mrs. Poyntz and her daughters could watch the course of the boat. They were doing so one fine day, in the summer of 1815, when, to their horror, they beheld the boat upset and disappear. A sudden gust of wind had capsized it, and the whole of the occupants were struggling in the water. Allen was a first-rate swimmer, and, seizing hold of Mr. Poyntz, he was able to sustain him until help arrived; but the two unfortunate youths perished beneath the eyes of their parents.

In the mausoleum we have before spoken of, at Easebourne, are two modern pieces of sculpture: one (the figure of a mourning female, by Chantrey) raised in 1840 by her husband to Mrs. Poyntz, "as well (so runs the inscription) to commemorate her virtues and his own affliction as to record the untimely death of their two only sons, unhappily drowned, in the flower of their youth, under the eyes of their parents, in the year 1815." The other (that of a man in a bending position, by Monti) was erected in 1848 to their father by his three daughters: Frances Isabella, Lady Clinton; Georgina Elizabeth, Countess Spencer; and Isabella, Marchioness of Exeter.

Of Mr. Poyntz it is recorded that he never afterwards could endure the sight of the sea. He survived Mrs. Poyntz, the last member of the Browne family, eight years. Her memory is still cherished in the place of her birth and death as that of a noble, a pious, a generous, and a tender-hearted woman. In spite of the melancholy associations of the spot, her affections still clung to Cowdray, and at her wish her body was placed in a coffin made of those noble trees which grew on the estate, and was thus exposed to the weeping eyes of those among whom her family had lived for nearly three centuries.

This is a melancholy episode in the annals of Midhurst. Let us get back to the trees. The avenues and the "close walks" of Cowdray far surpass anything of the kind that can be found at Arundel, at Goodwood, or in any other Sussex Park. The whole Park is belted in by them. Starting from the Midhurst Gate, an avenue of splendid limes—one mass of sweet-smelling blossom in Spring—takes one to the Easebourne gate, and here commences an avenue of Spanish, or sweet chestnuts, which extends for three-quarters of a mile to a wicket-gate, leading from the Park into the other extremity of the village of Easebourne. The fruit of these splendid trees is given to the poor of the place, and it is no slight boon; as many chestnuts as would produce £7 or £8 have been gathered from one tree, and there are some hundreds of them. From the other chestnut trees with which the Park abounds, 400 bushels of fruit have been frequently gathered, and sent into the London market.

Extensive and delightful as are the walks open to the public in Cowdray Park, those portions reserved for the use of the family vie with, and in some respects excel them—not in the extent of the avenues, or the magnitude of the clusters that crown the highest points, or in the gigantic proportions of the patriarchs of the Park that here and there stand alone and apart, the last remnants of a race which has long been transformed into those floating leviathans that bore England's thunders at the Baltic, the Nile, and Trafalgar.* Not in these respects could the more open part of Cowdray Park be surpassed; but in the private walks, that reach from the old ruins to the kitchen-garden—some half-mile or more in length—the foliage is of a different character: less grand and massive, but more sylvan. Light and elegant, interlacing their branches in every direction, the rarest trees of the forest shoot up high into the heavens, the light of which struggles

---

* The gardener of Cowdray, speaking of these old oaks in 1860, told us that he had it from Mr. Poyntz, his old master, that the Park and its vicinity once abounded with them; but that in 1793-4-5 they were felled and sent to Portsmouth and Plymouth for Government use. They have done their work !

down in broken patches through their feathery foliage, or
darts through some distant vista. Walks, bordered with
rhododendrons, of a tropical growth, ten and twelve feet
high, and rich with ferns and feather-grass, wind in every
direction, now touching on the Park above; now leading to
the brook below, which divides the walks from the meadows,
through which flows the Rother, and from the neighbouring
corn-fields, where the reapers are now at work. To paint
such scenes as these would baffle the most skilful artist in
words or colours. To enjoy them, ah! how short a time was
ours! Here lies the pity of it. These delightful walks,
which once resounded with the laugh of the young and
beautiful,* are now deserted and neglected; their only
denizens—the rabbits that run across your path at every
moment, and the squirrels that leap from bough to bough
above your head. Nothing can destroy the charms of this
sylvan spot; but there is something melancholy in the
reflection that the race for whom these walks were formed,
and by whom they were enjoyed for so many ages, had, by a
series of remarkable calamities, become extinct. The owner
of Cowdray in 1870 was the Earl of Egmont, a nephew of
the ill-fated Minister, Perceval. He acquired the property
by purchase, and only visited it in the shooting season.
Dying in 1874, the property descended to his nephew, the
present Earl, who has no family.

We have spoken of the village of Easebourne, which, for
a mile or more, in scattered cottages, skirts the Park wall. A
prettier village, or one with a fairer air of prosperity, is not
to be found in Sussex. The flower-gardens in front of the
cottages here make up for the deficiency at Midhurst. It is
astonishing how strong is the love of flowers in our English
peasantry. Garden or no garden, they fill their windows with
them, and train them up their walls and over their porches,
until their cottages, as some of these at Easebourne, are

---

* They were fully kept up by Mr. Poyntz when his house was the home of three
beautiful young women—all heiresses—and the resort of the noblest of the land, who
came as suitors.

masses of vegetation. And yet along the road-side the
honeysuckle and wild rose and briony and wild convolvulus
overgrow the hedge ; in every field are to be found the fox-
glove, the hare-bell, and a hundred other wild flowers ; and
if you wander over the Common, it is to tread upon heath of
every hue and to breathe an air impregnated with the perfume
of the camomile.

But the Common does not lie upon the side of Easebourne.
The river flows and the town stands between the Park and the
Common—those rural antagonisms.   And to which shall we
give the palm of beauty ?   In the one, our warmest admiration
is subdued and overshadowed by a sense of restraint.   No
one overlooks us, and yet we are not quite free.   The very
trees, in their stately order, seem to say " Profane not the spot
by vulgar talk or silly laughter.   We were planted by patrician
hands.   Admire us, and pass on."   Not so on the Common.
There we are free indeed.   The features, indeed, are very
different.   Here, a sand-pit, only half-filled up by the fern
and heath ; there, a grassy swamp, formed by a gurgling rill,
that has lost its way ; take care, or you have wet feet for the
rest of the day.   How hot the sun comes down !   And how
delightfully cool does that cottage look, its brown roof peeping
from a little wood, with such an orchard at its back !   Ah,
Master Common, there has been pilfering here !   And the
little enclosure of barley and turnips at the bottom—was not
that once the domain of the goose and the donkey ?   But
these are legitimate thefts.   They only diversify—do not
destroy the Common.   But how about those fir-woods growing
up over its sides ?   Well, we suppose *they* are legitimate, too
—at all events, they are legal, and, what is better, smell sweet
—which legal deeds sometimes do not.

The Common on the west of Midhurst lies in three
parishes : Midhurst, Woolbeding, and Bepton.   It is one of
the most extensive and picturesque in Sussex.   The heath is
peculiarly rich, and in all varieties—even to the white, which
seldom grows wild in England.   The Common almost reaches

to the foot of the hills which rise to the south-west and west, and the wooded heights of Harting and Up-Park are clearly visible on that side, whilst on the other those of Cowdray raise their stately heads.

We have not touched upon, much less exhausted, half the beauties of Midhurst or of its twin-sisters in beauty—Easebourne and Woolbeding. We leave in despair the winding Rother, with its deep-worn bed and over-hanging woods, that divide the water beneath between the dominion of light and shadow ; we can only bid the poet and the artist enter the " close walk," and fall into ecstasy, or yield to despair. The town of Midhurst itself—with its quaint old houses, projecting their gables into the street, or its substantial modern red-brick structures, slumbering so peacefully in the sun—we cannot dwell upon. We can only bid our readers go and judge for themselves. It is now easy of access by the railway. But we must linger awhile over the scene presented by the adjoining village of Woolbeding.

Woolbeding is like a beautiful jewel in a beautiful casket. The places which surround it are all beautiful : Midhurst, Easebourne, Cowdray, Iping—not one is without its element of beauty—its river, its heath, its hills, or its woods. But the beauties of all these places only prepare you for the excelling beauty of Woolbeding ; for here the attractions which struck you separately are so charmingly mingled—so harmoniously blended—that you feel you have hitherto only been going through a work of initiation ; you have been educating your eye and your taste for the scene which lies before you ; and now, gazing at its perfection, your sense of the beautiful is satisfied.

From whichever side you come upon Woolbeding, the approach is in harmony with the place itself—whether it be by Iping, by Easebourne, or by Midhurst. But the last is our favourite route. There are few more charming roads than that from Midhurst to Petersfield. Skirted on one side by the high Heath, with its rich-smelling plantations of firs, its quaint Swiss-built cottages, and its pretty gardens and orchards—fringed with the graceful silver birch, the oak, the lime, the beech, and the ash—it overlooks, on the other side, the rich valley of the Rother, which gradually widens until Sussex is lost in Surrey.

But, in our walk from Midhurst to Woolbeding, it is only the first half-mile of this delightful road that we have to tread; for having passed the Schools and the turnpike-gate, we must quit the highway to plunge down this shady road to the right: an arch of foliage—a leafy tunnel, with its high banks full of strangely-twisted roots, overgrown with ferns and ivy, primrose and violet and wild strawberry, and its rows of rounded oaks, that bend in stately guise to greet each other. For some hundred yards or so you are plunged into a half-light—more or less broken according to the time of year, and then you come upon a stone-bridge across a stream, that tempts you equally to look up it and look down it—so pleasant are its winding waters and its wooded banks. But you do not long look up or down, for there, right before you, lies a scene that few can gaze upon for the first or the fifty-first time and not exclaim "How lovely! how exquisitely beautiful!"

How describe the spot?—how, in fact, describe in words *any* spot that Nature has clothed with beauty? Feudal castles, monastic ruins, high-reaching cathedrals—any work of man's hands—may be described. But fields, woods, rivers, meadows, uplands, these cannot be described; for whilst, in the infinite variety of Nature, the scene changes a thousand times—assumes a thousand hues and aspects—excites a thousand tones of feeling, the words that we employ to describe them remain the same: they are but "trees," "meadows," "uplands"—not *the* trees, *the* meadows, *the* rivers, and *the* uplands that we have in our mind's eye and desire to present to the imagination of others.

Yet, to an English mind, Woolbeding may be made in some slight degree palpable even by the ineffectual medium of words ; for Woolbeding is essentially English in its beauty. Those two square-built, grey-roofed mansions, relieved by their numerous white-framed windows—looking out from foliage that gives to them at once an air of beauty and comfort—those are essentially English ; so are the rich meadows on each side of the broad, even road on which we walk from the bridge towards the village church— meadows only separated from the road by wooden railings, so that you are really, for all purposes of enjoyment, walking in the meadows themselves, where cows and horses are grazing on rich herbage or sleeping under fine old trees. Those are English. So are the pretty cottages, with their neat gardens and hawthorn hedges, that skirt the road. And let the eye make a wider range, and take in the wooded uplands that rise behind the mansions, and the fields of corn and turnips that lie under those wooded heights—and all this will be felt to be English. And then the air of repose and comfort and happiness that reigns over all—the sense of completeness in this little world—of its having something of all those essentials which make up the ideas of comfort and beauty ; that, too, is English. For, if there be mansions, and church, and cottages, there are also the farmer's solid-looking house, and out-buildings, and garden ; and if there be grounds and gardens, there are also corn-fields and turnip-fields and clover-fields ; and the peculiarity of Woolbeding is, that you cannot tell where the grounds terminate and where the farm begins : there is no sharp line of division—no park-wall or high fence to divide the one from the other ; but from grounds to orchard, from orchard to paddock, from paddock to corn-field or turnip-field, you glide from the useful to the purely ornamental, until, without being sensible of the change, your eye passes from the farmer's fields to the gentleman's grounds. And so, in the roads and paths which take you through the spot, they never separate you from the place—they are always in it, and of it, and associate you completely with the beauties you are gazing at and passing through.

There is this peculiarity, too, in the beauty of Woolbeding. It is fully matured—ripened—has all the richness and fulness that ages of careful tendance alone could give it; and yet it has no touch of age—none of its decay or neglect. In Spring the road from the bridge of which we have spoken is skirted by cherry trees which are one mass of blossom, and almost outvie the May itself; but side by side with them stand gigantic Scotch firs, with their smooth ruddy stems, and their smooth ruddy branches, scarcely less grand than the stems themselves; and when these have ceased to draw our eyes aloft, we come upon the still richer and more solemn foliage of the cedar, with its tier upon tier of spreading level branches. With these oriental and northern giants, too, are mixed the pride of English forests: the oak in its sturdy strength and well-rounded symmetry; the yew, with its deep rich green and its waxen berry—the lime, the beech, and the chestnut—and all these go to make up the roadside shade and the roadside beauty: with pleasant meadows stretching down to the river and pleasant uplands running up to wooded heights; the road, after passing by the church, anon plunging into another leafy tunnel that you cannot see the issue of, but about which you need not trouble yourself, but follow these broad steps to the right—get over this low stile, push open that loose gate, and you are out of the road and in a paddock at the back of the two square mansions and the little low church; you are "doubling" the village: taking it in the rear—not less beautiful than the front; and, with the river still with you—for it clings to Woolbeding, and winds round it on every side, as if it could not bear to leave it—and with the hills before you, which recede from the village as if they left it with reluctance, and with trees and hedges always by your side, and rich herbage at your feet, and with the cry of the cuckoo or the cock-pheasant, as the case and the season may be, in your ear, you walk round Woolbeding, turning at every step to look back at it—leaning over every gate to take in the wider prospect around it—loitering at every hedge to gather some new wild-flower or some tempting berry.

And so, imperceptibly, you pass from Woolbeding and are once more entering Midhurst—not by the Petersfield, but by the Easebourne road. And whether you come again and again, or come no more, you take with you the impress of a scene which years cannot efface. True, you have only seen material beauty: you have looked upon a fair scene as you might upon a fair face, with only the power to guess at the kind of soul which dwelt within it. You might pass on and never know what kind of inner life possessed that spot: whether it was grovelling or soaring, rough or gentle, earthy or celestial—"Pagan, Turk, or Jew." Yet even with this ignorance of its higher attributes, or with a knowledge that there were none, the beauty of the scene would not be without its influence upon you for good. You would feel, as Miranda felt when she gazed upon the face of Ferdinand—

> "There's nothing ill can dwell in such a temple.
> If the ill spirit have so fair a house,
> Good things will strive to dwell with't."

In the creation of such a spot, good influences, you feel, *must* have been at work. In the peace, the repose, the softness, the beauty of the scene—in the absence from it of anything to jar upon the feelings, or to vex the mind, there must be the working of "good things." And in the calmness that comes over the mind in the presence, or in the recollection, of such a spot, is there not a proof, even to the merest wayfarer, that, in the conflict of good and evil in this world, good has won a victory in the village of Woolbeding?

But it does not follow as a matter of course that the gazer at this scene should only be touched by its external features. His sense of its material beauties may be heightened by a knowledge that it has another and a higher beauty: that it has a moral and a spiritual beauty—a heart and a soul.

We do not speak in a Pagan sense: the "great God Pan" has long been dead; our woods are without dryads as our fountains are without naïads. We have discarded these fancies, and settled down to realities. In an English village the heart

of the community—nay, frequently, of the natural beauties of
the spot—is a resident Proprietor; and the soul is, an earnest,
zealous, Christian Pastor. From these two sources, if they
exist, flow fertilising and quickening streams, which develop
their fruits in a hundred pleasing forms; if they do not exist,
Nature may still put forth her riches—the river may flow as
clearly—the trees blossom as luxuriantly—the birds sing as
sweetly—the hills will not be less rounded, the valleys less
wooded; but there will not be wanting certain signs—certain
touches of neglect or lethargy or rudeness—to indicate that
all is not quite right: that some active energy—some softening influence—is absent, which ought to enter into the village
life.

But let it not be thought for a moment that such is the
case with Woolbeding.   Without trespassing upon the sanctity
of private life, the visitor has only to cross the threshold of
the village church to feel that the upper links that bind society
together in this rural England of ours are not wanting. There
you have a picture that must surely resemble the primitive
assemblies of Christians in this country, when these little
sacred edifices were erected. The church is not capable of
containing much more than a household, such as households
used to be, and still seem to be here: with the Lord and
Dame, stately and venerable in their age: their sons and
daughters, grandsons and granddaughters—the very embodi-
ment of "six thousand years' traditions of civility;" their
more immediate personal retainers; then a farmer or two
with their wives and children, with unmistakeable signs of
"well-to-do;" and then a good filling-up of villagers—clean,
healthy, strong, sober-looking men, and neat and happy-
looking women. You might put the whole congregation in a
drawing-room, and then the majority of them would be sadly
out of place. But here, in this neat, cheerful little Place of
Worship, they are all in their places—all at home; and even
the stranger who drops into a vacant place in one of the open
pews, feels that *he*, too, is not an intruder: that there is a
place for him, which the stately and courteous Heads of the

Family* would, if need were, find in their own family seat; and that he has a silent welcome from all—from the comely old dame who meets him in the porch to the clergyman who takes his place at the reading-desk.

The first moments of his first visit to Woolbeding church will, probably, be given by the stranger to the same kind of superficial review that engaged his attention out-of-doors. There, all was harmony and beauty; and here all is order and decorum: and, if you were in a theorising frame of mind, you might take the elements of the landscape one by one and find a parallel for them in the elements of the congregation. But you have not time for these speculative subtleties; your thoughts are diverted from the persons and scenes around you to the words of the Service, which is as simple as simple can be—no music, except the singing in unison of the children, led by one clear female voice: no clerk, unless the owner of that tremulous old voice, slightly predominant, can lay claim to the post: nothing which could give "effect" to the words of the minister or the responses of the congregation. And yet how solemn they are in their simplicity! how much more directly do they go to the heart! how strong a hold do they take upon the attention! And if this be so during the Service, it is still more so when, the Service over, the same minister ascends his simple pulpit, scarcely raised above the heads of those occupying the ground-floor, and proceeds, in the simplest of language, to address the congregation. In the simplest of language—so simple that not a sentence can fail to be as intelligible to the most uninstructed mind there as the names of the implements with which he does his daily labour—so simple that a child can understand both words, sentences, and the whole scope of the address; and yet so pure, so earnest, so deeply-rooted in truth and in love, that the more cultivated the ear which listens to it, the greater, in

* These types of the old English nobility (the Hon. Mr. and Mrs. Ponsonby) have, since this Paper was written and first published, in the *Brighton Herald*, passed away to their rest, and the minister referred to (the Rev. F. Bourdillon) left the scene of his early but still cherished ministration for (owing to delicate health) a foreign land.

all probability, will be the force of the lesson conveyed—the more complete the recognition of the preacher's power, and the deeper the sense of the value of his teaching.

Singular is the effect which such preaching in such a place produces on the stranger who here listens to it for the first time. It throws him into a fit of thinking, in which all kinds of questions suggest themselves. How, in a place apart, as it were, from the world—where Nature seems so much, and man so little, how is it that such earnestness can be kept up? where can the food of such zeal be found? Amidst large masses of men—with human passions and weaknesses and sufferings and errors constantly under the eye, we can conceive that Halls and Robertsons and Kingsleys—men with large and loving hearts—can rise up and devote themselves to their fellow-men—that their zeal can never slacken—their eloquence never die out. But here, in this happy, tranquil valley, there is nothing to arouse anxiety for others—nothing to keep alive that earnest zeal for truth—that strong desire to elevate ourselves and others above the world's temptations, which, in this quiet place, scarcely seem to have an atmosphere to live in. How is it that, in such an unpolluted sphere as this, so zealous a labourer is to be found?

The answer is easy: there is no such thing as an unpolluted sphere; to the zealous labourer, there is ample work, whether the sphere be a large town like Brighton or a small village like Woolbeding. The talents of a Robertson would not have been lost here any more than those of a Bourdillon are. Why, with similar gifts—with equal earnestness—with equal power to speak to the hearts and consciences of men, one should have been destined to address thousands of men of cultivated minds, and the other a few simple villagers, we cannot resolve: but that each, in bringing to his work the utmost powers of his being, works out the largest amount of good to humanity, we cannot doubt. The fervid eloquence of one affected thousands during his life, and after his death makes itself felt wherever men speaking the English tongue crowd

together in the Old or the New World. The simple words
of the other work within the circle of a little village, which
few beyond its immediate vicinity have even heard the name
of. And yet, in the composition of English society—in the
ingredients of our national greatness—the village is as essential
a part as the greatest of our towns. The village is the deepest-
rooted of our institutions—the lowest stratum of our English
soil, out of which rises all that is good, and all that is bad, in
the larger after-growths of society. Let the village community
become corrupt, and life would be corrupted in England at its
very source. If the child be contaminated, how can the man
be healthy, strong, or good? It is well, then, that the village
is entrusted to such good hands—that we see it developed,
materially and spiritually—to the outer and the inner sight—
to such perfection; that the affections of our higher classes
cling round these secluded spots; that from them men go
forth to fight in our armies and rule in our senates—that, in
such humble structures as this Woolbeding Church, we read
the names of soldiers who have fought and fallen in the Crimea
—of statesmen, whose names are associated with the history
of their country; it is well, also, that men of deep learning
come to these places and hold that learning as nothing compared to the task they have undertaken of expounding the
grand but simple truths of religion and morality. Thus it is
that village-life preserves its purity in England, and, doing so,
remains the source and well-head of England's strength and
beauty; for without this crowning excellence—this highest
work of the highest spirit—even the charms with which Nature
clothes our villages might become a mere snare for sensual
pleasures, and a Woolbeding, instead of being a Una, fair
without and fair within, might be a Duessa—fair without and
foul within.

Trotton, the Birth-place of Otway.

HE fate which poets share with prophets—a denial of honour in their own country—seems to have fallen with unusual severity upon Otway. In the various biographies which we have consulted, we have found his native-place set down as Midhurst, Woolbeding, and Trot*ting;* and though, in the better-edited works, Trotton is rightly named and correctly spelt, yet we will venture to ask how many of our readers, even those who are native-born to Sussex, and heritors of Otway's fame, know where Trotton is—whether in the east or west of Sussex—on the Ouse or the Arun, the Adur or the Rother? How many of them know in what year Otway was born, his parents' station of life, how he died, or where the mortal remains of so much fine genius lie interred?

We claim little credit in these respects over our neighbours. Our knowledge, such as it is, and it is but meagre, as to the birth-place and the resting-place of Otway, dates back but to a recent period. We never paid a visit to Trotton, or knew in which part of Sussex Trotton lay, until some few years ago; but having filled up the gap, and having found that in the birth-place of Otway a tardy act of justice has at length been paid to his memory, we deem it but right to place our readers, or to enable them to place themselves, on an equal footing with ourselves.

The act of justice to which we refer is a brass, newly

affixed to the wall of Trotton Church, just above the pulpit, and of which the following is a transcript :—

Hoc monumentum, quantumvis simplex,
Memoriæ sacratum sit
THOMÆ OTWAY, Armigeri,
Poetarum Tragicorum qui in Britannia enotuerunt
Facile Princeps,
Hoc Pago natus anno 1651.
Eheu! egestate acerrima gravatus,
Naturæ concessit 1685.
Abi, Lector amice!
Et, vicibus præcellentis ingenii prospectis,
"Quamcunque Deus tibi fortunaverit horam,"
Æternitatem cogita.

Which we venture, with all diffidence, to render as follows :—

Let this monument,
Simple as it is,
Be Sacred to the memory of
THOMAS OTWAY, Esquire,
Beyond dispute the first of Tragic Poets
Who have been famous in Britain,
Born in this Village in the year 1651.
Weighed down, alas! by extreme indigence,
He succumbed to Nature, 1685.
Go, friendly Reader,
And, seeing the unhappy lot of this surpassing genius,
"Every hour that God blesses you with life,"
Think upon Eternity.

The record of the time and place of Otway's birth, and this touching reference to his fate, are due to a gentleman who was at one time a resident of Trotton, William Jolliffe, Esq., now of Hammerdown Park, Somersetshire.

A few particulars of Otway's life may here be not inaptly given. Though born in Trotton, his father, Mr. Humphry Otway, was the Rector of Woolbeding, an adjacent parish (described in a preceding paper). The period of his birth was in the very death-throe of the struggle between Royalty and Republicanism, and a doubtful and dangerous time for all members of the Anglican Church. However, Otway's parents do not seem to have suffered: perhaps they were too remote from the chief scene of conflict to be disturbed; at

R

all events, they regained their original station at the Restoration, and in 1669 Thomas Otway—an only child, as he himself tells us in his "Complaint of his Muse"—went (like Collins, at a later date) from Winchester School to Oxford, and was entered a Commoner of Christ Church. Of his University career we know nothing; but he left Oxford—like Milton, Shelley, and Byron—without a degree, and seems to have proceeded at once (in 1672, when he was only twenty years of age) to London, and essayed his talents as an actor in the Duke of York's company. The attempt does not seem to have been a successful one, and from play-acting he turned to play-writing, and, in his twenty-fifth year, produced the tragedy of *Alcibiades*. This was followed, in 1677, by *Titus and Berenice*, by a translation of Moliere's *Fourberies de Scapin*, by a comedy, *Friendship in Fashion* (which was revived at Drury Lane in 1749, and hissed off the stage for its obscenity), and by another tragedy, *Don Carlos*, which was so successful as to have kept the stage for thirty successive nights : a fact so unprecedented as to lead Johnson to doubt its correctness. At this period of his career (in 1678) Otway left the Muses for a time for the more adventurous calling of arms. A cornet's commission was procured for him (by the Earl of Plymouth, one of Charles II.'s natural sons) in some troops sent out to Flanders. But these troops never reached the scene of action : the money voted for them was diverted by the King to other and more congenial purposes, and Otway returned to his pursuits as an author, and, in a comedy called *The Soldier's Fortune*, thus, it is supposed, refers to his own disappointment :—

Fortune made me a soldier, a rogue in red (the grievance of the nation); Fortune made the peace—just as we were on the brink of war; then Fortune disbanded us, and lost us two months' pay. Fortune gave us debentures instead of ready money ; and by very good fortune I sold mine, and lost heartily by it, in hopes the grinding, ill-natur'd dog that bought it may never get a shilling for't.

It was in the succeeding year—1680—that *The Orphan* was produced : a play that still keeps the stage, and which has at least the merit of touching the heart by scenes and poetry drawn from the ordinary sphere of life. *The History and Fall of Caius Marius* (chiefly remarkable for the introduction into it of whole scenes from Shakspeare's *Romeo and Juliet!*) followed: and then, in 1685, after a couple of forgotten comedies, came the poet's last and greatest work—that which makes his name "familiar as a household word" to all lovers of the drama—*Venice Preserved*. The advance in Otway's powers, displayed by this powerful and touching drama, is thus borne witness to by Dr. Johnson:—

> By comparing this with his *Orphan*, it will appear that his images were by this time become stronger, and his language more energetic. The striking passages are in every mouth; and the public seems to judge rightly of the faults and excellences of this play, that it is the work of a man not attentive to decency nor zealous for virtue, but of one who conceived forcibly and drew originally by consulting Nature in his own breast.

All this, as the same writer remarks, was performed before Otway was thirty-four years of age; and it held forth a promise that in an age of corrupt manners, and with a stage pandering to those manners, one writer at least would uphold the dignity of the drama and continue that race of dramatists which boasts of such names as Shakspeare, Fletcher, Jonson, and Massinger.

But this promise was not to be fulfilled, and Otway was destined to swell the long list of English poets who have been cut off at the very moment when their powers were ripest and their country was about to enjoy the fruition of their genius. Two different accounts have been given of the circumstances under which Otway died at the early age of thirty-four years: one, the more popular and harrowing, and which Johnson unwillingly adopts, as throwing a stain both on Otway himself and on the age in which he lived; the other, the more truthful and the more honourable to all parties. The first account, as given by Johnson in his life of Otway, is this:—

> Having been compelled by his necessities to contract debts, and hunted, as is supposed, by the terriers of the law, he retired to a public-house on Tower Hill, where he is said to have died of want; or, as is related by one of his biographers, by swallowing, after a long fast, a piece of bread

which charity had supplied. He went out, as is reported, almost naked in the rage of hunger, and, finding a gentleman in a neighbouring coffee-house, asked him for a shilling. The gentleman gave him a guinea; and Otway going away bought a roll, and was choked with the first mouthful.

The other and more authentic account, as given by Dennis, is, that an intimate friend of the poet (Blakeston or Black-stone) having been shot in the street, Otway, to avenge the deed, pursued the assassin, who fled to France. Otway followed him on foot as far as Dover, and on his return thence the fatigue he had undergone brought on a fever, aggravated by drinking a quantity of cold water while in a heat; and by this fever he was quickly carried to the grave. The place where he drew his last breath is stated to have been the "Bull" on Tower Hill; the day, April 14th, 1685. His remains were interred in a vault under the church of St. Clement Danes.

Pope (in Spence's *Memorials*) corroborates this latter version of Otway's death, with this difference, that he was in pursuit of a thief who had robbed one of his friends, not of a murderer. But the fact remains that Otway died in the discharge of a duty to friendship, and was not choked by a piece of bread flung in charity to a starving man.

That he was poor was no disgrace, and certainly has nothing surprising in it when we know how authors were paid for their work in those days. The profits even of a successful play, like *Venice Preserved*, was at the most £100; and for the copyright of that tragedy the poet received £15!

Besides his plays, Otway wrote several poems, but none of striking merit; and the best known of these, "The Poet's Complaint of his Muse," is chiefly worthy of preservation because it contains some facts respecting the author himself.*

In one account of Otway with which we have met, it is stated that he was buried at Woolbeding. But we have made enquiries on the spot and can find no foundation for this state-

---

* These lines will be found in the 1st volume of "Glimpses of our Ancestors in Sussex" under the head of "Sussex Poets."

ment, which, most probably, arose from the circumstance of his father having been rector of Woolbeding, though, it would seem, resident at Trotton. In our enquiries into this subject we were indebted to the courtesy of the then Rector of Woolbeding, the Rev. F. Bourdillon, for permission to search the Parish Register, and on the very first page of this old record, singularly enough, occurs the signature, "Thos. Otway," and immediately above it the motto, twice repeated, "Mors omnibus communis." Beneath the name are several dates—"1600," "1600," and "1649," the first partly erased, but whether intended to have reference to the name, it is impossible to say ; and equally so whether the name, "Thos. Otway," was written by the Poet himself, or by his parents, or by a friend. There is little doubt that the melancholy motto above it is intended to have reference to it. In this same record we alighted upon two other entries which are interesting in connection with our subject. Under the date 1670 occurs the following: "Mr. Humphry Otway, Rector of Woolbeding, was buried February 9." At this period the Poet was only nineteen years of age, and the loss of his parent, and, with him, probably, the extinction of his chief means of maintenance at the University, afford a reason for Otway's abrupt departure from Oxford, and an excuse for his adoption of the profession of a player. The mother of the Poet long survived her son, for it was not until we reached the year 1703 that the Register supplied us with the following entry :—"Mrs. Elizabeth Otway, widow of Mr. Humphry Otway, formerly Rector of this Parish, was buried." The parents, therefore, of Otway lie buried, we may assume, at Woolbeding.

These are the chief recorded facts of Otway's brief career. If the reader of them is tempted to pay a pilgrimage to Trotton, he will be well repaid : not, indeed, by finding that the memory of Otway is "freshly remembered" there—for the fact of Otway's birth there has so died out that old people of eighty, native-born to Trotton, had never heard the name, and even tradition cannot point to the house where he first saw the light*—but by the natural beauties of the spot, well fitted to have been the birth-place of a poet. Trotton is a very small village, four miles from Midhurst, on the road to Petersfield. Before reaching the church and the few houses and cottages near it, the traveller crosses a bridge over the Rother, here a rapid, gurgling stream, flowing over a pebbly bottom; and he will scarcely cross it without pausing to look at the pretty house and grounds which face him—the Rectory—or to look at the winding course of the river on each side, or to gaze at the more distant view of the beautiful hills which rise and sink to the south and the west—Harting Comb pre-eminent amongst them. It is not, however, from the bridge that the finest view of the scenery round Trotton can be obtained. To take in this, the lane round by the smith's forge must be followed, until, gradually rising, it opens upon the whole extent of surrounding country; and then the beholder must needs confess that Trotton, obscure as it is in topography, and with little music in its name, is not unworthy to have given birth to a poet.

The key of the church may be easily procured at the Rectory close by. It consists simply of a nave and chancel, in the latter of which stands the sarcophagus of Sir John Camoys and his dame, Elizabeth, well-known to archæologists for the beauty and antiquity of the brass effigies, which have defied all attempts to remove them. There are other antiquities in the building; but, of course, to the Otway-pilgrim the memorial to the poet will be the chief object of curiosity. To this, as we have said, has been assigned a place of honour on the wall near to the pulpit; and to Mr. Jolliffe the thanks of all lovers of poetry, and especially those of Sussex birth, are due, for thus marking the place where Otway was born.

---

* The Marsh, a spot some distance from the church and modern village, is named by tradition as the site of it; but with little authority.

Up the Arun: Houghton, Amberley, &c.

WHAT tracts of unenjoyed beauties lie at our very threshold in this pleasant county of ours! How many mazy, leafy streams pour forth their waters to the sea, and draw them back again in a full flood, passing and re-passing in their course nooks and corners of surpassing loveliness, without bearing upon their tides a single heart to throb in unison with the swift river-pulse—to sympathise with the soft, fleet flow of water; to listen to the sylvan choristers that answer each other from bank to bank; to look at the still-changing picture of hill and wood and level mead, still grouping themselves in some new order; to mark the play of light and shade upon the clear bosom of the stream—mirroring back some jutting point, now lustrous in the full flood of sunlight, and now dark with o'ershadowing trees. And still the little boat, floating with the tide, goes on its smooth, noiseless path, with no visible barrier, and no law save the rower's will to stay its easy, careless course.

What a change is such a river-trip as this to all ordinary modes of locomotion in this noisy, bustling world of ours! What a contrast to the rail or the road—-or even to the sea, such as steam has made it! Of all our primitive modes of movement, only the river—and such rivers as our Sussex Arun or Adur or Ouse, whose deities have not been scared by the paddle or the screw—seem to have been left unchanged, unmarred. They still preserve their original features, and are almost as quiet, as solitary, and as sylvan in these days of crowded population as they were when the half-naked Celt paddled up them in his hollow tree.

If any reader doubt our word, let him do as we did a short time back—"take the rail" to the Arundel Station, foot it up to the bridge, and there hire a boat, and having so timed his movements that the tide is flowing in, launch himself on the little stream and let it float him, as it will do, with little troubling of the oars, "up the Arun."

As he leaves the town behind him, the towers and turrets of the castle, set in a dense mass of wood, will rise up in all their picturesque beauty, and shape themselves to the very idea of feudal grandeur.   In the town itself you only see the castle piece-meal ; from the high road you are too much on a level with it ; but from the river you behold it in all its "pride of place," crowning the height on which it stands. And so it fills the eye, and stirs the imagination, and wakens the memory, until the same flowing stream that called up the vision gradually steals it from the eye, and the stately pile and its surrounding woods sink into the water.

But look ahead, and see where the boat is taking us. We have issued forth from the "cold shade of aristocracy" and are now approaching the constellation known in the pic-nic "system" as the "Black Rabbit." It is a sign of popular pleasures—of pleasant little plebeian parties from Brighton, from Worthing, from Arundel—from every part within a circuit of thirty miles ; for no place within that limit has enjoyed so long a reign, or so well deserves it, as the house known as the "Black Rabbit."

The spot on which it stands is one of the most picturesque in Sussex. Before it flows the Arun ; behind it rises a hanging wood, a path through which leads you to the Park—one of the most romantic walks that can be conceived. The higher you rise, the finer becomes the view over the plain through which the Arun flows to the sea, and the more imbedded you find yourself in glorious forest trees, until you tread the soft herbage of the Park itself, and are entranced by the sylvan beauties of the Swan Lake : a piece of water through which the surrounding hills drain themselves into the Arun, and the chief charm of Arundel Park.

But we must not wander so far from the banks of the Arun. Let us get back to the "Black Rabbit": a spot all the dearer to the Arundel people because it is associated with a great triumph of public right over aristocratic usurpation : for, some forty years ago, an unwise Duke of Norfolk conceived a desire to close the road to the Park by way of the "Black Rabbit," and some spirited individuals of Arundel upheld the public right of way, and there was a great trial at the Quarter Sessions, which ended in the ignominious defeat of the Duke; and, since that day, the "Black Rabbit" stands higher than ever in the affections of all true Arundelians. The house itself is an unpretending one—a mere cottage, standing in a little garden and orchard, where children may swing themselves, and their elders sit or walk, or try to catch a fish, or knock down nine-pins, or do something equally impossible; winding up with "tea in the arbour."

We can do none of these things at present. There is a landing-place at the "Black Rabbit," as there is at Whitehall; but our way is onwards with the flowing tide, which soon swallows up the plebeian inn as it did the princely castle, and takes us on "to fresh woods and pastures new." For, as we ascend the river, it becomes more and more winding, and every turn brings us into presence of some new beauty: now an ancient chalk-pit scooped out of the bosom of the hills, and serving as a foil to the green woods that surround it; now the swelling hills of the Park, dotted with stately timber; now a nearer sight and sound of leaves, as we find ourselves carried under the o'erhanging foliage of giant aspens, which almost span the river with their drooping boughs; or now a village spire shows itself, or a farmer's homestead, or we shoot under a bridge, or pass a lazy, creeping barge, or come

upon some solitary angler, whom we watch in vain in hope to
see that oft-talked-of, never-witnessed, phenomenon, "a bite,"
till he fades from our view. Or perchance a solitary boatman comes along, sculling his ancient-looking craft against
the stream with marvellous perseverance. And him, too, we
watch, trying to think what his business and desires are—for
"every man hath business and desire, such as it is"—till he,
too, goes by, and leaves the mystery unsolved.

At length we reach the end of our voyage. It seems to
us that we might go on for ever, floating along with the
stream. But it is not so. By-and-bye the tide will stop, and
to go further we must have recourse, as on the dry land, to
the labour of our arms. Or, by-and-bye, the tide will turn,
and then, if we do not profit by it to regain our starting-point,
it will be night before we see the castle and the town again.
So, wise betimes, we come to an anchor—that is, we bring
our boat alongside the river-bank at Houghton, some eight
miles up the Arun, and where, on landing, the first objects
that strike the eye—in a mass of pickaxes, spades, wheel-
barrows, planks, and broken ground, with a straight line
running through all, like order out of chaos—furnish
incontestable evidence that the "navvy"—that greatest of
modern revolutionists—is here. Houghton, in fact, is, or will
be in a month or two, a Station of the Mid-Sussex Railway,*
which, by connecting Ford with Pulborough, opens to West
Sussex a new road to London. The village has no pretensions
to beauty of any kind in itself; but it is surrounded on every
side by bold hills, which rise and sink until they are lost in
the far distance.

Let us leave the river here and walk over to Amberley—
some three-quarters of a mile onward. It is in every respect
a more interesting spot than Houghton, and so little frequented
that in the West of Sussex it enjoys the somewhat profane
soubriquet of "God knows" Amberley: the reply to an

---

* The Railway has been completed and the Station opened some years since this
was written.

enquiry after the village being invariably conveyed in the exclamation "God knows." You may, indeed, gaze at Amberley at your ease from the back of Arundel Park, where the ruins of the old castle seem to lie at your feet. But the river runs between, and round the river lies a low marshy ground, that is frequently overflown, and so makes access from this side difficult, if not impossible; and from any other quarter the road is such a roundabout one that Amberley cannot dispute its title to the singular prefix that it enjoys in West Sussex.

But this, like other vestiges of the past, is doomed to disappear before the advancing tide of improvement, represented by that rude son of civilization, the "navvy." By his labours even Amberley is brought within that iron embrace which links villages, towns, and cities in one great bond of union. Standing on the ruins of Amberley Castle, you see the thin straight iron line run across the low land between you and the hills to the south, crossing the river by a light and rather handsome iron bridge hung upon arches. That straight iron line stands forth as the assertor of present Power: the ruined walls above and around you speak of a Power that has passed away, but which is imposing even in its ruins. Not that Amberley Castle ever belonged to the great feudal fortresses of the Norman aristocracy, by which they held a conquered race in subjection. It never could take rank with Lewes, Arundel, Hastings, or Bramber. It was raised at a later period, in the 14th century, and by a Bishop of Chichester, with the somewhat modern name of Reede, whose effigy, in one of the transepts of Chichester Cathedral, long proclaimed, in barbarous Latin, that the foundations of Amberley Castle were laid by him. *Why* they were laid, *why* Willielmus Reede, Bishop of Chichester, selected this out-of-the-way spot for the site of a stronghold, we leave to some future chronicler of the Bishops of Chichester to find out. In the 14th century the communication between Chichester and Amberley must have been by no means easy. The spot itself has few recommendations; it is

the southern extremity of a long ridge running up the valley
of the Arun, till it ends in Pullborough Mound; in a wet
season it must have stood in a swamp, the overflowing waters
of the river washing its walls and cutting it off from the
surrounding country. Perhaps this swampy position, and
the safety it gave, was its recommendation; perhaps its
isolation from the world was its chief merit in the eyes of
its right reverend builder, who was not likely to be troubled
by any spying eyes or wagging tongues in that remote corner
of his diocese.   Perhaps here, amidst the milkers of the rich
kine that fed on the banks of the Arun, some bright-eyed
and ruddy-cheeked damsel—but we are treading on dangerous
ground, and, in these days of spirit-rappings, the ghost of
Bishop Reede himself may give some audible reproof of the
scandalous insinuation that he came down to Amberley for
aught but sacred and ecclesiastical purposes!

Jesting apart, the castle was not a fortress like Lewes or
Arundel, erected to keep an army at bay, but rather a strong
house raised to shelter within its thick walls a personage of
importance who did not choose to be intruded upon. There
are no lofty towers, or deep donjons, or barbicans, or covered
way. You enter by a gentle ascent, now planted with ever-
greens, beneath a solid archway, and find yourself on a
beautiful piece of greensward enclosed within solid walls and
containing the ruins of a chapel, and other portions of a
great man's residence in the 14th century, now in part
converted into, or adapted to, a comfortable farm-house, to
which the ancient court-yard serves as a lawn and flower-
garden, where children and nurse-maids have taken the place
of grave churchmen and tonsured monks.   From the ruined
outer wall, still solid, and rising to a good height, there is a
fine view of the woods of Arundel Park and of the adjacent
hills—Bury and others—which rise and fall in rounded beauty
till they are lost to sight in the west. Over this fine view
how often must the old Bishops have looked towards
Chichester, the seat of their power and dignity! In one of
the ruined nooks a cozy smoking arbour has now been

formed, and trees overshadow the ivy-grown wall, whilst, on the side sloping towards the village street, peas and potatoes are grown, and, altogether, we are tempted to exclaim, in Shakspearian language,

" To what base uses we may return, Horatio ! "

Having surveyed the ruined castle, and its peaceable adjuncts, let us pass through the solid oak door at its northern extremity. It leads into the churchyard, in which there is nothing remarkable ; but the church is evidently an ancient structure—at least, the tower and nave are—and it boasts of an archway, dividing the chancel from the nave, which is a fine specimen of early Norman architecture. Arch, pillars, and capitals are all in a perfect state of repair, and contrast curiously with the other parts of the plain and unpretending edifice, almost provoking the suspicion that they belong to a structure of greater pretensions. There are also a font—of Sussex marble—of great antiquity, and a brass of an armed knight, in the act of prayer, in good preservation. These relics of ancient art suffice to repay a visit to Amberley.

But Nature also has been munificent to Amberley, if not in the picturesqueness of its site, at least in the rich beauty of the surrounding scenery—in the glorious hills which rise and sink around it—not in a bare ridge and sharp line, like that which meets the eye at Brighton, but hills above hills, with hollow coombs, and wooded sides, and rounded tops, with lines softly blended together and leading on the eye from point to point till the mind loses itself in the vain attempt to take in Nature.

But we must not rhapsodise. " Time and tide wait for no man." What Time can do we behold in the ruins of Bishop Reede's Castle ; and the tide has turned, and is now ebbing rapidly to the sea. Woe to the boatman who fails to take advantage of it ! So back to Houghton, with many a lingering look at the glorious hills, behind which the sun is now sinking,

and then, once more in our little craft, back to the "Black
Rabbit," that famous baiting-house for "weary, fainting,
thirsty travellers," and the cravings of thirst assuaged, back
to Arundel as fast as the tide can carry us—not less than six
miles an hour, and with oars scarcely touching water—and
then, finally, back to the rail—having reached which, we give
up all individuality, and are once more a mere atom in a
fortuitous congregation of other atoms: thinking how
different our jumbled existence now is from that strictly
definable position in the world which we but now enjoyed
when floating, in our solitary grandeur, full of Nature and
our own thoughts, "down the Arun !"

"By the Rail" to Pulborough, and "by the River and Road" to Fittleworth.

I T is but a year ago, gentle reader, that we floated lazily "up the Arun," following all its windings and spying out all its beauties with a quiet soul and with loving eyes—floating with the tide and content to go as fast as that went and no faster—having a destination, indeed, before us, even as we had had a point of departure, but very indifferent to the particular minute or hour at which we reached that destination, contented as we were with the pleasant medium by which we were being borne to it—now under the shadow of the castle, now losing its turrets and towers behind some wooded height, and anon, as the river doubled, seeing them rise again in new beauty, and mirrored in the glassy stream ; at one moment beneath over-hanging trees, at the next between open meadows ; now rounding some wooded point, with the white gleam of a chalk-pit setting off the dark mass of foliage above and around it ; now opening on a wider tract, where, beneath the Down-side, nestled a little hamlet, with its farm, its parsonage, and its rising spire.

The river is still flowing under the castle, beneath wooded heights, and between open meadows. There is still the smooth, easy, noiseless highway, on which Celt and Roman, Saxon and Norman has travelled, each in his turn, and each leaving traces on its bank of his sojourn. But we travel by it no longer. Another spirit has come upon the scene—a swift, strong, eager spirit, that waits not for ebb or flow, but is running a race against time as if the stock of time was getting low—that never pauses, like the river, to dally with Nature or catch a new beauty from Art, but sweeps remorselessly by church and castle, mound and tower, cleaving the earth and water with as direct a flight as the eagle does the air—only bent on one purpose: to arrive at its journey's end.

The Rail now runs up the Valley of the Arun, often side by side with the river, spanning it with many a bridge, and linking its villages together in a tight iron grasp. For the noiseless flow of water there is a rush of fire and smoke and steam, and the grating of iron upon iron. For the easy meeting of scattered friends at Arundel bridge or Arundel boat-house, there to take water with bag and baggage, scrip and scrippage, careless as to minutes and hours, with no perplexities of time-tables to break up the smooth surface of the imagination—for this easy river-meeting there is the hurry, the excitement, the bustle of the Railway Station—the dissolution of self in a crowd—the muddying of the clear fancy by all kinds of disturbances, in the shape of parcels, tickets, change of carriages, &c., &c., until the mind reflects nothing but a host of insignificant troubles, jostling each other in the most unpleasant manner, and shutting out every thing but the dim image of some future event at which we are struggling to arrive.

But wherefore, then, do we leave the river and go by the Rail?

Ah, reader, do you live in the 19th century and ask this question? Do you wish to "get into the country" and ask this question? Have you ever been tramping it on the road and seen a carriage-and-four sweep by you—and can you ask this question? When there was no rail, nothing was more delightful than to go to Amberley by the river. We did it and are grateful. Had we postponed our trip "up the Arun" for another year we should never have made that trip, any more than our children will know the delights of travelling by a stage-coach. There is a law of attraction in

these matters, as well as in more material ones. We follow
each other, in these particulars, as bees follow their queen.
There is a Railway from Ford Station to Pulborough Mound.
The Arun is close to that Station, and it would be as easy
to step into a boat as it is to jump into a carriage. Both run
to the same point. But nobody does step into the boat, and
thousands jump into the railway carriage. We amongst the
rest.

Will you jump in with us, gentle reader? You have never
penetrated before into Mid-Sussex, or, if you have, not by
this road. You have doubtless gone to Petworth or to
Midhurst; but it has been by way of Horsham to the north,
or by way of Chichester to the west. You never heard of
the existence of such places as Houghton, and Amberley,
and Pulborough—much less of Fittleworth, and Stopham,
and Bedham—or, if you heard them named, you listened to
them as we do to the names of places at which a Speke or a
Livingstone take up their night's quarters on the banks of
the Nile or the Niger—places which we are never destined to
see and care not to picture to ourselves. Those who did
penetrate to such remote places—now and then an artist or a
pedestrian or a boating-party—were privileged to talk and
write of their achievement and magnify the beauties or
wonders of the places as they pleased—they could safely
indulge in all the traveller's privileges; for who would follow
on their track to check and compare?

Well, these remote places are now as near to Londoners
or Brightonians as Brighton itself, or Hurst or Lindfield, or
any other village not a mile from a Railway Station. The
Valley of the Arun has, in very truth, been " opened up."
The sacred ground round about Arundel Park has been
invaded by the navvy. The train screams and smokes and
grates along beneath the windows of the Duke's Castle. A
few years ago a mad kind of attempt was made by a certain
Building Society to fly in the face of the Duke by buying a
bit of land in the valley overlooked by the Ducal abode.
The lurking idea of the projectors was, we believe, that the

s

said Duke would give any sum of money rather than see independent plebeian abodes—abominations in the shape of villas and cottages *ornées*—rise up beneath his castle's eye. So the ground was laid out in building plots, and people took shares, and walls were raised and gates put up. And then people paused for a result. But the Duke was not frightened. He did not take alarm at the projected town. There was no road within a mile of the site; it was a long walk to Arundel along the river bank. The view was delightful, looking as it did straight up to Arundel Castle and its glorious woods. But a man does not build for views alone, and so, with one solitary exception, not a building plot was built upon; people sold their shares for what they could get, and the Society, we suppose, was "wound up." The attempt to build upon one of the most beautiful spots in West Sussex was a dead failure; for, though close to a river, it was three miles from the Rail, and thus, to modern notions, out of the world.

We refer to this little building episode because, in making our first railway trip by the Mid-Sussex Line, after leaving the Arundel Station, and glancing out at the lovely views which met our eyes, where should we find ourselves—for one brief railway instant—but in the very midst of our old friends—the Arundel Building Society's building plots! By one of those freaks of fortune which are so common in these days of Railway Bills, the Line of the Mid-Sussex had gone right through the estate, imparting to it a vitality such as that which a galvanic wire gives to the frame of a paralyzed man. There was death-like torpor, or what Shakspeare calls " cold obstruction " before—now all the signs of life were visible. The gates had become, or were becoming, houses; pig-styes were developing themselves into villas; bare walls had gardens within them and conservatories to boot. In a few years the almost-abandoned site of the Arundel Building Society will, in all probability, become a little town—a suburban colony—the genteel retreats of Arundel citizens or the summer lodgings of burnt-out Londoners and Brightonians!

This sudden change in the fortunes and prospects of a small spot does but typify that which awaits the whole of Mid-Sussex, now "opened up" to the world. It is one of the richest and most beautiful districts in England—rich in sylvan scenery, in wood and water, in agricultural and in dairy produce, and in the still larger blessings of pure and balmy air—not deficient, either, in the manners and morals of its inhabitants: a primitive and simple race—good-looking, hard-working, and civil-spoken.

But we get on slowly with our journey. We loiter on the way, as though we were floating on the river and not flying by the rail.

Whilst we have been looking "before and after," we have passed the resuscitated Building Society's Estate; we have daringly puffed steam and smoke in the very face of the Hereditary Earl Marshal of England; we have passed that curious mound at Burpham, by which our British forefathers sought to cut off the high ground from the marauders who came up the river in their shallow barks; we have issued upon a wider part of the valley, with level meadows on each side of the river, in which feed sleek slow-moving kine, on whose backs is slowly accumulating the best of beef for Christmas tables; and now the white gleam of the Houghton chalk-pit tells us that we are close upon Amberley and are about to issue from the narrow valley — at Houghton, almost a pass — by which the Arun makes its way from the Southdowns to the sea—we are issuing from this gorge or pass into a more open country, into which the Southdowns send their long chalk spurs until between them and the sandstone hills of the Weald there is but a division of a few miles. Amberley, and the ruins of its old Bishop's Castle, stand on one of these long chalk spurs—a narrow ridge in the low country through which the Arun, not yet compressed by the hills, winds and doubles at its will, and, in rainy seasons, often overflows until it looks like a vast lake. Pulborough, the next station to Amberley, and but five miles further on, stands on a mound of red sandstone.

The Arun has accompanied us thither; but it flows through
a new soil and through a new kind of scenery. We have bid
a final adieu to the chalk and are under the milder dominion
of sand. The change is palpable to the eye in the richer,
warmer tone of the soil—in the greater luxuriance of vegetation—in the almost tree-like appearance of the waving fern
and the rich purple of the heath; and we almost think it is
sensible to the feelings in the greater softness of the air and
the absence of that stimulating quality which, on the chalk,
"braces" us up until the o'er-wrought soul threatens to wear
out its scabbard, the body. If, reader, you are ever suffering
from this chalky influence, take our advice: foreswear the chalk
and all its blessings for a season, and do not pause until you see
that the roads beneath your feet are as red and sandy as these
we are treading between Pulborough and Fittleworth.

For at Pulborough we leave the rail.

So far have we come with the world and the world's wife;
so far we have been looking at river and fields, and trees and
churches, and castles, old and new, through that most lowering
of all mediums, the windows of a railway carriage. What
the world was to Dickens's young gentleman who boasted that
he had seen it—through the bar-windows of a public-house—
such is country to one who thinks he sees it from a railway
carriage! He does see something that looks like the country,
as the other saw something that looked like the world; but
the point of view—the hurry-scurry, the associations, and the
mental tone that arises from all these, raise a screen between
the country and that man's soul. Some of its external features
may strike his eye; but its essence never penetrates to his
heart.

No! to taste the true flavour of the country, he must quit
the railway carriage; turn his back on the railway; thank it,
if he please, for having brought him so far on his way, but
eschew all further connection with it until, having taken a
full pure draught of the country, he wishes to enter the
world again.

To carry out our own theory, let us quit Pulborough station as quickly as possible. Let us not, at this moment, be even tempted to turn our footsteps to Pulborough church, a fine old structure, standing on a mound, once, it is believed, crowned by a Roman fort. Let us resist for a time the temptation of Pulborough church and its famous brasses, and, turning to the right on leaving the station, pass under the railway bridge, and then, as we walk along the highway, discuss the important point whether we will march to Fittleworth by the road or the river.

Both ways are beautiful. If we select the river-road, we must get over a five-barred gate, which presents itself on the left-hand side, about a third of a mile from the station, and looking over which we see, a short distance off, a curious wooden bridge rising sharply above the Arun. We cross this bridge, and, keeping to the right, follow the towing-path until we come to another bridge—this time a stone one, immediately in front of Stopham House, the residence of Sir William Bartelott, M.P. for West Sussex, and a gentleman who can boast that his family has owned the same estate from the days of the Conqueror. There is nothing in Stopham House to attract attention: it is a plain, modern structure; but it overlooks a beautiful country, watered by the Arun and the Rother, whose waters are here united by a short canal, along the banks of which, crimsoned with flowers, we pursue the river-path to Fittleworth. We have bidden good-bye to the Arun; the canal takes us to another Sussex river, the most beautiful, to our thinking, of all our Sussex streams, the Rother, which—the canal having done its work of junction— proclaims its pleasant presence by a water-fall, and thence it leads us, along its flowery banks, to the bridge and water- mill which stand for Fittleworth on the river-side.

But, before we get to this point of our road, let us halt a moment to look at that old grey-looking farm-house which overlooks the river to our right. It is on our side of the stream, and so we can walk up to it through the fields. It is

well worth a visit, and we will answer for it that a proper
request to inspect the premises will be courteously granted.
Lee House—formerly the residence of Sir William Stanley,
of Lee—is one of the numerous instances in which a family
mansion has been converted into a farm-house, even as many
a farm-house has been cut down into a home for labourers.
This shifting of one class into the habitations of another and
a higher class is still going on; but it must have been much
more common in by-gone times than it is now. New mansions,
new farm-houses, and even new labourers' cottages, we rejoice
to say, are now built, specially adapted to the wants of the
class destined to occupy them.   But enquire into the history
of many of the old farm-houses in Sussex—and doubtless it
holds good of other counties—and it is astonishing how many
can trace back their origin to founders who belonged to the
noble, the ecclesiastic, or the class which we now call gentry.
Such is the case with Lee House.   Even as it stands, it is a
fine, solid old structure, with walls of immense thickness,
spacious rooms, wide staircases, and splendid cellarage.   But
it is only a "poor epitome of former greatness."   The ground-
plan of the original House can still be partly traced by broken
walls above or beneath the surface, and even the outbuildings
present indubitable marks, in fine old arches and stone
mullioned windows, of having been applied at one time to
higher purposes than barns and cow-sheds.   The date of the
house—1492—is inscribed in two places on the outer walls,
and in each case the Arabic numerals are used, and it is, we
believe, one of the earliest instances of their use in England.
The second figure, by-the-bye, the 4, more nearly approaches
in its shape to 1 than to the modern 4, a peculiarity which
some of our Sussex antiquarians may be able to account for.

   Independently of this literary curiosity, Lee House would
well repay a visit as the well-preserved remains of a Sussex
gentleman's residence of the transition-period of Henry VII.,
when the jealousy of the Crown, fresh from the Wars of the
Roses, forbade the construction of those strong castles which
could "laugh a siege to scorn," in which rebellious nobles

could bid defiance to Royal authority; and when the higher
classes were compelled to content themselves with residences
like this at Fittleworth, capable of defence against the attacks
of wandering predatory bands, but not to be classed under the
category of fortified places. If there be "sermons in stones,"
there is also history in bricks and mortar, and a little chapter
might be written from the evidence supplied in Lee House of
the change from an unsettled to a settled period, and, again,
from a period when the gentry were content to live in these
strong but somewhat rude and primitive dwelling-places to a
more wealthy and luxurious era, when they began to build
themselves splendid palaces, like Petworth House, sham
castles like Cotes' Castle—the castellated towers of which
can be seen in the distance between us and the Southdowns—
Italian villas, like Mr. Prime's at Warbleton, or solid English
mansions, square and ugly, like that at Burton Park: all
widely differing from this specimen of English architecture
in the 15th century—Lee House—which, no longer suited to
its purpose, was handed over from the noble to the farmer.

But we have tarried long by the road, and must find our
way to the river again. A few more windings and we are at
Fittleworth—'tis but a field or two further on, and we can see
the bridge and the water-mill, and almost hear the rush of the
water over the wheel. Of the village itself, we see from
this point little or nothing; the best approach to that is by
the road—the same road that we left to get over the five-barred
gate, but which we will now pursue, over Stopham bridge, by
Stopham House, and through beautiful hedge-rows until it
brings us to the head of Fittleworth Heath or Common.

Up to this point the Southdown hills have been gradually
opening upon our view, and now they rise and sink before us
in all their glory. From Chanctonbury, with its leafy crown,
on the extreme east, sweeping round through the headlands
of Arundel, Bury, Graffham, Lavington, and Dunction, to the
wooded heights of Harting, which look down on Hampshire,
the Southdowns of West Sussex form a magnificent amphi-

theatre—seen in its full perfection from this central point of Fittleworth. At other points of Mid-Sussex we see this or that portion of the Downs—this headland or that coomb— this or that range or projection; but here they sweep along from east to west, closing in the southern horizon like the sea itself on the other side—far enough from us to be viewed in all the completeness of their outline, but also near enough for us to distinguish now a wooded crest, now a smooth expanse of Down, now a coomb, hollowed in the steep hill-side, now a hanging wood, or a still darker mass of foliage marking a park, or, perhaps, a tall column such as that which rises at Lavington on the estate of the Bishop of Oxford. And it is not merely a hill-view. It is also a background to a nearer picture. In front of the village runs the Rother, making for some distance a silver chord to the hilly arc we have described, and, rising from the valley of the Rother, meadows, fields, and woods slope upwards to the foot of the hills, leading on the eye through all varieties of sylvan and rustic beauty until the Southdowns close in and perfect the picture.

But we have been dwelling on the distant features of the picture. There is a nearer one, and, if not so grand, still scarcely a less beautiful one, lying at our feet. We are at the summit of Fittleworth Heath—at the commencement of the straight bit of road which runs down to Fittleworth Common. Heath or Common—it is all one, only the higher part of the red sandstone hill, from which we are looking, is clothed with rich purple heath and yellow gorse, with a few scattered firs on its side, whilst at the foot of the hill there is a broad level margin of turf, sacred to cricket and other rustic sports. There is a booth now standing on it, and two country elevens are contending for the glory of Stopham and of Fittleworth. Yesterday there was a "harvest home," joined in by all the farmers of the district; and whenever anything is to be done at Fittleworth, that piece of pleasant turf called the Common is the scene of it. The high-road winds close round the verge of this country cricket-ground, and on the other side—on the slope of the hill facing us—runs the village-street, leading to the church, the tower of which peeps forth from a wood that rises just behind it.   Closely adjacent to the church is the vicarage, in a charming situation, and, not far off, another good house (the residence of Captain Montgomery, head of the West Sussex Constabulary)—both of which look towards the Heath on which we stand.   The village itself is scattered, but chiefly runs up, in a line of cottages, to the church.   Other cottages skirt the Common and follow the road, which, after the sharp descent we have named, turns round the Common to the left and makes its way—where every road ought to make its way—towards the village inn. It is, in fact, the common point to which the river-road and the turnpike-road lead us, and, in this instance, a most comfortable point.   The "Swan" at Fittleworth is not, indeed, quite so tall as the Grand Hotel at Brighton.   It is, in fact, just one storey high, and the occupant of that upper storey might safely drop out of his bedroom window into the road if he saw just cause.   But that cause would not, we venture to say, lie in the want of comfort and cleanliness, or even of that spaciousness which contributes to "quiet breathing."   In all these essentials to a night's repose the "Swan" is most rich. To all outward appearances only a roadside inn, it has all the comforts which, we rejoice to say, still hold their ground in the quiet little English country inn.

But we are "taking our ease at our inn" when all our senses should be given to out-of-door beauties.   Take a few steps from the "Swan" on any side you please, and you are in the midst of them.   The "Swan" itself is, of course, as its name implies, by the river—in the valley—within sound of the water-mill.   But hills rise on each side of it: rich, warm hills, covered with purple heath and yellow gorse, with, here and there, high broken banks or winding roads, showing the deep red sandstone which gives such a richness and warmth to the landscape.   Climb up any of these hills, and from the easily-gained elevation you look over a beautiful picture on every side.   Of course the Southdowns, with their beautiful slopes and summits, now smooth with turf, now dark with woods, first take the eye, and then the sight falls on the valley where the Rother runs, and then passes to the inner line of hills, no longer of chalk, but of red sand, which, running parallel with the chalk hills, indicate another character of soil and give rise to another kind of scenery. Look from the low ground at the Southdowns, and these latter would not be less beautiful, but their beauty would end with themselves. Such is the case at Amberley, where you pass from the chalk-hills into the river valley. But at Fittleworth you reach an inner line of hills—not so grand as Chanctonbury, Bury, and Lavington—not so grand in their outline, not so wide-sweeping in their extent, but very beautiful in their soft sides and rounded summits, and objects of beauty in themselves besides serving as points of view for more distant beauties. On one side—the Fittleworth side—of these red-sand hills you see the Southdowns; on the other—at Bedham, about three miles inland—you overlook the Weald of Sussex, take in the Surrey hills, and can easily get a peep of Kent. If we could compare any part of East Sussex with the scenery of Fittleworth, it would be Hayward's Heath, where the sweep round is so extensive and is closed to the south by the Southdowns. But then the hills are more distant from Hayward's Heath than from Fittleworth Heath, and the eye cannot so plainly distinguish their special forms, or take in so wide a sweep to east and west. The East Sussex view is as extensive, but not so bold, so rich, or so varied in its features as its fellow one of West Sussex. It is more map-like, whilst the other is a succession of pictures, if taken separately, or one magnificent view, if taken as a whole; and you may do which you please.

We might, however, write for ever, and then the reader would not have seen, even in his "mind's eye," the beauties of Fittleworth— the pleasant winding turns of the Rother through level meadows and under high sandy banks, shaded with woods—the heath-covered sand-hills, with winding and broken roads, now shutting out the view between high banks, now showing you distant church steeples and castellated buildings, with many a wooded height and soft, sleepy hollow —all these delights of Nature are only to be compassed by the actual sense of sight. The imagination may strain to conceive them; the writer or the artist may labour to bring them home to us. But let us go and look for ourselves, and, if we be honest, what is our confession? " It is quite different from what we supposed—we never conceived such a scene as this." The most that the writer—the artist—can do is to raise the desire in others to go and see what must be seen to be known; and this is what we have tried to do—very imperfectly, we know, and so the reader who goes to Fittleworth will say. But so that he *does* go, we care not what he says. The responsibility will be off our shoulders. It will be an affair between Man and Nature, and if they do not make a loving compact with each other, and part good friends for ever, *tant pis* for Man !

Bosham: Its Past and Present.

HERE is a very equal division both of historical incidents and of picturesque beauties between East and West Sussex; Brighton standing between the two as a kind of neutral ground, belonging rather to England—nay, to Europe—than to Sussex, so colossal are its proportions and so cosmopolitan is its character. But, looking to the east or to the west of Brighton, we meet with ground which has been illustrated in a pretty equal degree by great events in our national history; and in going over this ground, we note that, while its titles to the picturesque are pretty equal, they are based on very opposite characteristics. The chalk cliffs of Albion rise to the east of Brighton, and extend, more or less, along the Sussex sea-border till Kent is reached. There are none to be seen west of Brighton. East of Brighton the Downs are, to use a Shakspearian word, "unshrubbed." A little to the west of Brighton—almost as soon, indeed, as we cross the Adur and enter the Western Division of the county—they are crowned by magnificent woods, which extend along the heights of Arundel, Slindon, Goodwood, Dale Park, West Dean, Cowdray, and Harting, until we enter Hampshire.

Then, again, looking from the hills of East Sussex, at Lewes or Hastings, our eyes fall upon an almost unbroken sea-line; the division of land and water is sharply marked; there is no intermixture of the two elements or confusion of outline, but the sea-wave either flows up in an unbroken line to the base of the tall cliff, or it sweeps round the smooth curves of Pevensey Bay, or rolls in on the unbroken beach which its own action accumulates on the shores of Rye and Winchelsea, filling up the old harbours of those ancient

Cinque Ports, and converting into green fields the watery spaces where once rode the navies of the Edwards, the Henries, and of Elizabeth.

Turn to the west of Sussex—ascend the Goodwood hills, and what a different scene presents itself! The eye can hardly tell whether it is looking upon earth or water, so intermingled are they with each other and so equally divided; it is difficult to discern where the one begins or the other ends; it is a beautiful confusion of the two elements; creeks, estuaries, harbours, watery inlets, river-like channels, with bays, islands, of all shapes and sizes—the water now running in faint lines up into the country or collecting in larger and lake-like basins, with nothing to give it a defined or decided character: all mixed up in the most picturesque confusion. It is beautiful, but very bewildering, to look at; and he must be a skilful hydrographer, who can follow all these water lines and give to each its proper name and character.

Of course, each of these lines of water *has* its proper name and character: that, which winds so irregularly up nearly to the City of Chichester, is Fishbourne; that deep bay that comes next is the so-called Harbour of Bosham— an inland harbour, that has its proper sea-outlet further south in Chichester Harbour; or, if the navigator prefer it, he may "hug the shore" all round the inner side of Hayling Island and either find a way into the sea at Langstone Harbour (Chichester Harbour being to the east and Langstone Harbour to the west of Hayling Island), or he may still pursue his back way, round Southsea, into Portsmouth Harbour, and reach this point from Fishbourne without once going into the open sea. Up how many creeks and through how many channels he will have to sail or row, we will not say. Looking down from the Goodwood Hills or from Stoke Clump on the watery maze, landsmen would be tempted to think that the unhappy navigator, like the metaphysical Angels in Pandemonium, would "find no end, in wandering mazes lost." But, as an element of scenery, it is full of beauty, and forms, as we have said, a strong contrast to the smooth line of sea-coast in East Sussex—as strong as that of the wooded to the unwooded Downs.

Each of these strongly contrasted tracts of country has played its part in the history of this kingdom. Hastings and Lewes, Pevensey and Winchelsea belong to the one, and Arundel, Chichester, Selsea and Bosham to the other. Celt, Roman, Saxon, Dane and Norman have appeared at each, now as foes, now as defenders—crossing the scene like actors on the stage, playing their parts as barbarians, civilizers, warriors, seamen, priests, legislators, conquerors and conquered, and anon, like the landscape of sea and inland water we have been gazing at, losing their individual features in a mass that mixes and mingles until we cannot tell which is Celt, Dane, Saxon, or Norman—conqueror or conquered. To the learned ethnological eye there are still lines of division which might be mapped out; but it is best to be not overwise in this respect, and to take all the fine specimens of humanity that haunt and habit these shores of West Sussex as pure Britons or "true-born Englishmen," whichever the reader likes best!

But to return to our history. Whilst Pevensey, with its remains of Roman Anderida, and its Norman Castle, famous for its defence by Dame Pelham—whilst Hastings and Lewes, with their great historical battles, and Winchelsea, with its traditions of the Edwards and Elizabeth, seem to stand out more prominently on the scroll of history; on the other hand, Arundel, with its traditions of Sir Bevis and its two sieges; Selsea, the seat of the first Sussex See; Chichester, the ancient Roman Regnum and the city-camp of Cissa; and Bosham, the residence of Vespasian, Canute, and Harold—these West Sussex places challenge comparison with their rivals of East Sussex on historical as well as on picturesque grounds.

The Romans seem to have given an equal attention to both districts. The remains of their great road from Regnum by Pulborough, Hardham, Billingshurst, and Horsham (called

by the Saxons the Stane Street), to London can still be traced;
and at Bignor and Bosham remains of their Villas and
Basilicas have been found. The Danes and Saxons followed
in their footsteps—at Bosham built on their sites, and sailed
their light vessels up the creeks and through the narrow sea-
channels into the inner harbours which had seen the heavier
galleys of the Romans ride in them. Here, at Bosham,
Canute, the greatest of the Danish kings, resided in the old
Palace of Vespasian, and here, according to tradition, he lost
and buried a youthful daughter, whose tomb is supposed to
have been discovered in our own days. At all events, in the
year 1865, whilst the church, which dates back to Saxon and
even Roman days—for it is supposed to stand on the site of
a Basilica—was undergoing repair, the then Vicar, the Rev.
H. Mitchell, directed the masons to "sound the spot which
tradition had pointed out as the site of the child's grave,"
and "the iron bar at once struck upon a stone, and, on
removing the mould which covered it, a stone coffin was
presented to our delighted gaze. The mason, in raising the
lid, which was firmly fixed to the coffin by concrete, broke it
in two places, but, when it was raised, the remains of the
child were distinctly visible." They lost their form, we believe,
almost immediately. But the coffin was replaced in its old
resting-place, and he will be a bold archæologist who will
venture to dispute—at least at Bosham—that it contains the
remains of the daughter of Canute!

What is better founded is the close connection of Earl
Godwin and his son Harold with the port of Bosham.
According to some authorities, Godwin's first wife and the
mother of Harold was a daughter of Canute. And it is
certain that Godwin, like Canute, had a Palace at Bosham—
not the Roman building, but one nearer to the church; east,
says Mr. Mitchell, of the present Manor House. And here
also Harold, the guardian of the south coast of England,
came sometimes to reside; and here occurred that strange
incident in his career which had such a disastrous influence
on his after-fate. It was from Bosham, the chief port in the

11th century for communication with the opposite coast, that Harold sailed when he made that ill-starred visit to France which threw him into the power of Duke William of Normandy. There are doubts as to the object of that visit— whether, as some authorities say, it was made by order of Edward the Confessor to inform William that he—Edward —had made him heir to the English throne ; or whether it was made in opposition to the Confessor's wish * in order to obtain the release of Harold's young brother, Wulfnoth ; or whether, as some assert, Harold, whilst on a fishing excursion off Bosham, was driven by a sudden storm on to the coast of Ponthieu, and was there made prisoner by the Count of the country and ransomed, for his own purposes, by William. However this may be, it is certain that Harold fell into the hands of the Norman Duke, whose claims to the heirship of the English throne were in direct opposition to those of Harold. This fact, and the succeeding incident of the oath that Harold took to support William's pretensions, are all set forth in the famous tapestry of Bayeux which records the main facts of the Conquest. Here we see Harold, "Dux Anglorum," and his soldiers, riding to the church at Bosham, the edifice depicted as such being a fancy-sketch on the part of the fair weavers ; Harold and a friend entering the church on bended knees, in order to offer up their vows for a safe passage to Normandy. They are next seen refreshing themselves at the Manor House previous to embarking ; a messenger summons them to the ships in Bosham harbour, and stripping themselves of their lower garments, they wade to the vessels, with their dogs under their arms, and are soon under full sail to the opposite coast.

Such is the description in the tapestry of the embarcation of Harold for that fatal voyage. It was the starting-point of that tragic history which ends at Hastings. Commencing on the western coast of Sussex, "the cradle and the grave of

---

* This, it will be recollected, is the view taken by Tennyson in his drama of " Harold."

Harold," it has its climax on the eastern shore. At Bosham
Harold is "Dux Anglorum," the great English chief—the
warder of the English coast—the destined king and champion
of the sturdy race.   His star is in the ascendant.   At
Pevensey, or Sanguelac, or Hastings—the spot now known
as Battle—he lies dead and unknown amongst a heap of
slaughtered Saxons and Normans: the last of the Saxon
kings.

From this time Bosham, the western port of Sussex, seems
to sink out of sight. It figures no more in history. The
port and the adjacent waters, which we have attempted to
describe, were well adapted for the vessels of the Romans,
the Danes, and the Saxons, and all these races have left
numerous traces of their presence on the adjacent hills and
plains, in masonry and earthworks. But the Normans seem
to have preferred the more eastern coast, as being nearer,
perhaps, to their own country, or having harbours better
adapted for their larger vessels. The Cinque Ports, and
Newhaven and Shoreham (at the latter of which King John
so often embarked and disembarked in his rapid visits to
Normandy) were the favourite ports of the Normans in Sussex.
Bosham sank to what it is now: little more than a fishing-place,
with a church of which the Saxon remains constitute the
greatest point of interest, and with traditions of Roman and
Danish and Saxon days that still give it a place in history and
archæology. But the harbour is a mere inland bay made by
the water that sweeps in round Hayling Island at Chichester
Harbour and Langstone Harbour. At high tide it will only
float vessels of small tonnage; at low tide it is a mere mud-
bank, round which lie the houses on each side of the "harbour"
that make up modern Bosham. What strikes the visitor to the
place as singular is the wooded appearance of the country all
round Bosham. On every side, seaward and landward, there
are clumps of trees — fine high trees, though somewhat
weather-beaten trees—so different from the bare appearance
of the eastern coast of Sussex. The soil, too, is deep and
rich, yielding capital crops. It is, indeed, an old and fruitful

T

soil, that early tempted the invader, but which now seems to
have been left by the tide of modern progress; for, with all
its wealth, or rather waste, of water, it lacks that capability
of navigation which is a necessity for modern commerce.   If,
instead of the shallow Lavant, which only flows by Chichester
a few months in the year, or instead of the little mill-stream
that runs into Bosham Harbour and still fills the moat which
marks the site of Godwin's and Harold's Palace—if, instead
of these insignificant streams, a real river had flown from or
through the Southdowns into the sea, Bosham, or some
contiguous spot, might have been a great port, and Chichester
might have rivalled Liverpool or Southampton or Portsmouth
in maritime greatness.   As it is, Chichester, relatively to the
rest of England, is a less important city than it was two
thousand years ago, and Bosham, instead of being the
chief port for communication with France, is a mere
fishing hamlet, rich only in the traditions and associations of
the past, and with little pretensions to picturesque beauty,
except as viewed, with the neighbouring wood and land and
water, from the Downs that rise behind it.

Middleton: The Fight of Sea and Land.

THE interest of a spot does not always lie in its natural beauties, in its triumphs of Art, or in its associations as a theatre of great events. The parish of Middleton, on the West Sussex coast, is deficient in all these elements of interest. It is dull, flat, and only not unprofitable in a farming point of view. And yet there is a great interest attaching to this patch of coast, for here is to be witnessed in full operation one of those grand, if gradual, agencies by which, in course of time, the whole surface of the earth is changed : the sea made dry land, the dry land sea; the channel of commerce diverted ; the seat of Empire transferred from one people to another; islands thrown up, or re-united to the mainland ; harbours converted into meadows, and meadows made harbours. In this poor unattractive parish of Middleton we see land and sea opposed to each other in a contest which never ceases for a single moment, but in which sea is always victorious.

We do not suppose that Middleton is known to many even of our Sussex readers, or, if known, it is chiefly by the sonnet which, as so many of our poetical collections tell us, was written in Middleton churchyard, by Mrs. Charlotte Smith. The sonnet has outlived both church and church-yard.* The spot on which they stood is now one of the

---

* It is a fine one, and will bear repetition :—

Press'd by the Moon, mute arbitress of tides,
  While the loud Equinox its power combines,
  The sea no more its swelling surge confines,
But o'er the shrinking land sublimely rides.
The wild blast, rising from the western cave,
  Drives the huge billows from their heaving bed ;
  Tears from their grassy tombs the village dead,
And breaks the sacred Sabbath of the grave !
With shells and seaweed mingled on the shore,
  Lo! their bones whiten in the frequent wave;
  But vain to them the winds and waters rave,
They hear the warring elements no more ;
  While I am doomed, by life's long storm opprest,
  To gaze with envy on their gloomy rest.

most dreary on this dreary line of coast. The church, when it existed, as it did some forty years ago, must have stood like an advanced guard against the encroachments of the sea, and to the sailor and fisherman it must have been a prominent and welcome beacon on a low and dangerous shore. But the space between the edifice and the sea became less and less, and the garden which, within the memory of people yet living, fronted the churchyard, was swept away. Then, bit by bit, the churchyard itself followed, with all its memorials of past generations. At last the fabric of the church was assailed. Efforts were, of course, made to preserve this, and bulwarks were raised on the sea-side to strengthen and uphold it. But the work of undermining went on, until, one night, in a fierce gale of wind and rain, the church came toppling down, and the sea swept triumphantly over the ruins. For several years these were visible at low tide; but all vestiges have now disappeared. There used to be a broad carriage-road—a coast road—leading to the church from the villages to the east. The sea now rolls where carriages and waggons used to roll. The only approach to the site of the church is by a lane from an upper or inland road, through a farm-yard (Mr. Coote's) down to the sea-shore; if the piece of ground which we come to at the end of the lane is to be dignified by the name of sea-shore.

A more melancholy spot—more eloquent of ruin past and ruin yet to come—it is difficult to conceive. And the effect upon the mind is the more powerful because it is not prepared for it. The upper road, though running parallel to the sea-coast, and not more than 200 or 300 yards from it, is nevertheless a purely country road—not very picturesque, certainly, for the fields on both sides are flat, and the hedges are without timber, and the ditches are wide and deep, and there are no road-side cottages. But there are no sea-signs such as usually meet you near the sea-coast. For aught that the eye can discern, you might be travelling in the heart of the Weald. You meet with none of those marine indications which speak so indubitably of the near adjacency of salt water along the greater part of the sea-shore: there are no broken boats —no wandering sailors—no road-side "Ship " or "Jolly Fisherman," with its marine loungers—no smell of tar or sound of a beating surf. All is still and quiet and country-like. And yet follow any of these country lanes which strike to the south out of this country road, and in a few moments you are on the very skirts of the ocean itself. You are in the presence of that mighty rival of the solid earth, and you come upon it without any change of ground. Your approach has been by a dead-level: you have not to mount even such a ridge as banks in one of our Southdown ponds. Nor, on the other hand, is there any fall from a higher ground, such as characterises the coast between Worthing and Brighton. Along this West Sussex coast-line, and especially at Middleton, the land runs as flat as a bowling-green to the very edge of the ocean, and approaches the monster as little prepared for resistance as a naked child is to do battle with a crocodile of the Nile. No beetling rock—no towering chalk cliff—no shelving shore on which the shingle may accumulate—nothing but the loamy surface of the wheat-field—the soft flesh of the earth, into which the sharp teeth of the old Sea Monster penetrates at every tide, tearing away whole mouthfuls of the delicate food and swallowing it up with utter remorselessness. Even when the old tyrant is calm and quiet his waters wash the base of the rich, soft soil, and sap and undermine it; lubricating it for a future gulp as a boa-constrictor does a rabbit. But when his fury is provoked by the wind, or when the moon draws out his strength, then he tears and rends and mangles it, and leaves behind such staring gaps and such masses of ruin of wood and brick and stone and earth as meet the eye here at Middleton.

For Middleton is the extreme left of a series of groynes, extending from Pagham on the west, by which the land-holders and householders of Aldwick and Bognor and Felpham and Middleton have endeavoured to protect their property. These groynes, though insignificant in bulk when compared to our Brighton groynes, are vastly more numerous, occurring at every twenty or thirty yards, and sometimes much smaller intervals, along a sea-frontage of some five or six miles. They are to be counted by hundreds, and make the shore black with their long straight lines, running a greater or less distance into the flat sand. And yet the shingle which they arrest in its course from west to east is nothing like the mass which collects against the Brighton groynes, and makes the Brighton beach so solid and so impenetrable to the sea. And the reason is, that here, on this West Sussex coast, the land does not shelve down to the sea. The fall ceases at the base of the chalk hills, some six or seven miles inland; or if there still be a fall to the sea, it is so slight as to be imperceptible to the eye, and scarcely to affect the flow of fresh water, which collects in a stagnant fashion on the very borders of the sea. Thus, having nothing to rest on—no back-stay, no *point d'appui*—the shingle is a mere ridge, more or less wide, separating the sea on the one side from a meadow or field, often below the level of the sea, on the other. So that, if the ridge be broken through by the fury of the sea, the water pours through like a deluge and the land is inundated. Such was the case a few years ago at Felpham, when the Blockade Station-house there was swept away and the people of the village had to be taken out of their houses in boats. Even now it is only by continual efforts that the narrow ridge of shingle which protects Felpham can be kept up; the shingle is continually thrown into the meadows which lie under its lee; and the ultimate fate of these fields and of the village itself can scarcely admit of a doubt.* But at Middleton, where, as we have said, the system of groynes ends, there is no ridge of shingle at all. The sea comes up without impediment to the yellow earth, depositing a few black-looking flints at its feet, which black-looking flints are no protectors, but the *avant-courriers* of destruction: the *carte de visite* by which Ocean signifies to Earth his near approach!

* Since the above was written, in 1875, much in the way of protecting Felpham has been done by the efforts of Mr. F. Sparkes, the intelligent officer of the Commissioners of Felpham Levels.

The groynes ended, there is nothing to stop this unpleasant visit: the sea at once sweeps some fifty yards round the last point of resistance; and then revels in the soft mould, which, now higher, now lower—now six feet, now twelve feet high—yields itself, whether high or low, an easy prey to the invader.

It is on the jutting point formed by the last groyne to the east that the best idea is given of the ruin which follows a conflict of sea and land when sea is strongest. Here stands* a kind of wooden barn, and in front of this, as we are told by men still in the prime of life who attended Divine Service there as children, stood Middleton church. All around is a mass of *débris*—a mixture of earth and shingle, with bricks, chalk, and black logs of wood, the remnants of shattered groynes. A little in the rear are broken stone-walls, built solidly enough, but undermined and fallen into ruins on their sea-side. They are the vestiges of barns which once stood here. Still further in the rear are two or three cottages, in bleak desolation. The whole place is full of a melancholy interest. It looks toil-worn, exhausted, and shattered, as by an unequal contest—ready at any moment to give way in despair. We can fancy the sea mumbling to itself, " One good rush, and this old rotten piece of earth must tumble into my jaws." It looks so jaded, so broken, so time-worn everywhere, like a fine old man whose constitution is breaking; whilst the sea before it is fresh and young and strong, and knows not what Time is, and smiles at the talk of ruin, and is insatiable in its demands: no sooner swallowing up one foot of earth, than, like some barbarous invader of a feeble people, it asks for two more, and makes these a resting-place for still further demands. So that, as it creeps on and eats into the rich mould of West Sussex, and as every year has to count its loss, in inches, in feet, or in yards, the mind, in its desire to anticipate the end, rushes to that period when the whole of the fertile expanse between the sea-coast and

---

* Or rather, it should now be said, stood; for, since the above description was written, a considerable inroad has been made by the sea on this point of land.

the chalk-hills, now the garden of Sussex, shall have sunk into the arms of the sea, and fleets shall float where now cattle pasture and the green corn grows.

The absorption of Middleton churchyard into the smooth clear bed of the Ocean was not a very pleasant process. Ever and anon, as the sea made a fresh inroad into the soft soil, coffins "cropped out," and still more ghastly evidences were given of the nature of the spot which the tide was washing away. To the villagers round about, the place, lonely at all times, now became invested with supernatural terrors, and the traveller who found himself benighted near the old ruinous church and the crumbling churchyard, hurried by as fast as he could, and breathed more freely as he left them behind. A friend of ours tells a story illustrative of the feelings excited by Middleton church at this phase of its existence. He had been out on a shooting excursion along the coast, and was returning home rather late at night—a moonlight night—when the ruins of Middleton church rose up before him. He knew them well, and was not given to superstitious fears. In fact, as a medical student, the churchyard had been rather useful to him in a scientific point of view: it was a very store-house of human bones. Perhaps he may have felt a twinge of conscience as this thought came over his mind; it is certain he did not think of arresting his steps at this moment for the purpose of increasing his collection of the osseous remains of mortality. He shouldered his gun, began to whistle a lively tune, and was about boldly to pass the old ruins, when he was startled by perceiving an out-stretched object in front of the high but tottering wall that faced the sea. He stopped and looked again; his fancy might deceive him. No—there was no doubt about it. In the bright moonshine was something plainly discernible in front of the church wall; fixed, immoveable there, but still with a certain air of life and motion. Our friend was startled, but not daunted. He took up a stone and flung it at the some-thing. His aim was true: a dull, hollow sound came forth as the stone hit its mark, and the object moved—visibly moved—

but still retained its place and shape—that shape being after the fashion of a human form with threatening, outstretched arms. Our friend now drew nearer—for there was only a narrow path left by the receding tide between the ruins and the sea—but, as he did so, he cocked his gun, and, in modern Volunteer phraseology, came to the "ready." He now drew slowly to the object, which was again perfectly motionless, but not less threatening in its gesture: so threatening, indeed, that our friend, presenting his gun, shouted out "Speak, or I'll fire," "Speak, I say, or I'll shoot you," and so keeping up his courage by the sound of his own voice, and with his gun to his shoulder, he drew nearer and nearer to the object of his fears, which never stirred—made no reply, and was just about to receive a charge of No. 1 duck-shot, when a voice came thundering on the ears of my friend—not from the tottering wall, nor from that strange appearance on it, but from a neighbouring groyne—" Halloa, there, friend, what are you up to ? Don't you be a peppering my great coat !" Our friend dropped his gun in a moment, and his head, too, declined a little from the erect. He didn't know at the moment whether he was most relieved or ashamed. The spokesman from the groyne was a coastguardsman. The day having been wet, he had hung his great coat on the old church wall to dry! That was the spectral appearance which had so puzzled, not to say alarmed, our friend ; and it is, we believe, the only well-authenticated ghost story connected with the ruins of Middleton church !

Pagham and its Harbour.

F Middleton, which stands at the eastern extremity of the system of groyne-defence on the West coast of Sussex, is a dreary spot of earth, only invested with a melancholy interest by the fact of the losses it has suffered, the peril which threatens it, and the inevitable doom which awaits it, Pagham, which stands at the western extremity of that same system of groynes, is a match for it in the absence of all picturesque beauty and in the presence of an equally active agency of destruction.

Pagham, however, differs from Middleton in two very important particulars: its church still stands, and it has a harbour. The church, too, is a fine one, and in admirable preservation. It was restored some thirty years ago, when in a state of absolute ruin, by the efforts of the then incumbent, Mr. Goddard, and enriched with handsome painted windows, a fine rose window, brought from Rome; a font, piscina, reading-desk, &c., either ancient, or formed upon ancient models. The church itself is of spacious dimensions, and has all the architectural properties of a village church of the first order: nave, chancel, aisles, transepts, tower, and spire. If only exposed to the fair action of Time, Pagham church, as restored by Mr. Goddard, might stand for centuries—a monument of that spirit of restoration which has marked the present age. But Pagham church stands in presence of the same redoubtable enemy who has triumphed over Middleton. If we want to understand what the position of Middleton church was forty years ago we have only to go to Pagham churchyard and cast our eyes over the low wall which bounds it to the south. One solitary green field, low and flat, with a few weather-beaten trees, and then comes a vast expanse of mud and sand, which the sea overflows at high tide, bringing its waters, in spring-tides, or in a gale of wind from the south, to within a few yards of the churchyard wall—nay, it is said, in some cases, washing the very wall itself.

As the visitor overlooks this low, flat, dreary waste of sand and mud, he naturally puts this question to himself, "And where is Pagham Harbour?" For Pagham Church and Pagham Harbour go as naturally and inseparably together as Goodwin Sands and Tenterden church-steeple. Arrived at the church you expect to see the harbour, and instinctively look for some sign of pier, ship, channel, or lighthouse, to mark its presence. Not one of these haven-like appearances can you discern from Pagham churchyard; and yet, notwithstanding, you are overlooking Pagham Harbour in all its glory. Whatever of a harbour there is, lies before you; and you, like the unfortunate mariner who happens to be caught in a gale on the eastern side of Selsea Bill, must make the best you can of it.

As for ourselves, distrusting our powers of discerning a harbour where signs of a harbour there was none, we, on leaving the churchyard, modestly enquired at the first cottage we came to on the road-side "the way to the harbour?" A little girl was our informant, and the information she gave us was not beyond her powers: "It is down the road, sir, just opposite." We turned round and saw a farm-road, with a swing-gate and a turnstile which would have been in admirable keeping as an approach to a barn or a farm-yard, but constituted about as strange an approach to a harbour as is, we should think, to be met with in all England!

At the bottom of the lane thus guarded stand a few cottages, with that indispensable accompaniment of cottages —children— to whom the appearance of "a gentleman" was evidently no slight source of interest. Both the cottages and the children belonged to a colony of Coastguardsmen stationed here, as on other parts of the Sussex coast, with no other apparent object than to cultivate potatoes and walk up and down with large telescopes under their arms. Let us, however, do justice to these fine, healthy-looking fellows: they have always a civil answer to a civil question; they are ever ready to satisfy the curiosity of the passer-by with all the information they possess, and, in case of need, to give every assistance in their power, whether it be called for on sea or on land: whether it be to rescue the crew of a stranded ship or to help the weaker "vessels" of another kind over the muddy tracks of such spots as Pagham Harbour.

A few words from one of these fine, civil, intelligent British sailors satisfied us that our little cottage guide had not deceived us; that the lane and the turnstile *did* lead to Pagham Harbour; and that the muddy bank on which we ventured, after passing the Coastguard cottages, *was* the harbour pier; so that the vast expanse of mud and sand which stretched for miles to the west, up to Selsea—to the north, up to Sidlesham—and as far as our eyesight could reach to sea-board—that this dreary waste of mud and sand was Pagham Harbour: extensive enough to hold all the navies of the world, if only mud could do the work of water! But water there was none—only a vast expanse of muddy bottom, furrowed here and there by narrow channels, in which, when the sea pours in, the water flows a little deeper than over the surrounding banks and drifts of sand which make up the greater part of what is called the harbour. By dint of diligent research and toilsome marching over the very heart of the harbour, we did at length detect the mouth of the channel in direct communication with the sea—a gap in the long line of beach which stretches in front of the harbour. This gap, which constitutes the mouth of Pagham Harbour, has about six feet of water at high tide; it is constantly shifting to the eastward, and, as it shifts, the sea, running in and out of its new channel, ravages the land which lies on its track along the shore. The vast expanse of mud to the westward of the present channel represents the land which has been devastated by this process: converted from green meadows and waving corn-fields into sand-banks and oyster-beds. Of course, the greater this territory of mud and sand, the shallower is the water which covers it at high tide: scarcely enough in parts to swim a boat in safety. It is a glorious place for wild-fowl and shell-fish and sea anemones; but for the usual uses and purposes implied by the title "harbour," Pagham is, in Carlyle phrase, a sham and a simulacre.

Pagham Harbour is, in fact, a mere breach of the sea through the shallow ledge of shingle which is thrown up along this part of the Sussex coast, and which, without the continual efforts of man, and the aid of art, would afford as inadequate a protection against the encroachments of the sea in many other parts as it has done here at Pagham. For tradition tells us that this breach in the beach at Pagham was effected by a sudden eruption of the sea in the beginning of the 14th century, when 2,700 acres of land were devastated and converted into a muddy waste. How many more thousands of acres have since shared the same fate it would be difficult to say. Not a year passes without twenty or thirty acres being added to the waste. Our companion, who had visited the spot a few years ago, recollected at that time seeing the ruins of a farm-house, the deserted garden in the rear of which was still putting forth its spontaneous growth of fruit and vegetables. Both farm-house and garden were gone, and many a broad acre besides. The church is now the nearest building to the sea, which almost reaches to it, and it seems to stand next in the order of ruin. What expanse of firm earth once stretched between the edifice and the ocean it is impossible to say; but in a field to the south-east of it—now a briny morass—are still to be traced the foundations of a Palace which the Archbishops of Canterbury occupied here in the Norman times, before they removed their residence to a safer spot and higher ground at Slindon. Anselm was consecrated at Pagham in 1108, as was a Bishop of London, Richard de Belmers, in 1267.* Thus another

---

* Thomas à Becket, when Archbishop of Canterbury, frequently came to Pagham with a large retinue; and it was concerning a manor within this lordship that the dissension arose with Henry II., which terminated in the assassination of Becket and entitled him to a place in the Roman calendar.

instance can be added to those which are furnished by the
residence of Godwin and Harold at Bosham, by that of
Thomas à Becket at Tarring, and by the fact of Selsea having
been the original seat of the Sussex Diocese, to show how
much more important these little, neglected, and almost forgotten sea-ports on the southern coast of England used to be
in the days of the Saxons and the first Normans, when the chief
commerce of the kingdom was carried on with the opposite
coast of France; when the Norman nobles naturally loved to
be in close vicinity to their possessions in that kingdom;
and when, in all probability, the tract of land between the
Southdowns and the sea—now the garden of Sussex—represented the most advanced tillage of the age: for here we
know, by the remains at Bignor and by the stations which
crown the encircling range of the Southdowns, that the
Romans had taken a firm hold of the soil and held it in
peaceful possession; and the height of the fields above the
roads, and the width of the ditches into which those fields
drain themselves, speak to the antiquity of their cultivation.

To those who care about the past these associations give
an interest to such spots as Pagham, desolate as they may
now be. And to those who prefer looking forward to
looking backward, the continual work of change which is
going on along the West Sussex sea-board, from Pagham to
Middleton, the disappearance of one Parish Church, the
critical situation of another, and the yearly swallowing up of
meadows, corn-fields, gardens, and farm-houses, will supply
a source of interest which will probably excuse in their eyes
the space which we have devoted to this description of the
battle of sea and land on the South-coast of England.

*   *   *   *   *   *   *

The foregoing paper was written in 1862, and it must
now be read in the past tense; for a great change has since
taken place on this part of the West Sussex coast. Pagham
has no longer a harbour. On this side of Bognor (Middleton
lies on the other or eastern side) a march has been stolen

on the sea, and the breach made 500 years ago through the beach has been stopped. The harbour created by the flow of water through this breach, and which at high tide reached up to Sidlesham, was never, indeed, a very useful or safe one. It was at all times, by the shifting of the harbour's mouth and the uncertainty of the channel through the mud, a very dangerous place even for small vessels, and of late it had been practically disused, so that, a few years ago, a scheme was started, and sanctioned by the Government, for stopping up the harbour-mouth and restoring the submerged land (some 3,000 acres) to its old agricultural uses. And this scheme has been successfully carried out. Pagham Harbour exists no longer. Two vessels full of shingle were first sunk in the gap in the beach as a *point d'appui*, against which other material was accumulated until the breach was stopped up; the line of shingle is again intact; and an immense piece of ground to the northward of it has been recovered. This, the old bed and shores of the so-called "harbour," is dreary enough to the eye at present. Some 600 acres (in popular estimate, 800) have been actually "reclaimed," and are now farmed as pasture and arable land; a great deal more is still half mud, half sand, with pools and channels of water, dotted by the trucks used by the Reclamation Company. But this will, doubtless, be drained in course of time, and will help to repay the expense of reclamation. Six hundred acres, at £100 the acre, are worth £60,000, and there must be three or four-fold this quantity of land to be reclaimed. But, independently of this actual gain to the Company and the country (for, of course, this reclaimed land employs labour and pays taxes), there is the defence of the adjoining land to be taken into consideration. Before the "harbour" was stopped up, every year—almost every tide—saw some fresh land "wasted"—converted into mud or sand. A few years ago (as described in the earlier part of this paper) the waves swept up to the wall of the churchyard on the south, and all beyond was a waste. Now there is a green field, and beyond that arable land, in which men are ploughing; and the bank, with tamarisk on it, that had been thrown up as a sea-barrier, is considerably inland. Pagham Church has no longer to dread the fate of Middleton Church, which once threatened it—how nearly may be judged from the words of an old man named Robinson, who lives in a cottage by the roadside near the church. "I have seen," said he to us, "100 acres that I ploughed swept into the sea, and I have seen the sea run up that lane (pointing to one adjoining the church) and over the road into this cottage." The sea is now full half a mile off, and there is a high bank of beach between it and the land which, three or four years ago, it overflowed at every tide.

Here, then, Land has gained upon Sea in the great struggle of earth and water. But, for the most part, along that portion of the Sussex sea-front which extends from Worthing Point to Selsea Bill, the victory has lain with the sea.

Within the historical period of this country the long reef of black rocks disclosed at low tide, and running from the beach at Aldwick (on the west of Bognor) some three or four miles into the sea in a south-easterly direction, was a portion of the main-land.* It would seem to have been a barrier raised by Nature herself to cover Bognor—then called by the barbarous and to us unintelligible name of Bucgrenora—from the heavy seas that roll in from the Atlantic. Whilst this barrier existed there was a good line of defence, which, by a little human skill or industry, might have been made as impregnable against the sea as the lines of Torres Vedras were by Wellington against the French invaders of the Peninsula. But in past ages the inhabitants of the South-coast of England seem to have been very indifferent to the loss or gain of a few thousand acres; land in those days was not valued as now by tens of pounds sterling at per square

---

* In a return made in 1340 by Sussex parishes of their assessable value, several of them explain a falling off by reason of land laid waste by the sea in the previous 48 years. Amongst those parishes is Pagham, 2,700 acres; Hoo, 400 acres; Hove, 150; Goring, 150; Lancing, 70; Felpham, 60; Middleton, 60; Rottingdean, 50; Brighton, 40—in all, 5,500 acres. The submerged Pagham land included the Park round the Palace which the Archbishops of Canterbury had at this place.

foot. There is good reason to believe that, so far from strengthening the natural barrier which Nature had given them, the people of those days assisted the sea to overcome it by removing the rocks. These consisted in a great degree of pyrites of iron, and works for the smelting of this ore were erected on the coast; and whoever wanted material for a cheap wall went to " the rocks " for it, as may be seen now by the remains of these walls at Bognor; and the roads were mended with them; indeed, everything was done to weaken instead of strengthen the line of defence, and at length the sea swept over and through the rocks instead of against them, and, finding nothing on the other side but green fields, it has been annexing these ever since. " Bognor rocks " now show their black tops twice in the twenty-four hours to the people of what once was Bucgrenora and now is Bognor, in silent reproach of the short-sighted folly of their ancestors. The older Bognorians, as they look at their battered sea-front and shallow fringe of shingle, shake their heads as they tell their visitors of the fields and hotels and rows of cottages which used once to stand where now the sea sweeps along in sovereign masterdom.

Nor are the people of Bognor of the present day, as it seems to us, much wiser than their progenitors of Bucgrenora. They do not, indeed, now "kill their goose" by removing the rocks that assist to shelter them; that is prohibited by a superior authority; but they carry on a divided, spasmodic, and piece-meal defence which is utterly ineffectual. To an eye accustomed to the high, strong, but not long-reaching groynes of Brighton—now made of concrete instead of wood —which "hold" the beach that is constantly being swept in from the south-west, nothing can be more absurd than the low, thin, long-reaching groynes that run along the sands in front of Bognor and the adjoining parishes. Between Middleton and Pagham—a distance of some six or seven miles, Bognor lying in the centre—you may at low tide walk over hundreds of these sham-groynes, so closely do they lie to each other; and the sand on each side of them is of the

v

same level, and the great majority of the groynes are now nearly level with the sand ! They rise a little—a very little—towards the shore ; but, with one or two exceptions, nowhere do they approach to the dimensions or solidity even of the old Brighton groynes. And the consequence is, that the beach which constantly drifts in from the west, instead of being " held " by them, is washed over or past or through them, and the sea is constantly gaining ground in its Fight with the Land. For the most part the works of defence are of a stop-gap, piece-meal character, carried out spasmodically and by different bodies, not by joint action, and upon an uniform principle. Now it has been the owners of the soil, and now the occupiers of it ; now Commissioners of Levels ; now a Local Board ; now a Reclamation Company who have taken the work of defence in hand ; and thus, whilst the sea attack has always gone on under one chief, Neptune, and upon one set of principles, and those the very best in the world—the laws of Nature—the land-defence has been disjointed and on divergent principles, and under a variety of Generals. No wonder, therefore, that, as we return at different periods to this part of the Sussex coast, we see the same scene of desolation—the same process of destruction, even in an accelerated degree ; the same unsuccessful attempt to repel the unwearying assailant ; the same waste of money and loss of soil. At any moment we should not be surprised if, in this 19th century, with all its science and capital, the scene of 500 years ago were repeated by the sea breaking through the thin line of shingle at Felpham, Bognor, and Aldwick, and re-making the harbour which has ceased to exist at Pagham !

A Sussex Sporting District.

USSEX is, and always has been, in some form or another, a hunting and a shooting county. Its unwooded Downs abound with hares and rabbits, with peewits (or lapwings) and larks, as they used to abound with the great bustard and with wheatears—now almost extinct. And whilst the rich gorse with which they are dotted gives shelter to these, the woods which diversify the western range of Downs afford shelter for that favourite object of pursuit of English sportsmen, the fox—to say nothing of the victims of Master Reynard, pheasants and partridges.

With these inducements to sport it is not to be wondered at that the Sussex Squire is a fox-hunter; the Sussex farmer a keen sportsman; and, we are afraid we must add, the Sussex labourer an inveterate poacher! At least, a good many of them "that way incline."

Whilst this sporting character applies to every part of Sussex, uplands and lowlands, Downs and Weald, there is no district which possesses it in a stronger degree, or has done so for a longer extent of time, than that which lies half-way between Chichester and Midhurst, including Charlton and its Forest, Singleton, East and West Dean, and Goodwood. From the 17th century to the present day this district has been famous in a sporting way—if not in the same way or on the same spot, in some way and on some spot. · The chalk hills which rise to the north of Chichester and divide the Weald from the sea-coast are ornamented rather than covered on their southern slopes by woods and "hangers" and copses, leaving the springy turf of the "unshrubbed Down" to the horseman, and admirably suited for racing and coursing. On their northern side extend the thicker woods of what is still dignified by the title of Charlton Forest, some 800 acres in

extent; and in the very centre of these Western Downs, and
nestling under some of their boldest eminences, lie the
villages of Charlton, Singleton, and East and West Dean—
the first-named famous for many a long day as the point to
which the boldest riders of Sussex, nay, of England and of
France, gathered in "the season of the year," in order to
pursue their much-loved sport of fox-hunting.   Hither
William the Third, an ardent lover of sport, but who
ordinarily preferred the hunting-fields of his own country,
and hunted the boar instead of the fox, is recorded to have
come once, with his guest, the Grand Duke of Tuscany; and
the associations of the ill-fated Duke of Monmouth with
Charlton are still stronger.   He and Ford, Lord Grey (who
took a conspicuous part in the rising against James II. which
ended in the defeat of Monmouth's followers at Sedgmoor,
and cost Monmouth his life), both kept packs of fox-hounds
at Charlton, and it was Grey's master of the hounds, a
gentleman named Roper, who, in happier days, returned to
the spot from a temporary exile, and, in association with the
Duke of Bolton, brought the Charlton fox-hunt to its highest
point of celebrity.   It was now that some of the chief nobles
of the land began to take up their abode at Charlton for the
fox-hunting season, and that some of them, as the Dukes
of Devonshire and St. Alban's and Lord Harcourt, built
themselves what we should now call hunting-boxes in it,
whilst others accommodated themselves as best they might
in the farm-houses and cottages of the place.   For the
convivial meetings of these noble sportsmen, after the day's
sport was over, a banqueting-room was designed and built by
the Earl of Burlington, which was called Fox Hall, the front
of which displayed the gilt figure of a fox, which was given
by the Duchess of Bolton (the daughter of Monmouth) to
show, as remarks Mr. T. J. Bennett (from whose paper in the
Sussex Archæological Collection we borrow these facts),
"the southerly wind so dear to fox-hunters."

The Charlton Hunt flourished during the lives of the two
first Dukes of Richmond (the Goodwood Estate having been

purchased by the first Duke, a son of Charles II. and his mistress, the Duchess of Portsmouth, of the Compton family, as a hunting-seat); and it was in the time of the second Duke that the most famous " run " took place which Sussex, or, perhaps, any other county, has ever witnessed. It was so remarkable in its incidents as to be not only " writ down " at the time, but to be framed and "hung up for monument" in Sussex mansions and farm-houses. In one of these (Mr. Wise's, at Funtington, originally built, and occupied for nearly 400 years, by the old Sussex family of Scardeville, to one of whom the authorship of the description of the " run " is, doubtless, due) it was found in 1854 by Mr. T. J. Bennett, of Chichester, and by him thought so worthy of preservation that he sent it, with a few illustrative facts about Charlton and its Hunt, to the *Brighton Herald*, in which it appeared on March 11, 1854, and from which we will now copy it:—

A FULL AND IMPARTIAL ACCOUNT OF THE REMARKABLE CHASE AT CHARLTON, ON FRIDAY, 26TH JANUARY, 1738.

It has long been a matter of controversy in the hunting world to what particular country or set of men the superiority belonged. Prejudice and partiality have the greatest share in their disputes, and every society their proper champion to assert the pre-eminence and bring home the trophy to their own country. Even Richmond pack has its Dymoke. But on Friday, the 26th of January, 1738, there was a decisive engagement on the plains of Sussex, which, after ten hours' struggle, has settled all further debates and given the brush to the gentlemen of Charlton.

Present in the Morning :

The Duke of Richmond,	Cornet Philip Honywood,
The Duchess of Richmond,	Richard Biddulph, Esq.,
The Duke of St. Albans,	Charles Biddulph, Esq.,
The Lord Viscount Harcourt,	Mr. St. Paul,
The Lord Henry Beauclerk,	Mr. Johnson, ⎫
The Lord Ossulstone,	Mr. Peerman, ⎬ Of Chichester.
Sir Harry Liddell,	Mr. Thomson,
Brigadier Henry Hawley,	Tom Johnson,
Ralph Jennison, Esq., Master of	Billy Ives, Yeoman Pricker to His
His Majesty's Buck Hounds,	Majesty's Hounds,
Edward Pauncefort, Esq.,	David Briggs, ⎫ Whippers-in.
William Farquhar, Esq.,	Nim Ives, ⎬

At a quarter before eight in the morning the fox was found in Eastdean Wood, and ran an hour in that cover ; then into the forest, up to Puntice Coppice through Heringdean to the Marlows, up to Coney Coppice, back to the Marlows, to the Forest West Gate, over the fields to Nightingale Bottom, to Cobden's at Draught, up his Pine Pit Hanger, where His

Grace of St. Albans got a fall; through My Lady Lewkner's Puttocks, and missed the earth; through Westdean Forest to the corner of Collar Down (where Lord Harcourt blew his first horse), crossed the Hacking-place down the length of Coney Coppice, through the Marlows to Heringdean, into the Forest and Puntice Coppice, Eastdean Wood, through the Lower Teglease across by Cocking-course down between Graffham and Woolavington, through Mr. Orme's Park and Paddock over the Heath to Fielder's Furzes, to the Harlands, Selham, Ambersham, through Todham Furzes over Todham Heath, almost to Cowdray Park; there turned to the limekiln at the end of Cocking Causeway, through Cocking Park and Furzes; there crossed the road and up the hills between Bepton and Cocking. Here the unfortunate Lord Harcourt's second horse felt the effects of long legs and a sudden steep; the best thing that belonged to him was his saddle, which My Lord had secured; but, by bleeding and Geneva (contrary to Act of Parliament) he recovered, and with some difficulty was got home. Here Mr. Farquhar's humanity claims your regard, who kindly sympathised with My Lord in his misfortunes, and had not power to go beyond him. At the bottom of Cocking Warren the hounds turned to the left across the road by the barn near Heringdean, then took the side to the north-gate of the Forest (here General Hawley thought it prudent to change his horse for a true-blue that staid up the hills. Billy Ives likewise took a horse of Sir Harry Liddell's); went quite through the Forest and run the foil through Nightingale Bottom to Cobden's at Draught, up his Pine Pit Hanger to My Lady Lewkner's Puttocks, through every meuse she went in the morning; went through the Warren above Westdean (where we dropt Sir Harry Liddell) down to Benderton Farm (here Lord Harry sunk), through Goodwood Park (here the Duke of Richmond chose to send three lame horses back to Charlton and took Saucy Face and Sir William, that were luckily at Goodwood; from thence, at a distance, Lord Harry was seen driving his horse before him to Charlton). The hounds went out at the upper end of the Park over Strettington-road by Sealy Coppice (where His Grace of Richmond got a summerset), through Halnaker Park over Halnaker Hill to Seabeach Farm (here the Master of the Stag Hounds, Cornet Honywood, Tom Johnson, and Nim Ives were thoroughly satisfied), up Long Down, through Eartham Common fields and Kemp's High Wood (here Billy Ives tired his second horse and took Sir William, by which the Duke of St. Albans had no great coat, so returned to Charlton). From Kemp's High Wood the hounds took away through Gunworth Warren, Kemp's Rough Piece, over Slindon Down to Madehurst Parsonage (where Billy came in with them), over Poor Down up to Madehurst, then down to Haughton Forest, where His Grace of Richmond, General Hawley, and Mr. Pauncefort came in (the latter to little purpose, for, beyond the Ruel Hill, neither Mr. Pauncefort nor his horse Tinker cared to go, so wisely returned to his impatient friends), up the Ruel Hill, left Sherwood on the right-hand, crossed Ofham Hill to Southwood, from thence to South Stoke, to the wall of Arundel River, where the glorious 23 hounds put an end to the campaign, and killed an old bitch fox, ten minutes before six. Billy Ives, His Grace of Richmond, and General Hawley were the only persons in at the death, to the immortal honour of 17 stone, and at least as many campaigns.

This famous run was, doubtless, the crowning glory of the Charlton Hunt. The third Duke of Richmond, indeed, was a fox-hunter like his predecessors, and built some fine kennels for his hounds at Goodwood, to which they were removed from Charlton ; but this change was detrimental to the latter place; the hunt declined; from being cosmopolitan it became local, and on the fourth Duke of Richmond going to Ireland as Lord Lieutenant, the hounds were given by him to George the Fourth, and symptoms of madness showing themselves afterwards in them, they were destroyed.

But, after all, the glories of the Charlton Hunt were to be "translated" rather than extinguished. They sprang up afresh, though under new auspices. Previous to the destruction of the Goodwood pack an attempt had been made by a neighbouring potentate, the owner of Petworth (then the "proud Duke of Somerset"), to set up a rival pack. But, springing not so much from love of sport as provincial jealousy, it failed, and deserved to fail. "Whose hounds are those," enquired the Duke of Sir William Goring, of Burton, one day, "who so frequently come near my house?" "Mr. Roper's, the Charlton Pack," was the reply. "Mr. Roper's! The Charlton Pack ! Who is he? Where's his estate? What right has he to hunt this country? I'll have hounds and horses of my own," cried the irate Peer, and on the word he built kennels and stables, and took to the field, and did his best to tempt the fox-hunters to his meet. But they would not desert their first love ; the hounds were eventually given away, and Petworth had to wait another century before it supplanted Goodwood in the hunting-field. The time came at last—"the day and the man." The late Earl of Egremont prepared the way by building the splendid stables now attached to Petworth House, which came to him by succession from the Percies and the Seymours. But it was his son, the first Lord Leconfield, who, when simple Col. George Wyndham, laid the foundations of the present hunt, whilst the occupant of "The Drove" at Singleton (an appanage of the Petworth Estate). The kennels here are of the most perfect kind, fitted for three packs, the dogs, "the ladies," and the young hounds ; and here resides the

huntsman of the pack, Mr. C. Shepherd, under whose skilful
care and guidance they are bred, trained, and hunted. To
see these packs in their own quarters, as we have done, or
"at work," after cubs or an old fox, is a treat which only a
sportsman could sufficiently appreciate, but which has its
attractions even to an unskilled eye. The hounds are "as
one compact." With as many wills as there are dogs, and
all ready to burst out, at the voice of the huntsman they
become "one and indivisible." We confess it was with a
certain degree of nervousness that, at the opening of the
kennel-door, we stood in the midst of an eager and restless
set of animals, any one of which was able to pull down a
man, and, once down, what would become of him ?* But, at
the voice of the huntsman, all was quiet and order ; every
eye fixed on his eye, and limbs motionless, though trembling
with excitement. Each animal sat on its haunches, covering
the smallest possible space of ground. The name and the
value, deeds and qualities of each animal were related, and,
as this was done, the animals seemed to be aware of the
fact! Their genealogies are as carefully kept, too, as are
those of race-horses, and each year has its printed list of the
various packs, with names, age, sires and dams, from the
hounds of seven years to those of one year. These
comprehend in all some 60 couples, or 120 dogs, and they
are the sole property of the owner of Petworth, now the
second Lord Leconfield, and are kept up at his sole expense.
The cost of doing so is enormous (some £20,000 or £30,000
a-year), comprehending as it does not only the keep of the
hounds and their numerous attendants, but of the large
stud of horses which are so necessary to mount these, and
for the use of the Master and his friends. These fill the
splendid stables of Petworth. The country hunted by the
Petworth Pack is virtually the same as that over which the
Charlton hounds hunted, and many a fox takes the same

---

* There is a tradition that, in one kennel (not the Petworth one), an unfortunate
wretch, employed as a feeder of the hounds, disappeared one day bodily, and, on
enquiry, no doubt was left but that the hounds had set upon him and eaten him up—
to the very bones.

line, and meets at last with the same fate, as that of the "old bitch fox," which held her own so stoutly for ten hours in the great run of 1738. But the glory of the hunt no longer shines forth at Charlton. The quiet of the old village between the Leven Down and the Trundle (two beautifully rounded prominences of the Southdowns so-called) is now unbroken by the excitement and revelry of the noble fox-hunters of England. A "Fox Hall" is still pointed out at which the Dukes of Richmond used to lodge; but it is not the original banqueting place built by the Earl of Burlington. That was pulled down long ago; so were the kennels and stables; and the residences of Dukes and Earls have disappeared, or been converted to humbler uses. There is nothing, indeed, to show that Charlton was, for nearly 100 years, the great "meet" of noble fox-hunters, and a trysting-place for rank, wealth, and beauty. With the exception of a good farm-house, and of the residence of the owner of a steam saw mill, the village is occupied by labourers, the tenants of the Dukes of Richmond, whose tenements are, indeed, so numerous that, for convenience sake, they are numbered not as rows or streets, but in catalogue fashion, from 1 upwards.

There is, however, one week of the year during which even the quiet of Charlton is broken, and still more that of its neighbour village, Singleton, from which Charlton is only divided by a few minutes' walk through pleasant fields; and that is the week of Goodwood Races. Then a wonderful social revolution is effected in Singleton, Charlton, and all their vicinity. They are invaded by the fashionable world— by Princes, Dukes, Earls, and Lords, with their fair partners, who, with their cooks and ladies' maids and valets, take possession of farm-houses and cottages—anything in the shape of a house—and literally set up their tents, living a kind of *fête champêtre* life amidst most rustic scenes and scenery. With these, too, come a host of jockeys and stablemen, and other "horsey" gentry, with studs of race-horses, for the accommodation of which the cottagers are

turned out of their homes, with their families, to manage as
best they can for some five or six days. A good many
cottages at Singleton are, indeed, let under this condition.
They are labourers' cottages for 358 days in the year, and for
the other seven they are stables or horse-boxes. So severe,
indeed, is the pressure in the Goodwood week in Singleton
and Charlton that a guinea for a bed, and that of the
humblest, is a common price, and it is a golden harvest for
the farmers (who "take in" Princes and Duchesses) and the
villagers. Of course this inundation of race-folks into the
rustic world has its drawbacks. It is a kind of saturnalia for
a term. But, after it has passed, the villagers settle down very
quickly to their usual life, and that is of the quietest.

Into the glories of the Goodwood week, its rise, under the
presiding genius of Lord George Bentinck, from a mere
country-side day's sport into national importance as the
most aristocratical races of England, it is not our cue to
enter. But it is singular how sport of the highest class
gravitates to this rural corner of the Southdowns. If there
is a secluded spot in England it is Charlton or Singleton,
or East or West Dean. If a man want solitude let him go
here—let him take his strolls up the Leven Down or the
Trundle, or to Stoke Clump, or in Charlton Forest, or over
Cocking Hill, and, beyond the sight of a shepherd or of a
ploughman,

" Who homeward plods his weary way,"

he will not be disturbed by man or beast. Always save and
except that the " view hallo! hallo!" does not break upon
his ear, with a whirlwind of dogs and horses and men in
red coats, or that an Arab-like steed, with a boy in drab
wrappings on its back, does not canter by him, swift, silent,
and mysterious. These are signs of the sport-life that still
flourishes round Charlton, and keeps up its olden associations.
Not far off from it, too, the name of another little village,
Duncton, calls up remembrances of another phase of sport,
if we may so term it. Duncton, the birth-place of James Dean,

"Dean Swift," the famous Sussex bowler, was long the centre of a cricketing district that supplied the Sussex Eleven with its best players. Its club could play and beat Brighton 50 years ago. From this part of West Sussex "hailed" the Broadbridges, the Lillywhites, Hawkins, Millyard, James Taylor, and a host of other crack players, who enabled Sussex, some 40 or 50 years ago, to "hold its own" against All England. Since then the star of cricket in Sussex has set, and Duncton no longer sends forth champions of the game. Cricket is still played, doubtless, on its common; but the North and West of England have entered the lists, and their strong battalions bear away the palm in this as in other respects from the South. It is the fight of the many against the few. Still, sport of all kind flourishes in Sussex, and in no part of it are its traditions stronger, or do its glories assert themselves more brilliantly, than in that part of the Downs of West Sussex where, in the hollow of the hills, nestle the villages of Charlton, Singleton, and East and West Dean.

Cricket in Sussex.

RICKET has been referred to in the preceding Paper as one of the characteristics of the Charlton district. In all probability it made its way into West Sussex from Hampshire, in which county it first took that form in which we now know it; and where the fame of the Hambledon Club—the first Cricketing Club ever formed in England, and which dates from 1750 to 1791— still survives. Two upright sticks, about a foot apart and with a third laid across them, were the original wickets, and the primitive bat consisted of a crooked stick, from which, by an easy corruption, the name of cricket is supposed to be derived.* The inconvenience of the ball frequently passing between the two upright sticks without disturbing them, or causing the fall of the stick resting on them, led to the addition, in 1775, of a third or middle stick, and, in course of time, to two smaller sticks or "bails" being laid on these. Other improvements followed upon the adoption of the game in London and other parts of the kingdom, and to its being played by the higher ranks of society, until cricket grew to what it now is: the national game of England.

In this process of improvement Sussex most certainly had a considerable share. It quickly followed in the footsteps of Hampshire as a cricketing county, and eventually outstripped it. It owed this superiority chiefly to the men of West Sussex —the Broadbridges, the Lillywhites, the Deans, &c., by whom

---

* The name cricket (says a writer in the *Encyclopædia Britannica*) is cognate to the Saxon cric or cryc, a crooked stick, which doubtless applied to the earliest bats, which were made with a sweeping curve at the base. The name first occurs in 1550, as a game at ball with a stick.

the style of bowling was revolutionised ; the old-fashioned under-handed bowling being superseded by the over-handed bowling which was adopted by the Broadbridges, and brought to perfection by their compatriot, Lillywhite, the "Nonpareil" bowler, as he came to be called.

We are, however, anticipating events. It is in East Sussex, and in the diaries of men living in that part of the county, that we find the earliest reference to cricket in Sussex, and almost, we might say, in England. Thomas Marchant, of Little Park, Hurst, sets down in his diary that in 1717 his son Willy "went to see a cricket match ; " and Walter Gale, the schoolmaster of Mayfield, chronicles in 1759 that he "left off school at 2 o'clock to attend a cricket match of the gamesters of Mayfield against those of Lindfield and Chailey."

This shows that cricket had taken root in the eastern parts of the county at a very early period.

Coming to more recent times, a contributor to the Sussex Archæological Collections, " C. F. T.," tells us that from " about 1790 to 1815 there was a very strong club at Oakendene, near Cowfold. Three brothers, named Wood, Marchant, of Hurst, Borrer, of Ditchling, Voice, of Hand-cross, were the chief players. William Wood, though he never played in great matches, was reckoned the best bowler in Sussex. He used to carry a ball as he walked about his farm, and trained a dog to pick it up and bring it back. He was always bowling at some object. Borrer and Marchant were great batsmen and hard hitters. Vallance, of Brighton, also belonged to this club. He and Borrer won a great match at Lord's, in 1792, for Brighton against Marylebone, the former making 68 and the latter 60 in the second innings, both 'not out.' The betting was heavy against Sussex when they began the second innings, as they had 131 to get ; and the spectators actually staked their watches and rings at last ; but Brighton won by nine wickets."

The scene now shifts to Brighton, where cricket was followed by Lord Barrymore and other associates of the Prince of Wales, though we are not aware that the Prince himself was a player. He is, however, credited by "C. F. T." with enclosing and levelling a piece of ground to the north of the then town for the purpose of a cricket ground, and this was subsequently perfected, if not, as we believe, originally formed, by an enterprising Brightonian, Mr. James Ireland, who invested his savings, as a draper and as the landlord of the Golden Cross, in the laying-out of the Royal Cricket Ground and the adjoining gardens, maze, ball-room, aviary, &c., to which was attached the Hanover Arms; and we are old enough to remember the opening of these in 1823 under the auspices of the Duke of York, but who failed to attend the public breakfast prepared for him on the occasion. The Prince of Wales's cricket ground was comprehended in the ten acres bought by Mr. Ireland of Mr. Thomas Read Kemp; and the work of enclosure was chiefly due to Ireland. On this spot, more generally known as Ireland's Gardens, the most famous matches ever played by Sussex, then in its palmy days, came off. Here the "great deeds" of the Sussex champions of cricket—the two Broadbridges, Lillywhite, Slater (the first wicket-keeper of his day), Lanaway (the old, steady under-handed bowler), Morley, Meads, Brown (the swiftest of bowlers), Pierpoint, Hooker, Duff, and Dale, or, later on in the day, of Box, Charles Taylor, Taylor of Northchapel, Hawkins, Hammond, Millyard, &c., &c.— were achieved. Have not we "assisted" at these games as reporter and spectator? Have we not often witnessed the pitched battles between Kent and Sussex, Sussex and Surrey, and the All England games, in which Sussex would challenge the players of all the rest of the kingdom—first with its native strength, and then with Fuller Pilch as "a given man!" Have we not, once and again, seen the small, active, light men of Sussex meet the big-limbed men of Kent, and treat them as the handy little vessels of Drake and Raleigh and Frobisher treated the huge galleons of the Spanish

Armada? Have we not seen Lillywhite bowling to Fuller Pilch, delivering over after over so true to distance and so dangerous in pitch and twist that the long-armed Kentish Prince of batsmen could do nothing but advance his bat to its full extent and block the ball as it began to rise? Over after over did this contest between perfect bowling and perfect batting go on, until the spectators grew well-nigh weary of it, perfect as it was, and sighed for a wide ball that might be sent to the wall or an opening to the wicket that might send the bales flying. In the meantime Box was crouching, cat-like, behind the wicket, eager, and sure, to catch a passing ball (but which seldom did pass Pilch) to right or to left—little mattered it to him which it was—and Hawkins was watching, hawk-like, only with hands distended instead of wings, at point, for the chance of a catch, with Charles Taylor, not less perfect in the field at slip or cover-point. And have we not listened to the "chaff" of that merry wag, Felix, when he and the Mynns and Wenmans and Pilches had beaten the best bowling of the Sussex men and began to find it safe even to take liberties with the balls of the "Nonpareil?" Have we not witnessed the varied feats of Jim Broadbridge, perhaps the most thorough all-round cricketer that ever went into the field—great as a bat, as a bowler, as a field, and as a captain of the game? Did we not see Jemmy Dean, the Sussex Plough-boy as he was first called, and afterwards, by a merry conceit, "Dean Swift," make his *debut* at Ireland's in a match of Duncton *versus* Brighton, in which he sent down wicket after wicket of the Brighton men at the first ball, and, as each wicket fell, leapt up some feet into the air, arms and legs spread-eagle fashion, as only a Sussex plough-boy could? It was the beginning of as successful and meritorious a cricketing career as the annals of cricket in Sussex can boast of. Too many promising careers have been defeated by that stumbling-block of Sussex cricketers—the love of drink. Jim Broadbridge set a baneful example in this respect. Witness the "half-pints" brought out to him again and again after successful hits; the game stopping whilst he "imbibed." The most brilliant hitter and fielder of Sussex—perhaps of any county—Hawkins—fell an early victim to the same pernicious habit. His free, easy style of batting, with the bat swung over the right shoulder, *à la* Jim Broadbridge, and the quick, sharp hit that caught the swiftest ball "to the leg" and sent it right away, was the pride and delight of a Sussex ground, and not less so the unerring certainty with which he would "take" the hardest-hit ball almost from the point of the bat. But these brilliant qualities, which, joined to youth and good looks, elegance of shape and grace of action (albeit marred by a few eccentricities, as that of touching his hat and other parts of his apparel three several times before coming to the wicket) made Hawkins for a time the pet and hope of the Sussex eleven—these qualities were soon dimmed, and at length destroyed, by habits of intemperance, and he died at the early age of 29.

In these "palmy days" of cricket in Sussex the largest proportion of the county eleven came from the western districts. It had not always been so. The Pierpoints, Dales, Slaters, Meads, Morleys, and Lanaways of an earlier day were eastern men; but with the rise of the Broadbridge school and the *debut* of Lillywhite as a bowler the balance inclined to the west. Lillywhite was born at West Hampnett, near Goodwood, and his first recorded appearance in a cricket match is on July 11, 1822, but not as a bowler. It was not until the following year, when he was thirty-one years of age, that his extra-ordinary merit in this department of the game was recognised; but, the discovery once made, Lillywhite came at once to the front, and he and Jim Broadbridge, with Lanaway for a change as an under-handed bowler, and Brown the swift bowler as a *dernier ressort*, soon carried Sussex to the highest point amongst the cricketing counties. Many stories are still told of the tremendous bowling of Brown, originally a tailor by trade, and a curious "tenth part of a man," for he was between six and seven feet in height and broad and stout in proportion. It was a common feat of his, at the

Royal Cricket Ground (which he, like Box, kept for a time), to bowl at a single stump, the cricketing officers of the regiments stationed in the town and other gentlemen staking so much on his striking it, which he constantly did; for his bowling (under-handed) was as true as it was swift. But it was only in the last resort, when a batsman had beaten all the other Sussex bowlers, that Brown was called out; for, if met, the result was disastrous. All the field might be, as they often were, placed behind the wicket, but if the ball was "tipped" (it could be scarcely struck "fore-right"), away it went like a cannon-ball, and not all the fielders in the world could stop it! One of the latest occasions that Brown bowled was in a game with Kent, when Felix had beaten the "Nonpareil" and other Sussex bowlers, and at length Brown was tried. But the experiment failed; the Kentish men were not to be frightened by the giant's bulk or pace, and he was soon taken off, after some very fast scoring. We do not remember his bowling in a county game after that. "In 1819," says "C. F. T." he "threw a 4½-oz. ball 137 yards on Walberton Common. This was, and perhaps is, the longest throw on record. 'Little Dench,' of Brighton, who 'stopped' to him, had always a sack stuffed with straw fastened to his chest. At Lord's a man once tried to stop a ball with his coat, but Brown bowled right through it, and killed a dog instantaneously on the other side."

It was a great blow to cricket in Brighton, if not Sussex, when the ground formed by Ireland, and which had been successively kept by him, Pierpoint, Brown, and Box, was closed in 1848, and eventually converted into a crescent (Park Crescent). The Sussex eleven had, indeed, previous to this lost its pre-eminence, and was now second to Kent and Surrey. But from this period dates a still more rapid decline. Other grounds were, indeed, found in Brighton—that on which Montpelier Crescent now stands (kept by Box for a time) and the Brunswick Ground at Hove, and the existing one in the same parish. New players also came forward from time to time to sustain the cricketing reputation of their county—notably, the sons and grandsons of the "Nonpareil," and "little Jack Wisden," the pupil of Box, and the Phillips', Bushby, Charlwood, the Humphreys, Fillery, Stubberfield, &c., &c.; also many gentlemen players, as the Rev. G. Cotterill, Mr. J. M. Cotterill, Mr. R. T. Ellis, Mr. C. A. Smith, the Rev. F. J. Greenfield, &c. But the places of the Broadbridges, the "Nonpareil," of Box, Hawkins, James Taylor, of North Chapel, and Millyard amongst the professional players, and of Mr. Charles Taylor and Mr. Langdon among the gentlemen players, have never been completely filled up; and whilst Sussex has retrograded, or, at all events, has not progressed as a cricketing county, other counties, like Gloucestershire, Yorkshire, Lancashire, once unknown in the cricketing-field, have made giant strides, and left the southern counties, Sussex and Hampshire, and Kent, and even Surrey, far behind. So the seat of Empire, in sport as well as in commerce and war, shifts its ground, and cricket has its Romes, its Venices, and its Genoas!

Farncombe & Co., Printers, Lewes.

Lightning Source UK Ltd.
Milton Keynes UK
UKOW07f1129070515

251063UK00009B/291/P